Reformed Ministry

Traditions of Ministry and Ordination
in the United Reformed Church

Tony Tucker

ISBN 0 85346 217 8
© The United Reformed Church, 2003

Published by The United Reformed Church
86 Tavistock Place, London WC1H 9RT

The
United
Reformed
Church

Produced by Communications and Editorial, Graphics Office

Printed by MCPGOLDIES Limited, Units B2 & B3,
Hatton Square Business Centre, London EC1N 7RJ

FOREWORD

The United Reformed Church has a unique history. It was born, by the grace of God, in 1972 from the union of the Presbyterian Church of England and the Congregational Church in England and Wales, the first union of churches from different 'families' in England since the reformations of the sixteenth century. It united again in 1981 with the Re-formed Association of the Churches of Christ, and then in 2000 with the Scottish Congregational Union. It is a church born of repentance for division within the body of Christ and committed to reconciliation. It promises in its Basis of Union to take '…wherever possible and with all speed, further steps towards the unity of all God's people.' Thirty years on that commitment remains undiminished, and is writ large in countless ecumenical ventures in the three nations. We have learnt something of the spiritual dynamics of reconciliation and unity in our short life. We know the frustration and the joy, the pain of failure and the wonder of resurrection.

Partners at the ecumenical table are gift givers. They bring with them the riches of God's bounty experienced in their particular histories and witness. The United Reformed Church's commitment to mission now and its enthusiastic willingness to work with others sometimes causes it to underestimate the value of the gifts it brings. Tony Tucker's timely study of *Reformed Ministry* will help us overcome our tendency to corporate amnesia, for he carefully and patiently chronicles the development of our understanding of ministry. Here is a record of what we have been given which will be of value not just to us but to those who gather at the ecumenical table.

Those who read it carefully will realise that the journey to which we were called has not been without its tensions and disagreements, but they will also recognise that the gift of God has been granted precisely as we have committed ourselves to seek the mind of Christ together. They will also realise that this book is but a cairn on the journey, for the God whose intent is 'to gather up all things' into Christ has not finished with us yet.

Many generations of ordinands at Mansfield College (myself amongst them) have reason to give thanks for Tony's ministry of encouragement and insight. This work simply extends that circle of indebtedness. We are grateful for it.

David Cornick

To Mary with love and thanks

CONTENTS

PREFACE

'The ministry of the whole people of God' has become something of a mantra for our times - the equivalent perhaps of 'the priesthood of all believers' to earlier generations of especially Protestant Christians. This book originated in a discussion with a group of ministerial students in which one student vehemently asserted – and without contradiction from other members of the group - that their priority as ministers should be to work themselves out of their jobs. The ordained ministry, it was argued, would be superfluous if all church members were exercising their corporate ministry. That discussion raised many questions. Is the ministry of Word and sacraments essential to church order, or is it merely decorative - or even a hindrance to the ministry of the whole people of God?

These questions are explored from the perspective of the traditions of Congregationalism, Presbyterianism, and the Churches of Christ which in 1972 and 1981 coalesced into the United Reformed Church. After an opening chapter on the Roots of the Traditions, attention focuses on the period from 1920 – a year of great significance for church relations in England and Wales. Against the backdrop of the winds of change which were to transform twentieth century society and its institutions, later chapters examine how Congregationalists, Presbyterians and members of the Churches of Christ wrestled with their understanding of ministry and ordination. This took place against the wider backdrop of another wind of change - the ecumenical movement - which was challenging the divided churches to forsake their comfortable separation and seek the Church's unity and peace. That search could not evade the question of how ordained ministry - often a sign of division in the Church - might become instead a focus of unity.

For most of the period under review the ordained ministry of Congregationalists, Presbyterians and Churches of Christ included few women. English Congregationalists ordained their first woman in 1917, but for many decades thereafter women ministers constituted a tiny minority. The Presbyterian Church of England accepted the principle of women's ordination in 1921, but the ordination of the first woman after normal training did not take place until 1965. For Churches of Christ the ordination of women presented graver problems of biblical interpretation and approval did not come until 1973. What Congregationalists and Presbyterians said about ordained ministry applied in principle equally to men and women, but they were slow to put principle into practice. Consequently ordained women were excluded from positions as church leaders and theological educators. No woman Congregational minister, for example, became a Provincial Moderator, and only men were appointed to the staff of recognised theological colleges until several years after the formation of the United Reformed Church. It is at least open to question whether some of the proposals for church unity, which are discussed in later chapters of this book, would have been presented differently – and in some cases have had a different outcome – if women had had an equal voice in their preparation. A new century will perhaps approach these tasks from a more inclusive perspective.[1]

I gladly acknowledge advice and help which I have received from many people. Arthur Macarthur, David Thompson, and the late Daniel Jenkins shared their knowledge of the three traditions and advised me in the initial stages of the project. Susan Durber and Elaine Kaye read and commented on the text. Martin Cressey and Donald Hilton lent material on the English Covenant, and Donald Norwood gave helpful advice on local ecumenical partnerships. Carol Rogers and Sara Foyle took the text through the process of publication. Two names call for particular mention. I wish to thank Elaine Kaye for the immeasurable benefits of her scholarship and friendship, and my wife Mary for her artwork and the unswerving support without which this book would long ago have been abandoned in favour of the enticements of retirement.

Tony Tucker
Oxford
January 2003

---

[1] These issues will be explored in a forthcoming book, *Daughters of Dissent*, by Elaine Kaye, Janet Lees and Kirsty Thorpe, due for publication in 2004.

Chapter One

The Roots of the Traditions

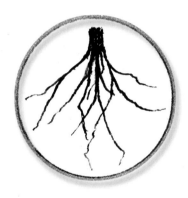

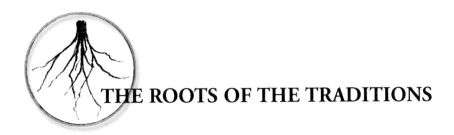

THE ROOTS OF THE TRADITIONS

Ordination has long been a source of controversy and painful division in the Church. For centuries arguments have revolved around questions of succession and authority. While it is tempting to dismiss these as bickering about secondary matters and a distraction from the Church's fundamental missionary task, serious issues are nevertheless at stake. The principal means by which the Church has through the ages shared its faith and endeavoured to transmit it from one generation to another have been preaching and teaching. From its earliest days the Christian community recognised the essential importance of guarding the purity and truth of what was taught in its name. What was to be handed on – the 'tradition' – must be true to the revelation of God in Scripture and to 'that faith which God entrusted to his people once for all.'[1] The exact nature of the faith was often hotly contested, as almost every page of the New Testament bears witness. Later it became the function of the great Councils of the Church to define the faith and to draw boundaries between orthodoxy and heresy. The ministry was the practical – and local – means by which the faith was proclaimed and taught. Questions of who should be authorised, how that authority should be conferred, and of its public acceptance throughout the Church have been, and remain, of paramount importance. The rite of ordination has been the means by which the Church has provided itself with officers whom it authorised to teach and transmit the faith.

This apparently straightforward objective has not been without its complications. The loss of a universally recognised and accepted ministry has been a major casualty of the historic fragmentation of the Church, from the major division of Greek and Latin Christendom in the 11th century, and later at the 16th century Reformation. One consequence was that the ordinations of churches which had separated from the historic episcopate were rejected as utterly invalid by those who had retained that episcopate. In their History of the Dissenters (1808) Bogue and Bennett rehearse the arguments against the Dissenters used by high church clergy in the reigns of William and Anne.

> the baptism of the Dissenters (they say) is no baptism, their dispensation of the Lord's supper is no sacrament, their prayers, as ministers of Christ, are no prayers, and have no influence, and their preaching is no preaching, and utterly destitute of effect; they are therefore all of them without the pale of the Church of God.
>
> Ordination (they continued) is absolutely necessary to make a man a minister. This ordination must be performed by the laying on of hands of a bishop; and that bishop must have derived his office and authority by a regular succession from the apostles.

---

[1]   Jude 3.

Such an ordination the dissenting ministers have not had; they were ordained by presbyters only, who have no right to ordain. Therefore their ordination was not valid: they are no ministers of Christ, but continue mere laymen, and all their ministrations are invalid, and have no effect.[2]

Three centuries later the language of church discourse has become more generous. Dialogue has replaced outright rejection. Churches standing within the historic episcopate have had to re-evaluate the non-episcopal ministries of churches which they now recognise as belonging to the one holy, catholic and apostolic church. These churches have had to face the issue of whether to accept the historic episcopate for themselves. Questions surrounding ordination remain crucial, and continue to present stumbling blocks in the quest for Christian unity.

This exploration is concerned with the story of one small, yet not insignificant, part of that quest, in which three denominations – the Congregational Church in England and Wales, the Presbyterian Church of England, and the Churches of Christ – united to form the United Reformed Church in the United Kingdom. The first part of that union was accomplished in 1972 with the formation of the United Reformed Church by the union of a majority of the Congregationalists and Presbyterians, and was extended nine years later with the accession of the Churches of Christ in 1981. The union was hailed at the time as a breakthrough in ecumenical relations which offered a sign of hope to the whole church in its quest for unity. To a casual observer it might seem that the union of three denominations of similar character was an unremarkable event. But that would be to underestimate the achievements of those who by a long process of negotiation in the Joint Committee, and consultation with the congregations and councils of the participating churches, brought into existence a new church out of three communions which were significantly different in their ethos and churchmanship. Within that wider story our concern is to discover how these participating churches understood ordination to the church's ministry, and to what extent, if at all, their understandings of ordination underwent change in the years preceding the opening of formal negotiations for union, and while the negotiations for union were taking place.

Our exploration will begin in 1920. But before we come to that we must first examine the traditions of the Dissenters, or Nonconformists as they were later to be called, and their understanding of ministry and ordination, for it was to their experience and writings that 20th century Congregational theologians in particular often turned in their deliberations.

---

[2]   Bogue, David and Bennett, James, *History of the Dissenters*. (London: 1808) Vol. I. pp. 419-20.

Martin Luther and the Priesthood of All Believers

On the matter of ordination the three denominations stood firmly within the traditions of the Continental Reformation and English Dissent. We need to look briefly at those traditions. Fundamental to their understanding of church order was their belief in the priesthood of all believers. This had its roots, as Protestant doctrine, in the polemic between the Papacy and the Reformers. Its origins however lay in the New Testament understanding of the Church. Martin Luther (1483-1546) argued from 1 Peter 2.9 that through their baptism all Christians are incorporated into Christ's royal priesthood. 'Our baptism consecrates all without exception and makes us all priests.'[3] Luther rejected the priesthood to which he had been ordained and dismissed his ordination as a 'man-made ceremonial.'[4] He argued that the priest's true ministry was to preach the Word, which in his view the Roman Church had abandoned and replaced with the 'vain repetition' of celebrating the Mass and reading the canonical hours. What people called priests were in reality 'ministers of the Word' who had been chosen by the Church. Ordination was the rite by which the Church chose its preachers. Luther agreed that ordination had been celebrated from the foundation of the Church, but he denied that it was a sacrament because there was no evidence that it had been instituted by Christ. It was an ecclesiastical ceremony by which the church provided itself with those who were to preach the word. The 'Frankfurt Ordinal' (1520) has the formula: 'We receive thee for a minister of Christ and a preacher of his holy gospel, and give thee with the laying on of our hands, according to apostolic and early Church custom, power and authority to preach the Word of God.'[5] He came close to thinking that ordination was unnecessary. In two typically forthright comments Luther declares that 'any one who has been called by the church to preach the Word, but does not preach it, is in no way a priest' and 'the sacrament of ordination cannot be other than the rite by which the church chooses its preachers'.[6] Faith was more important than order. Ordination did not therefore possess any 'indelible character'. A priest could revert to being a layman if he ceased to exercise the functions of ministry. Luther dismissed the claim that ordination conferred an indelible character as a ridiculous fiction, designed to enhance the power and authority of the Papacy.

The doctrine of the priesthood of all believers might appear to undermine the need for an ordained ministry. Luther comes close to this when he says that anyone may baptise or pronounce absolution. In his view there was no difference in status between laymen and priests, religious and secular people. The difference consisted in 'office' or 'occupation' rather than status. Luther rejected the concept of hierarchy which denied to the Church as the Body of Christ its corporate priesthood. But this did not mean for Luther that everyone had an unbridled right to celebrate the Gospel sacraments. All have the same authority, yet 'no one has the right to administer them without the consent of the members of his Church or by the call of the majority.'[7]

---

[3]   *An Appeal to the Ruling Class* (1520) *Reformation Writings of Martin Luther*, trans by Bertram Lee Woolf, Vol 1, (London: Lutterworth 1952) p. 113.

[4]   *The Pagan Servitude of the Church* (1520) ibid. p. 315.

[5]   Quoted in *The Apostolic Ministry*, ed K E Kirk, (London: Hodder and Stoughton, 1946) p. 467.

[6]   ibid. p. 314.

[7]   ibid. p. 318.

The enduring significance of the priesthood of all believers lay in its insistence on the equal status of all believers before God. The whole believing community had been formed into a 'holy priesthood' through their baptism as individuals into the death and resurrection of Jesus Christ.[8] Later interpretations tended to be influenced by a rugged individualism, to which Protestantism was sometimes vulnerable, which failed to do justice to the classic understanding of the priesthood of all believers as affirming the participation of the individual believer in the corporate priesthood of the universal community of saints drawn from 'every tribe and language, nation and race'.[9] The doctrine claimed that all who believed and were baptised were equal before God, and that priesthood had been given to the whole Church, but intended no statement as to function or office within the body of believers. The issue of whether those who were not ordained should be permitted to perform tasks which were normally assigned to ordained ministers was not a prime concern of the doctrine.[10]

Ulrich Zwingli (1484-1531) accepted the priesthood of all believers while preserving the place of distinctive ministerial orders within the church. 'It is true we are all fully ordained to the priesthood (sic. of all believers) … but we are not all apostles and bishops.'[11] This was later affirmed in the Second Helvetic Confession (1566) which stated 'The apostles of Christ indeed call all believers in Christ priests, but not by reasons of a ministerial office, but because through Christ all who are the faithful, having been made both kings and priests, are able to offer spiritual sacrifices to God. Accordingly, there are great differences between a priesthood and a ministry. For the former is common to all Christians, as we have just now said, but the same is not so with the latter. And we have not removed the ministry out of the midst of the Church when we have cast the papistical priesthood out of the Church of Christ.' Because belief in the priesthood of all believers did not exclude a special ministerial order, it was compatible with a high view of ministry, and therefore commanded wide assent within the churches of the Reformation despite their differing emphases.[12]

John Calvin and the 'Call'

A second influence came from Geneva and John Calvin (1509-1564). Calvin derived from scripture five classes of ministers. The first three – apostles, prophets and evangelists – were 'not instituted to be perpetual'. The other two classes – pastors and teachers – were the ordinary ministers of the church. In their case Calvin emphasised the importance of the 'Call'. The call to ministry was 'the external and formal call which relates to the public order of the Church', and is given by consent of the people. The office of Teacher is 'an office which consists in the ministry of the Word'. The Teacher however does not 'preside over discipline, or the administration of the sacraments…but the interpretation of Scripture only'.[13] Bishop, presbyter and elder were, for Calvin, synonymous terms. They provided a ministry which was essential to the Church.

---

8   I Peter 2.9.

9   Revelation 5.9.

10   For a Reformed discussion of the priesthood of the Church, see T F Torrance, *Royal Priesthood – A Theology of Ordained Ministry*, (Edinburgh: T & T Clark, 2ⁿᵈ edition, 1993)

11   Quoted by J L Ainslie, *Doctrines of Ministerial Order in the Reformed Churches*, (Edinburgh: Hodder and Stoughton, 1940) p. 7.

12   T W Manson, *Ministry and Priesthood – Christ's and Ours*. (London: Epworth Press, 1958), pp. 35-72.

13   *Institutes,* Book IV iii 4 (London: SCM Press, 1961)

'For neither are the light of the sun, nor meat and drink, so necessary to sustain and cherish the present life, as is the apostolic office to preserve a Church in the earth.'[14] The rite of ordination is closely linked at all times to the call and is entirely invalid without it. Ordination is to be performed by the laying on of hands of the pastors. This is not an 'empty sign', for, as Calvin explained, 'the Spirit of God hath not instituted anything in the Church in vain.' Nevertheless in the Ordinances, first produced in 1541, ordination was without imposition of hands. Pastors were first to be chosen and examined by those who were already pastors, and having then been approved by the civil authorities, would preach a trial sermon, and, if approved by the people, would be ordained.

The Scottish Church followed Geneva. An order of service of 1561[15] for the 'election of the superintendents' and 'all uther ministers' contained the following elements:

1. Sermon
2. Questions to the People
3. Questions to the candidate concerning motives, beliefs and acceptance of church discipline
4. A further question to the People and a 'word' to the nobility
5. Ordination Prayer
6. Giving of the Right Hand of Fellowship by other ministers and elders of that Kirk present 'in sign of their consente'
7. Blessing on the newly ordained minister
8. Exhortation of the duties of his office
9. Singing of the 23rd Psalm

In this order the giving of the right hand of fellowship appears to be a substitute for the imposition of hands, although later both were included. The imposition of hands has a more controversial history. It is found in early Reformed services, eg those of Zurich (1532) and in the First (1536) and Second (1566) Helvetic Confessions. Calvin omitted it in the Genevan Ordination Service of 1541 in order to avoid associations with papal superstition. He was not opposed to the imposition of hands in principle. 'It is certain that when the Apostles appointed anyone to the Ministry, they used no other ceremony than the laying on of hands.'[16] The omission of the laying on of hands did not invalidate the ordination which took place after the due processes of selection, 'trials' and call had been completed. It was important that those selected should be admitted to the ministry in an approved and recognised form, but ordination did not depend on any ritual act.

Nervousness over papal practice led to a cautious approach to the use of the imposition of hands. This did not initially form part of the ceremonies of ordination in the Reformed Churches in France, the Netherlands or Scotland. The first National Synod of the French Reformed Church in 1559 decreed concerning the ordination of ministers that 'their election shall be confirmed by prayers and imposition of hands by the ministers, yet without superstition of opinion of necessity'. The later Synod of Rochelle (1571) affirmed that 'although the usage of imposition of hands be good and holy, yet it should not be reputed necessary as if it were the substance of ordination.'

---

[14]   ibid.. *iii 2*.
[15]   J L Ainslie, op. cit. p. 155.
[16]   *Institutes*, Book IV iii 10.

The Scottish Church, as we have seen, followed Geneva, and in the 1561 order omitted the laying on of hands.

It was not long however before the imposition of hands became accepted as a standard element in ordination. By the time of the Second Book of Discipline (1581), it was authorised, though not enforced. Robert Bruce was an example of a leading minister who was ordained without the imposition of hands. It was not until 1597 that the Assembly, under royal influence, made the rite obligatory.

An important issue in the Reformed Churches of the 16th century was who had the power to ordain. In the Roman Church ordinations had been carried out by the bishop. In the Reformed Churches ordination now became the responsibility of a minister or ministers. There was variety of practice. In the First Helvetic Confession (1536), it is done by the 'ministerial elders'. In England the elders joined with the ministers in imposing hands. 'He (the minister) and the elders shall lay their hands on him (the candidate)'.[17] While there was variety of practice, and the participation of elders was included, it was essential that a minister or ministers should act.

English Separatism – Reformation 'without tarrying for any'

A third important strand was that of English Separatism. This was a multi-faceted movement with affinities with the 15th century Lollards and the continental Anabaptists who were especially to influence the English General Baptists. The mainstream of English Separatism however flowed from the Calvinistic Puritanism which sought to reform the Church of England during the reign of Elizabeth I, but which was not itself Separatist.[18] The Bishop of London, Edmund Grindal, writing on 11 June 1568, describes the growing influence of Separatism in London as seen from the point of view of the authorities. The Separatists are described as citizens of the lowest order, together with a small number of ministers 'remarkable neither for their judgement nor their learning'. They meet in private houses, in the fields, occasionally even in ships where they administer the sacraments. 'Besides this they have ordained ministers, elders and deacons, after their own way.'[19]

The Separatists believed that the Established Church was in a state of apostasy and had forfeited all right to be a church. In their view it was as if there were now no church in England. They believed they were commanded by God to renew the biblical covenant and to reconstitute the church in obedience to the pattern of church order which had been revealed in scripture. But they were Puritans before they were Separatists. They were not opposed to the principle of an established Church but aimed at its reformation on Puritan lines. Following the death of Archbishop Parker in 1575 and the translation of Archbishop Grindal from York to Canterbury, the Puritans hoped that the Church of England would be reformed as a manifestly Protestant Church. They urged the abolition of the popish ceremonial which had been re-introduced during the reign

---

[17]   Cartwright, *The Second Admonition to Parliament* (1572), see J L Ainslie, op cit p. 185.
[18]   M R Watts, *The Dissenters*, (Oxford: 1978) p. 14.
[19]   Quoted in B R White, *The English Separatist Tradition*, (Oxford: 1971) p. 26.

of Mary I and the establishment of a godly, ie Calvinist, clergy. The Queen quickly made it clear that she had no intention of giving free rein to Puritan ideas or practices. Grindal was ordered to suppress the popular meetings – or 'prophesyings' – which had sprouted for the study and exposition of the Bible, and drastically to reduce the number of preachers who were licensed for each county. Refusing to do this, Grindal was suspended from office. Other bishops however obeyed and began the silencing of Puritan preachers. This was the signal for Robert Browne, a leading Puritan minister, to repudiate the established Church which the bishops by their actions had polluted, and to set in motion a reformation 'without tarrying for anie'. Browne despaired of the parochial system and came to the view that 'the kingdom of God was not to be begun by whole parishes, but rather of the worthies, were they never so few'.[20] Though he later submitted under pressure to return to the Church of England, and was thereafter reviled by the Separatists as a traitor to their cause, Browne is rightly regarded as the founder of English Separatism. His separatism was born out of necessity because he believed that the civil power had failed in its duty to maintain pure and undefiled Church.

Browne's submission did not bring the end of Separatism. Further separations took place when Archbishop Whitgift, who had succeeded Grindal, continued Elizabeth's policy to establish uniformity and insisted that his clergy subscribe to the Prayer Book as containing 'nothing contrarie to the word of God'. A number of Separatists met in London, among them Henry Barrow, who had been closely associated with the Queen's court until his conversion to Puritanism. Barrow argued that 'the faithful being as yet but private men, ought by the commandment of God to assemble and join themselves together in the name and faith of Christ, and in all mutual duties orderly to proceed according to the rules of the word to a holy choice and use of such offices and ordinances as Christ hath ordained to the service and government of his Church'.[21]

A Separatist congregation was comprised of 'private men', yet obedience was possible. Their authority to act as a company of Christ's people derived from no superior ecclesiastical authority, nor from sacerdotal notions of succession in ministerial office, because they were competent in themselves. 'A true church could, therefore, exist without ministers, because at its first gathering the members would not, perhaps, know each others' gifts well enough to choose from among them elders and deacons'.[22] Barrow insisted that the gathered fellowship had power 'both to receive into and cast out of their fellowship....although they have yet obtained to have neither a ministry nor sacraments among them.'[23] This did not mean that the ministry was a matter of indifference among the Separatists. The point was not that a covenanted fellowship had no need of ministers, but that it could exist without them, if the lack of ministers were due to circumstances beyond their control. Barrow assumed that a church without ministers would not celebrate the sacraments, although the lack of sacraments did not mean that the congregation was not a true Church. The Barrowist congregation in London, for example, existed without sacraments until the appointment of Francis Johnson as pastor in 1592.

---

[20]   Watts, op. cit. p. 29.
[21]   Quoted in B R White, op. cit. p. 76.
[22]   ibid. p. 76.
[23]   ibid.

The judgement that the Separatist tradition undervalued the ministry is superficial. While the fellowship was primary in importance, and the ministry in that sense was subordinate to the fellowship, the ministry remained important. Barrow, Greenwood and the other Separatists firmly believed that the ministry belonged to the scriptural pattern of the Church. It followed that a covenanted fellowship should take all possible steps to appoint officers, and that until these had been appointed, no sacraments should be administered. This self denial emphasised rather than devalued the importance of the ministry.

From the beginning of Separatism, the appointment of officers emphasised the importance of relationships between different congregations. A church seeking to appoint a minister would assure themselves from the congregation to which the potential minister already belonged about his suitability for ministry. All members of the congregation declared their assent or dissent from the proposed candidate. Once the call had been issued and accepted, the new minister was to be ordained and received into membership of the congregation he had been appointed to serve. Ordination would be carried out by the elders of that congregation, or, if they lacked elders, by elders of another congregation. Thus the fellowship between churches was recognised and embodied. In extreme situations, where no elders might be available, the congregation had the spiritual power from Jesus Christ, as Head of the Church, to appoint members from among themselves to carry out the ordination. Ainsworth, the Separatist leader in Amsterdam, claimed strong support from the Old Testament, based on Number 8.9-10, for the ordination of ministers by the whole congregation. The Separatists retained the imposition of hands in spite of the hierarchical associations which they rejected.

The Westminster Assembly (1643-49) – A Presbyterian National Church?

During the ferment of political and ecclesiastical controversy of the mid-seventeenth century, the most powerful opposition to the Established Church came from the Presbyterians, who wanted the national church to be re-ordered according to Presbyterian polity. The Presbyterian movement in England had been initiated in the previous century by Thomas Cartwright (1535-1603), a leading Puritan divine and Cambridge scholar, who had been deprived of his professorship in 1570 on account of his Presbyterian views. In lectures on the Acts of the Apostles he advocated the abolition of the offices of archbishop and bishop in favour of the parity of ministers who should be chosen by their congregations. The failure of the Puritans at the Hampton Court Conference in 1604 to achieve their demands for the modification of episcopacy resulted in the eclipse of the Presbyterian cause until its revival in the controversies of the 1640s. The Westminster Assembly was convened by Parliament to effect a more perfect reformation in the liturgy, discipline and government of the Church, following the abolition of episcopacy by Parliament. The Assembly, which comprised 120 members together with 10 members of the House of Lords and 20 from the House of Commons, met for five and a half years from 1643 to 1649. The majority of the English members of the Assembly were Presbyterians. Since its political purpose was to cement the alliance between the Scots and Parliament, four ministers and two elders were appointed by the General Assembly of the Church of Scotland. Their participation was a reminder that the reformation of the Church of England on Presbyterian lines was a condition of Scottish financial and military aid.

The question of ordination was addressed at an early stage because of its urgency. The Civil War had disrupted the parochial system. Many churches were vacant, 'scandalous' and 'malignant' ministers having been deprived of their livings. It was not clear who had the authority to ordain their successors, or who was authorised to arrange settlements for those who had received some form of ordination. Related issues concerned whether congregations were competent to call a minister or whether the call by a congregation required confirmation by other ministers in the neighbourhood. These questions were hotly debated for several months. Independent members in the Assembly feared that the powers of the gathered Church would be usurped by 'ruling elders' in a new form of sacerdotalism. They argued that the ordination of individuals who had been gifted by the Holy Spirit 'lay in the suffrage of the people rather than the clerically-managed rite of the laying-on of hands'.[24] The issue was not about ordination as such but on who should be empowered to ordain. The principal concern of the Independents was to refute any suggestion that the apostles had possessed a power of ordination which had then passed to the officers of the Church by virtue of their office. This would be to replace episcopacy with a similar hierarchical system. The Independents however failed to win the arguments against Presbyterian polity.

Another debate in the Assembly was on whether a minister could be ordained unless he had been designated to a particular congregation or charge. Those who opposed this represented the large number of ministers who had been ordained 'sine titulo'. Some also took the view that as a man should not preach before being ordained, election to a charge before ordination would introduce the undesirable practice of preaching by unordained people - an argument strange to modern inheritors of the Reformed tradition.

There was also controversy over the proposal that a potential minister should be 'recommended' to the people of the congregation by the ordaining authority. To some this posed a veiled threat to the congregation's right to elect its own minister. Some thought the recommendation should come from the congregation to the ordaining authority rather than from the ordaining authority to the congregation. For the Independents, strongly supported by the Scots, the right to protest against a candidate, who to all intents and purposes had been chosen by the ordaining authority, was not an adequate safeguard of the rights of the congregation. The majority in the Assemby, however, were prepared to transfer to presbyteries the powers which had formerly been exercised by the bishops.

Difference of opinion emerged on what kind of presbytery should constitute the ordaining authority. Some took the view that the presbytery should be comprised only of 'preaching presbyters', while others argued that it should include 'preaching presbyters' and 'evangelists'. These argued from scripture that the power to ordain had been given to Timothy and Titus as evangelists, and therefore someone like Timothy 'must be present at least'. This was opposed by those who saw it as a covert means of reviving episcopacy.

---

[24]   R S Paul, *The Assembly of the Lord*, (Edinburgh: 1985) p. 203.

After lengthy debates the 'Form of Presbyterian Church Government and Ordination of Ministers'[25] was sent to Parliament for approval and was subsequently ratified by the General Assembly of the Church of Scotland. Ordination was described as 'the solemn setting apart of a person to some public church office'. Authority to ordain was to be vested in the 'preaching presbyters to whom it doth belong'. Those ordained were to 'be designed to some particular church, or other ministerial charge'. Ordination is to be 'by imposition of hands' (of the preaching presbytery) 'and prayer, with fasting'. It is thus the act of a presbytery, the document stating unambiguously that 'no single congregation, that can conveniently associate, do assume to itself all and sole power in ordination'. It is to be performed in the church where the minister is to serve.

Detailed rules were provided for the examination and approval of candidates for ordination, and for the rite itself. After examination by the presbytery, the candidate was to be sent to the church where he would serve. There he would preach 'three several days' and meet the people 'that they may have trial of his gifts for their edification, and may have time and occasion to inquire into, and the better to know, his life and conversations'. The congregation was then required to give its assent, or to state their objections. Following the giving of consent, the presbytery would proceed to ordination.

Significantly, the Assembly accepted the validity of previous episcopal ordination. Ministers designated to a congregation who had formerly been episcopally ordained were to be admitted without fresh ordination. Ordained ministers moving from Scotland or any other reformed church to serve a congregation in England were to bring testimonials of their ordination with other evidence of their fitness for ministry, and were to be admitted without further ordination.

The Westminster Confession represented the classic formulation of Presbyterian faith and order. It had a major influence on the development and expansion of the Reformed Churches, and was a major contributory influence to the understanding of ministry and ordination in the United Reformed Church.

An Alternative – The Congregational – Way

A significant minority in the Westminster Assembly were identified as followers of the Independent, or Congregational Way rather than of Presbyterianism. They were known as the 'Dissenting Brethren'. They had links with the earlier Separatists through spending time in exile in the Netherlands, though they are not accurately described as Separatists themselves. They, together with John Owen[26] and John Cotton[27] in New England were the effective founders of classical Congregationalism. Their ideas had influence during the Commonwealth and Protectorate and found expression in the Savoy Declaration of 1658.

---

[25] The Westminster Confession 1647 is included in *Stating the Gospel - Formulations and Declarations of Faith from the Heritage of the United Reformed Church*, ed D M Thompson, (Edinburgh: T & T Clark, 1990)

[26] John Owen (1616-1683) was Vice-chancellor of Oxford University during the Commonwealth and Protectorate and was a voluminous author.

[27] John Cotton (1584-1652) left England for New England in 1633 but kept in close touch with his English friends.

On the English scene those of the Independent or Congregational way were in positions of power and influence during the Commonwealth and the Protectorate of Oliver Cromwell. Two principles distinguished Congregational polity. The first, which we have already encountered, was that the church existed before the ministry and a church could exist, if necessary, for a considerable period of time without a pastor. This did not mean that early Congregationalists sat lightly to the ministry, but it was not essential to the church. The Church did not arise out of the ministry but existed prior to the ministry. The key words in comprehending Congregational polity were 'society', 'company', 'communion', 'fellowship', 'together', or 'one another'. Such fellowships fulfilled the scriptural injunction that God's people should bear one another's burdens and thus fulfil the law of Christ. The fellowships themselves were based on the scriptural concept of 'covenant'. Each fellowship was a covenanted community, and a newly constituted fellowship would often have a written covenant to mark its formation. At the time of its formation, if there was a minister among those who participated in the covenant, he might be invited to become pastor to the congregation. But even without a pastor, it remained a true church.

The second principle was that the congregation itself was responsible for discerning the gifts of ministry. Before calling a minister from another congregation, the congregation would seek experience of the potential minister's gifts and graces. Representatives of the congregation would be sent to sit under that minister to discover whether they recognised in him the charismatic gifts and abilities which were needed for their church. Congregations expected those whom they called to be their pastors to be equipped by the Holy Spirit with the gifts and graces needed for their ministry. Almost as important was that the congregations believed themselves to be capable, under the guidance of the Holy Spirit, of recognising the presence of those gifts. They understood the gifts of ministry in terms, for example, of Ephesians 4.7-16 with its emphasis on the grace given to the church by Jesus Christ, the Church's risen and ascended Lord. Order, rites and ceremonies had no value unless they were accompanied by the gifts of the spirit for building up the Body of Christ. John Owen was emphatic that 'To erect a Ministry by Vertue of outward Order, Rites, and Ceremonies, without gifts for the Edification of the Church, is but to hew a Block with Axes, and smooth it with Planes, and set it up for an Image to be adored'. 'Nothing at all can be done without these Spirit Gifts. And therefore a Ministry devoid of them is a Mock-ministry, and no Ordinance of Christ.'[28] It was better for a church to have no minister than to have one imposed upon the congregation who lacked the charismatic gifts of ministry.

It followed from these principles that the Church was antecedent to the ministry but not that the ministry was an unnecessary appendage. In the words of Thomas Hooker, 'there must be a Church of believers to choose a Minister lawfully... Therefore here is a Church before a Minister.'[29] While that principle was fundamental, the covenanted fellowship was under a duty to seek to provide itself with pastors and teachers. John Owen was emphatic that without a minister the members of a church 'cannot come to that perfection and completeness which is designed unto them. That which renders a Church completely organical' is 'the gift of Christ in the ministry.'[30] Ordination, far from a matter of minor significance, was of great solemnity and importance.

---

[28]   John Owen, *Two Discourses Concerning the Holy Spirit and his Work*, pp. 221, 232, 228, quoted by G F Nuttall, *Visible Saints*, (Oxford: 1957) p. 87.

[29]   Quoted by G Nuttall, ibid. p. 86. Thomas Hooker was minister of the First Church of Christ, Hartford, Connecticut.

[30]   ibid.

Ordination in the Congregational and Independent tradition was firmly based upon election by the people. The calling of a minister involved the will of God, the will of the people, and the will of the minister. It fell to the congregation to determine in the first instance whether the call, which the ordinand believed he had received from God, was genuine. The congregation was then responsible for deciding whether that call to ministry was to be exercised among them. The stress on election, which in modern times has become a secularised word, may appear to reduce the issue to a human level. But election in the religious understanding of the 16th and 17th centuries was not a matter of democracy but the church's response to God's primary act in calling a person to the ministry and bestowing the gifts for ministry on that person. Since election lay at the heart of ministerial calling, it is difficult to avoid the suspicion that ordination as a rite was held to be secondary in importance. Ordination was for the sake of order rather than of necessity. Ordination, said Hooker, 'doth not give essentials to the outward call of a Minister.' It 'presupposeth an officer constituted, doth not constitute; therefore it's not an act of Power, but Order.'[31]

Much of this rather grudging approach was in reaction to the situation in the episcopal Church of England in which ministers were imposed upon parishes without their consent and call. John Rogers rejected both 'Popish ordination…and also Presbyterian ordination' on the grounds that both were antichristian and disorderly, because they took place without the election of the minister by the people, and thus did not give 'the essentials to the call of a true minister of Christ.'[32] A principal reason at the Restoration why Independent ministers who had held livings during the Commonwealth refused to be episcopally ordained was not so much that this impugned their ordination but that they rejected episcopal ordination as such. John Owen welcomed the opportunity to disown his episcopal ordination when he agreed in 1654 to become one of the two representatives of the University of Oxford in the House of Commons, from which episcopal ordination would have disbarred him under the Clerical Disabilities Act 1642. This however should not be taken to imply that Independent ministers sat lightly to their ordinations. John Howe, asked by the Bishop of Exeter, what was wrong in being twice ordained, replied: 'the thought is shocking; it hurts my understanding; it is an absurdity; for nothing can have two beginnings. I am sure, saith he, I am a minister of Christ…; and I can't begin again to be a minister.'[33]

The Laying on of Hands

Among early Independents there was some difference of opinion about the laying on of hands because the act might be wrongly interpreted as conferring authority independently of the call of the minister by the congregation. In December 1657 a dispute took place between two London ministers, the Presbyterian Thomas Willes and the Congregational Thomas Brooks, both rectors of London parishes. Brooks accepted that he had been solemnly ordained by fasting, prayer and the laying on of hands, but that he dared not stand upon this Call 'for if I should I should stand upon the sands and quagmire.' Willes claimed, in a letter to Richard Baxter, that Brooks 'scrupled imposition of hands.'[34]

---

[31]   Thomas Hooker, II, 66, 52, 59, quoted by G F Nuttall, op. cit. p. 88
[32]   John Rogers, *An Idea of Church Discipline* 1653
[33]   Quoted By G F Nuttall, *The Early Congregational Conception of the Ministry and the Place of Women within it*, (Congregational Quarterly, Vol XXVI, 1948)
[34]   G F Nuttall, *Visible Saints*, (Oxford:1957) p. 91.

In 1647 the Norwich Independent Church, having elected Timothy Armitage as their minister, sought advice from the Independent Church at Great Yarmouth 'concerning ye manner of ordination, how they shall proceed in it, whether by imposition of hands, or by other ways'. To their enquiry they received the reply:

> If laying on of hands was significative as the ceremonies were, and for ye conferring of some immediate gift, it was not to be done. But if meerly demonstrative before ye church, noting ye man set apart for ye worke and office unto wch hee is set apart then it might well be done; onely with this caution yt such as were against it would not be offended with ye thing done.[35]

The imposition of hands was normal practice, but its omission did not invalidate the ordination If not essential, it was of the *bene esse* of ordination. Customary practice is evidenced by the account of the ordination of Richard Davis to be their minister by the Independent Church at Rothwell on March 22nd 1690:

> the said Mr Davis, by fasting and prayer of the church, and imposition of hands of the eldership, in the name of the said church, was set apart to and installed in the office of Pastor and Bishop of the said Church of Christ at Rothwell[36]

On this occasion only the elders of the local church laid hands on the ordinand. Other ministers were present but several left abruptly, saying 'there was no business for them'.

Isaac Watts (1674-1748) agreed that imposition of hands, while customary, was not essential to ordination. Writing to his brother Enoch Watts, he confirmed the earlier view of John Owen, ie '...that it is not absolutely necessary that a minister be ordained by the imposition of hands of other ministers, but only requisite that other ministers should be there present as advisers and assistants when he is ordained by the Church; that is, set apart by fasting and prayer.'[37]

In another letter Watts writes that 'the laying on of hands can never be proved from the Scriptures to be an essential requisite to ordination that I can find, nor that an office is thereby ordinarily conveyed; but it has been a sign in use in all ages, agreeably to, and derived from, the nature of things, as when a superior has prayed for a blessing on an inferior, or when anything has been devoted to sacred use; I could use it on all occasions with great freedom, or omit it, according as it might be most agreeable to the Church where I minister'.[38]

If there were scruples among the Independents, the Presbyterians had fewer. In 1656 John Brinsley of Yarmouth published 'The Sacred Ordinance of Ordination by Imposition of the Hands of the Presbytery'. He argued that imposition of hands conveyed grace and was not merely declaratory.

---

[35]   C B Jewson, 'St Mary's, Norwich', (*Baptist Quarterly* x 172), quoted by H M Davies, *The Worship of the English Puritans,* (London: Dacre Press 1948) p. 225.

[36]   N Glass, *The Early History of the Independent Church at Rothwell,* 1871, quoted by H M Davies, op. cit. p. 226.

[37]   Milner, *Life of Isaac Watts* (1834) p. 196f, quoted by H M Davies, ibid.

[38]   Milner, op. cit. p. 231, quoted by H M Davies, ibid.

But he went on to say, 'I do not say absolutely necessary, so essential unto this Ordinance, as that it should be null and void without it....But more than indifferent.'[39] Some of the Congregational persuasion were more easily able to identify with this. It would seem that in some Congregational fellowships ordination by imposition of hands was the norm while in others it was not observed. An entry in the church book at Bury St Edmunds noted that 'the church did by election and by holding up of hands, and by fasting and prayer, ordain Thomas Taylor', thus implying that imposition of hands had not taken place.

It would appear that during the Commonwealth the imposition of hands in ordination was optional. Prayer, preceded by fasting, was the essential element in ordination. 'The maine weight of the worke', said Thomas Hooker, 'lyes in the solemnity of prayer'.[40] The whole fellowship, members as well as officers, by participating in prayer in the calling and ordaining of ministers, were directly and immediately involved in the act of ordination.

Ordination was the act of the local fellowship of believers. But it also expressed unity and fellowship between neighbouring churches. Local churches invited neighbouring churches to send their ministers or other 'messengers' to be present at the ordination of their ministers. This was an important recognition that the ordination of a minister involved more than the particular fellowship in which it was taking place. It would be too much to say that the presence of members of neighbouring churches was essential, but it was certainly desirable. In an age of restricted communications, much correspondence passed between local churches. Great care was taken over the dismission and recommendation of members moving from one fellowship to another. The ordination of a minister thus provided a valuable opportunity for the fellowship between churches to be recognised.

The Savoy Declaration (1658)

The political, ecclesiastical and social upheavals of the Commonwealth and Protectorate provided the context for the Independents also to issue a public statement of their faith and order in the Savoy Declaration of Faith and Order (1658).[41] This emerged from a relatively brief conference of 200 representatives of around 120 Congregational Churches who met at the Savoy Palace on 29 September 1658.[42] This assembly was the first national gathering of Congregationalists, although local churches had numerous contacts for mutual support. They shared advice, for example, on the drafting of local church covenants; they regularly sent representatives to each others' churches on the occasion of the ordination of pastors, and communicated on the transfer of members.

---

[39] John Brinsley, *The Sacred Ordinance of Ordination by the Imposition of the Hands of the Presbytery* (1656), quoted by G F Nuttall, *Visible Saints,* (Oxford: 1957) p. 92.

[40] Thomas Hooker, *A Survey of the Summe of Church Discipline*, Part II. 74 (1648), quoted by G F Nuttall, op. cit. p. 93.

[41] The text of the Savoy Declaration may be found in *Stating the Gospel*, ed D M Thompson, (Edinburgh T & T Clark, 1990) pp. 61-117.

[42] The Savoy Palace housed various court officers and was a rendez-vous for Dissenters and Continental Protestants.

The Declaration of Faith was prepared in eleven days whereas the Westminster Confession had taken over five years. Its later influence in England was much less than in America. Watts[43] suggests that the Savoy Declaration was inspired more by the conservative Congregationalism of the Low Countries and Massachusetts than the Independent radical tradition in England. The Declaration of Faith was modelled on the earlier Westminster Confession. The second section 'Of the Institution of Churches and the Order appointed in them by Jesus Christ', containing 30 propositions, indicates a different understanding of church order among Congregationalists of the Commonwealth, who had good reason to believe in 1658 that the Congregational way would become the dominant form of churchmanship in England. R W Dale[44] said of these propositions that 'They represent the results at which English Congregationalists had arrived after a hundred years of controversy'…'In its fulness and precision it is, perhaps, the most admirable statement of the ecclesiastical principles of English Congregationalism.'

Proposition IV affirmed the competence of the local church to order its affairs, stating that 'Christ has given to the gathered Churches all that Power and Authority which is in any way needful for their carrying on that Order in Worship and Discipline which he hath instituted for them to observe'. This competence extended to the appointment of church officers, as in Proposition VII: 'a particular Church, gathered and completed according to the mind of Christ, consists of Officers and Members: the Lord Christ having given to his called ones…Liberty and Power to choose Persons fitted by the Holy Ghost for that purpose, to be over them, and to minister to them in the Lord'. In Proposition IX these officers are defined are 'Pastors, Teachers, Elders and Deacons'. They are to be '…chosen thereunto by the common suffrage of the Church itself, and solemnly set apart by Fasting and Prayer with Imposition of Hands of the Eldership of that Church'. (Proposition XI) The imposition of hands firmly places Congregationalists within the mainstream of church tradition and practice, while affirming the Congregational principle that ordination is the action of the local church, gathered and empowered to act by the Holy Spirit. Lest the imposition of hands should appear too prescriptive, and its omission be deemed to invalidate the ordination, Proposition XII offers an escape clause in its affirmation that 'the Essence of this Call…consists in the Election of the Church, together with his acceptation of it, and separation by Fasting and Prayer; and those so chosen, though not set apart by Imposition of Hands, are rightly constituted ministers of Jesus Christ'. Proposition XV emphasises that the rite of ordination, when conducted by those already ordained, is not effective without the minister being elected and called to serve a particular congregation. 'Ordination alone without the Election or precedent consent of the Church, by those who formerly have been ordained by vertue of that Power they have received by their Ordination, doth not constitute any person a Church-Officer, or communicate Office-power unto him'.

The Savoy Declaration is uncompromising in its adherence to the Congregational principle of the competence of the local church. It recognises the importance of Synods and Councils, and their value in assisting the churches to deal with difficulties in matters of doctrine or practice. This is spelled out in Proposition XXVI: 'It is according to the minde of Christ, that many Churches holding communion together, do by their Messengers meet in a Synod or Councel, to consider and give their advice in, or about that matter in difference'. But they are not to be given power.

---

[43]   M R Watts, *The Dissenters*, (Oxford: 1978) p. 168.

[44]   R W Dale, *History of English Congregationalism*, (London: Hodder and Stoughton, 1907) p. 386.

'Howbeit these Synods so assembled are not entrusted with any Church-Power, properly so called, or with any Jurisdiction over the Churches themselves, to exercise any Censures, either over any Churches or Persons, or to impose their determinations on the Churches or Officers'. The Presbyterian concept of church courts, in ascending order of importance, was firmly rejected. 'There are not instituted by Christ any stated Synods in a fixed Combination of Churches, or their Officers in lesser or greater Assemblies; nor are there any Synods appointed by Christ in a way of Subordination to one another'. Presbyterian and Congregational practice were to be fundamentally different. In the Presbyterian tradition ministers were to be under the authority of presbytery, as the ordaining authority, while in the Congregational tradition ministers were responsible only to the church which had elected and called them.

The Savoy Declaration has been described as 'a relic of the greatest period of Congregational history; a high-tide mark on the sands of time'.[45] It brought to an end the age of confessional pronouncements which had begun in Germany in the sixteenth century and included, in England, the Thirty-Nine Articles and the Westminster Confession. The Savoy Declaration was a public and political document as well as a statement of ecclesiastical principles. It was issued at a time when the Independents were prominent on the political stage and were making their bid to become the national Church. These hopes were dashed by the restoration two years later of the Stuart monarchy and the severe persecution of Dissenters which ensued. The Declaration's public influence waned, though its influence upon English Dissenters and American Congregationalists remained considerable. No new formulations of faith and church order would emerge from the Dissenting tradition for nearly two hundred years because there was no body competent or authorised to speak on its behalf.

A New Declaration

Nearly two centuries passed before the Congregationalists restated their principles in a new Declaration - the Declaration of the Faith, Church Order, and Discipline of the Congregational or Independent Dissenters which was first published in 1833.

The Declaration was drawn up to mark the inauguration in the previous year of the first national Association of Congregationalists in England and Wales.[46] Proposals for the formation of a national association of Congregational Churches had been under discussion since 1806 when the London Board of Congregational Ministers had passed a resolution to form a national Union. The arguments in its favour were that it would strengthen the churches in their mission by building chapels, providing financial aid towards the stipends of impoverished churches, and to evangelise neglected villages. Some of these tasks were already being undertaken by recently formed County Unions. Under the influence of the Evangelical Revival, there was a growing feeling in some quarters that the Congregationalists or Independent Dissenters now required a stronger denominational

---

[45] A G Matthews (ed) *The Savoy Declaration of Faith and Order 1658,* (London: Independent Press, 1959) p. 39.

[46] The Declaration was re-published in successive editions of the Congregational Year Book throughout the 19th and into the 20th century. For a discussion of the formation of the Congregational Union, see R W Dale, *History of English Congregationalism,* (London: Hodder and Stoughton, 1907) pp. 686-98, and R Tudur Jones, *Congregationalism in England 1662-1962,* (London: Independent Press, 1962) pp. 242-44.

identity. This initial Union soon collapsed, having failed to win general support, and it was not until 1829 that the proposal was revived. A provisional committee was established in 1830 to consider the formation of a General Union of Congregational Ministers and Churches; this was agreed in the following year and the Union was formally constituted in 1832. There was predictably vociferous opposition from those who feared that the proposed Union would threaten the equality of ministers and the independence of local churches. The larger view prevailed that the Union was needed to overcome the continued isolation of the Independent Churches which hindered their evangelistic efforts and the propagation of their ecclesiastical principles. The Declaration of 1833 was intended to re-assert those principles.

R W Dale[47] comments that this Declaration 'was not a creed to be subscribed to by ministers and Churches as a condition of membership of the Union. It was not even a confession of the belief of the ministers and delegates who adopted it. It was simply a statement "for general information" of "what is commonly believed" among Congregationalists'. It was descriptive rather than prescriptive, and the product of preachers rather than theologians. While lacking all authority, the value of the Declaration lies in the light it throws on contemporary Congregational belief and practice in the middle decades of the 19th century.

Under the Section 'Principles of Church Order and Discipline', paragraph 4 affirms the scriptural principle, as they understood it, that 'the New Testament authorises every Christian Church to elect its own Officers, to manage all its own affairs, and to stand independent of, and irresponsible to, all authority, saving that only of the Supreme and Divine Head of the Church, the Lord Jesus Christ'. According to paragraph 4 'bishops, or pastors and the deacons, are the only officers placed by the apostles over individual churches', and that these exercise their ministry 'subject, however, to the approbation of the church'.

The importance of the ministry is affirmed in paragraph XI. 'It is the privilege and duty of every church to call forth such of its members as may appear to be qualified by the Holy Spirit to sustain the office of the ministry.' The churches are encouraged to act together to maintain an adequate degree of learning as one of their especial cares, in order that 'the cause of the Gospel may be both honourably sustained and constantly promoted'.

Paragraph XII restates the Congregational conviction that church officers, 'whether bishops or deacons, should be chosen by the free voice of the church'. They are to be set apart to the duties of their office by 'special prayer, and by solemn designation'. Imposition of hands 'by those already in office' is noted as the 'custom of most of the churches'. The former emphasis on fasting has disappeared. Nor is the word ordination used in this paragraph or elsewhere in the Declaration. The solemn setting apart is described instead as 'dedication to the duties of their office'. It is difficult not to form the impression that a significant change in the understanding of ordination has taken place. However this may be to place too great a weight on the theological importance of the Declaration. R W Dale described it as the work of those who 'were for the most part popular preachers, children of the Revival', who lacked the leisure for deep research and cared little for the theological subtleties which had exercised their forbears.[48] A century later R Tudur Jones, unimpressed by the Declaration,

---

[47]   op. cit. p. 701.
[48]   op. cit. p. 704.

dismissed it as 'a disappointing document that suggests a bureaucratic memorandum passed down for information rather than a distillation in words of an august faith'.[49] For all its limitations, the Declaration was the best the newly-formed Congregational Union could offer. It was destined to last well into the next century until the emerging ecumenical movement required Congregationalists to undertake the preparation of new formulations of their faith and order.

---

[49]   R Tudur Jones, op. cit. p. 243.

Chapter Two

Questioning the Traditions

- A Call to Christian Unity

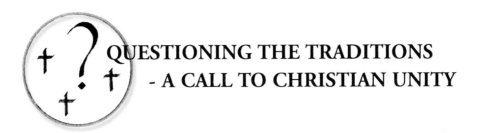

QUESTIONING THE TRADITIONS
- A CALL TO CHRISTIAN UNITY

The Great War (1914-1918) had exploded the belief in universal progress which had dominated the early years of the century. The shared sufferings of war had brought people together. The huge loss of young lives, to whom war memorials were being erected in every village, town and city, bore vivid witness to those sufferings. They also raised uncomfortable questions concerning the justice, mercy and love of God, which the churches were hard-pressed to answer. The separation of churches, which had seemed almost a matter of pride, because based on powerful conviction, now began to appear shameful and to impede the Church's witness to its Gospel of peace and reconciliation. As a result the churches became more sensitive to public criticism. A new vision was needed of the visible unity of the whole Church. Great efforts of imagination and sacrifice would be required to turn vision into reality.

The Lambeth Conference 1920

The Lambeth Conference 1920, which brought together the Archbishops and Bishops of that part of the Holy Catholic Church which was in communion with the Church of England, boldly appealed for the reunion of Christendom. In their Encyclical Letter 'To the Faithful in Christ Jesus'[1] they underlined the theme of Fellowship which had dominated the Conference. 'The secret of life', they said, 'is fellowship'. Reflecting on the recent war, they declared that 'Men never prized the universal fellowship of mankind as they did when the Great War had for a time destroyed it'. That destructive war, however, had also created new fellowship, and had brought to greater prominence fellowships such as the trade unions and other societies, which had come into existence before the war and were now seen by many as signs of hope for the post-war era.

The message of the Church is addressed to a world craving fellowship with God and with men. 'Fellowship with God', they said, 'is the indispensable condition of human fellowship'. The Church is itself a fellowship which has been called into being by God and is sustained by the Holy Spirit. The Church's object is to 'win over the whole human family to that fellowship (in God) by which alone it can attain to the fulness of life'. In order to pursue this object, the church must itself offer a pattern of fellowship. The divisions of the Church both weakened and hindered the Church in its mission. 'The weakness of the church in the world today', they declared, 'is not surprising when we consider how the bands of its own fellowship are loosened and broken… But the war and its horrors, waged as it was between so-called Christian nations, drove home the truth with the shock of a sudden awakening.'

---

[1]   Encyclical Letter, *To The Faithful in Christ Jesus*, (London: SPCK, 1920)

One of the immediate effects of the recent war had been to sharpen this awareness which had been dawning in Christian consciousness before the war. The birth of national churches on the Mission Field had begun to reveal the need for new structures to embody fellowship. The European conflict had brought it home 'with the shock of a sudden awakening', so that what had earlier seemed a desirable and even laudable dream had now become 'an imperative necessity'.

Lambeth 1920 took place therefore when a 'great wind was blowing over the whole earth'. Reunion dominated the conference and its outcome was an appeal for a new approach to reunion. The starting point was that unity already existed and did not have to be created. In a profound and moving statement the Encyclical declared that 'It is in God, who is the perfection of unity, the one Father, the one Lord, the one Spirit, who gives life to the one Body.' This one Body also exists - 'It needs not to be made, nor to be remade, but to become organic and visible.' The fellowship of members of the one Body also exists -'It is the work of God, not of man. We have only to discover it, and to set free its activities.'

The newness of the approach lay in the intention not to judge schemes of reunion on their success in meeting the claims of competing communions, nor of defining what might be the essential measure of uniformity which would be required, nor of reducing the rich variety of the different communions to a dull uniformity, but rather 'using their diversity so that the church can become all things to all men'. They must mean more, however, than joining 'in some vague federation'. The goal must be nothing less than 'one visible society whose members are bound together by the ties of a common faith, common sacraments, and a common ministry. It is towards this ideal of a unity and truly Catholic Church that we must all set our minds.' The vision of the Lambeth Conference was nothing less than the visible realisation of a universal fellowship 'in full and free activity'.

An Appeal To All Christian People

How was this vision of such a universal fellowship to be achieved? The Conference, in its Appeal to All Christian People,[2] offered a fourfold basis for achieving the goal by inviting the separated churches to offer their 'whole-hearted acceptance' of:

1. The Holy Scriptures 'as the record of God's revelation of himself to man'.
2. The Creed 'commonly called Nicene, as the sufficient statement of the Christian faith, and either it or the Apostles' Creed as the baptismal confession of belief.
3. The 'divinely instituted sacraments of Baptism and the Holy Communion, as expressing for all the corporate life of the whole fellowship in and with Christ'.
4. 'a ministry acknowledged by every part of the Church as possessing not only the inward call of the Spirit, but also the commission of Christ and the authority of the whole Body'.

This fourfold basis was a modification of the famous 'Lambeth Quadrilateral' which had been adopted by the Lambeth Conference 1888 to provide 'a basis on which approach may, under God's blessing, be made towards Home Reunion'.

---

[2] See G K A Bell (ed) *Documents on Christian Unity 1920-4*, (Oxford: 1924) pp. 1-5.

The Appeal continued with a claim that the Episcopate, rooted as it was in history and experience, was the one means of providing such a ministry. 'We would urge that it is now and will prove to be in the future the best instrument for maintaining the unity and continuity of the Church.' But recognising that this was a sensitive, and potentially divisive issue for the non-episcopal churches, the Appeal offered these communions an assurance that their ministries had been 'manifestly blessed and owned by the Holy Spirit as effective means of grace'. They recognised also that the office of Bishop needed to be exercised in a representative and constitutional manner, and should 'more truly express all that ought to be involved for the life of the Christian Family in the title of Father-in-God'. They generously offered that the Bishops and clergy would declare themselves ready to accept from the non-episcopal communions 'a form of commission or recognition which would commend (their) ministry to their congregations, as having its place in the one family life'. They expressed the hope that the same motive would lead non-episcopal ministers to 'accept a commission through episcopal ordination, as obtaining for them a ministry throughout the whole fellowship'.

Anticipating that this would raise the issue of re-ordination, the Appeal made it clear that their intention was that non-episcopal ministers should not be asked to repudiate their past ministry. 'God forbid that any man should repudiate a past experience rich in spiritual blessings for himself and others.' This would be to dishonour the Holy Spirit 'whose call led to our several ministries, and whose power enabled us to perform them'. What the Appeal envisaged was a 'new call to wider service in a reunited church'.

Nor was it the intention that one church, for example, a non-episcopal communion, should become absorbed in another. It was rather that 'all should unite in a new and great endeavour to recover and to manifest to the world the unity of the Body of Christ for which He prayed'.

A Congregationalist Response

In August 1920, their work completed, the bishops and archbishops of the Anglican Communion returned to their dioceses to await the response of the Churches to their Appeal. The first assembly of major importance following Lambeth was the Autumn Assembly of the Congregational Union of England and Wales, which met at Southampton from 27 September to 1 October 1920. The Chairman of the Union for that year, the Revd Dr A E Garvie, Principal of New College, London, had prepared his chairman's address on 'The Christian Church and the Social Problem' before the issue of the Lambeth Appeal. The Appeal could not be ignored, but neither was Garvie empowered to make more than a personal statement. Accordingly he added a few sentences to his address which he made into a new peroration:

> We welcome that Appeal heartily, as we too desire that the Church of Christ should make its unity of spirit manifest to the world. We recognise with gratitude to God, whose Spirit is leading His Church towards this goal, the advance in thought and feeling and aim of the Anglican Church towards the other Christian Churches, and shall meet that advance with all brotherly affection. We pledge ourselves to give serious, prayerful,

unprejudiced consideration to the definite proposals made, on which it would be premature to pass final judgment. We shall use every opportunity for fellowship and co-operation with our Anglican brethren. We pray that God by His spirit may so guide all our counsels, as we believe He has been guiding them, that at last we and they shall be guided in the unity of that same Spirit to realise without any hindrance or limitation our common membership in the one body of Christ, the fulfilment of Him that fulfilleth all in all to the glory of God, that God may be all in all.[3]

At the same Assembly a more robust contribution was made in a paper read by Dr A R Henderson, who was about to become Principal of Paton College, Nottingham, on the title 'The Lambeth Appeal and the Congregational Ministry'.[4] He welcomed the Lambeth overture and the spirit which informed the Appeal. Nonconformists could rejoice that they were no longer treated as schismatics who must cut their connection with the past and enter the one true Church. Episcopacy, however, even as commended in the Lambeth Appeal, remained an obstacle. 'Though no one was asked to repudiate his past ministry, their order could only be made valid with the larger church by re-ordination at the hands of a Bishop.' He averred that 'as to re-ordination...he would rather be ordained by a Presbyterian Synod than by an Episcopal Bishop'. Henderson envisaged the possibility of corporate unity between the Church of England and all the Evangelical Free Churches of England, America, Canada, Australia and other English-speaking countries. It would preserve the best elements of Episcopalianism, Presbyterianism and Congregationalism. Bishops would preside over Presbytery, and Presbytery would leave congregations to manage their own spiritual affairs. The price of such a corporate unity would have to be, in his view, that Anglicans should forgo their desire for union with the Roman Catholic and Eastern Churches. He believed that the Free Churches were ready for such an organic union as he had sketched, and 'it would be a step forward towards the ultimate goal of the one Church of Jesus Christ'.

The Assembly contented itself with a resolution, moved by the Revd Dr J D Jones, minister of Richmond Hill Congregational Church, Bournemouth, and carried unanimously, which gave a cautious welcome to the Lambeth proposals while pointing out their potential difficulties:

> That this Assembly of the CUEW, without recording any final judgement upon the definite proposals contained in the pronouncement of the Anglican Episcopate on the matter of Reunion, desires to express its appreciation of the brotherly and ecumenical spirit which breathes through the Appeal. It recognises in the growing desire for unity the working of the Spirit of God. It joins earnestly in the prayer that the unity which already exists among all who believe in the same Lord may become increasingly manifest to the world without. It declares itself ready to participate in every movement to promote religious intercourse amongst the various branches of Christ's Church, and it is especially desirous that all those who belong to the one Lord should be able to gather together at His table without restrictions or doubtfulness of mind. It thinks well, however, even at this stage, frankly to declare that there are proposals in the Appeal which, as at present understood, seem to set great difficulties in the way of that closer

---

[3] *The Congregational Year Book 1921*, p. 91.

[4] *The Christian World*, 7 October 1920. A R Henderson had been minister at Queen Street Congregational Church, Wolverhampton, since 1919, and was Principal of The Congregational Institute (later Paton College), Nottingham, 1921-37.

fellowship which it desires, difficulties which reach down to fundamental matters of faith, inasmuch as conditions are suggested to which this Assembly of Congregationalists, out of loyalty not simply to the history and traditions of the Congregational Churches, but to the Gospel entrusted to them, cannot agree.[5]

It is clear that the Congregationalists in 1920 took a less urgent view of the imperative of Christian unity than the Bishops who assembled at Lambeth. In proposing the above resolution to Assembly, Dr Jones commented on Dr Henderson's paper that he 'was not sure that he shared Mr Henderson's belief that a corporate union would be a good thing'.

The Congregationalists next met in Assembly in May 1921 under the chairmanship of the Revd A J Viner.[6] A section of his Chairman's Address included reflections on the Lambeth Appeal. He welcomed the 'courteous tone and brotherly spirit which pervades the appeal', and expressed satisfaction that it had stressed 'fellowship' rather than 'organisation'. 'Essential and effective unity amongst men must be spiritual and vital rather than institutional.' He saw difficulties arising from the Congregationalist understanding of the nature of the Christian Church. This emphasised the competence of the locally gathered fellowship 'to discharge for themselves all the functions, both priestly and prophetic, of their common Church life'. According to Congregational doctrine, the local church is empowered to select from among its members men and women to preach the word or administer the sacraments. Appointment by the local church entitles them to act. Ordination therefore 'is not a rite that makes a ministry valid and confers authority. It is rather a rite which recognises an authority resident in the Church and delegated by it to one who is to act with the Church and for it'. The Congregationalist conception of the Church, and whether this could be taken into the proposed fellowship, was a more important issue than the matter of re-ordination. The questions Congregationalists put to the proposals included, for example, whether credal tests, as in the Nicene or Apostles' creeds, would be a condition of membership. Would the proposed united church be the established church of the state? Would the church maintain a 'catholic' view of membership which recognised members of the Society of Friends and the Salvation Army as true members of the Church of Jesus Christ? Would it still be possible for any member to be appointed 'to serve the Church either in the pulpit or from the altar'? He insisted that these were not 'captious questions' but reached to the heart of what Congregationalists believed. But because of those beliefs, the Congregationalists were poised to offer the hand of welcome to all fellow Christians. 'We shall be glad to hear the clergy of the Episcopal Church speak their message from our pulpits, we shall delight to have them preside at the Lord's Table in our Churches. Our doors stand wide open. We are ready, more than ready, on terms of complete equality, for the fullest reciprocity.'

This Assembly effectively delivered the *coup de grace* to the Lambeth Appeal in its resolution of 10 May 1921.[7] There was fulsome acknowledgement of the spirit which had moved the Archbishops and Bishops to issue their Appeal. The Assembly insisted on its 'desire for a closer

---

[5]   *The Congregational Year Book 1921*, p. 52.

[6]   The Revd A J Viner served as Secretary to the Lancashire Congregational Union from 1909 to 1919 when he was appointed to the North-West Province as one of the first Moderators of the CUEW. He died in office during his year as Chairman of the CUEW.

[7]   Bell, op. cit. pp. 105-7.

fellowship among Christ's people'. They warmed to the emphasis on 'fellowship' – a word which could not fail to touch a chord in the Congregationalist breast. They embraced the vision of unity which was embodied in the Lambeth Appeal – a vision 'which we too greet and to which we would not be disobedient'. There were fervent promises of their intention to labour together for the goal of Christian unity and to keep open the door of conference and negotiation. But the cost of the Lambeth proposals was too high. Union, for Congregationalists, would only be possible on the basis of 'a frank acknowledgement of the full validity of one another's ministries', and should be achieved through intercommunion and the interchange of pulpits. Their second difficulty was that the Assembly could not accept 'a formulated creed' as a condition of union. 'We hold firmly and loyally the faith once for all delivered to the saints, but we believe that under the guidance of the Spirit, the expression of that faith may and must vary from age to age.' That conviction also led to the rejection of Lambeth's insistence on the necessity of the Episcopate. 'Our belief in that same freedom of the Spirit...renders it impossible for us to assent to any form of church establishment interfering as we believe it does with the Church's full spiritual liberty.'

The Resolution concluded with high-sounding language, affirming the Assembly's prayerful desire to be of one heart and one soul with their fellow-Christians, and united in one holy bond of truth and peace. This could not however conceal the fact that, although a final decision had not yet been taken, the Congregationalists were moving politely but unambiguously towards rejecting the Lambeth Appeal.

The Presbyterian Response to Lambeth

The Presbyterian Church of England cordially welcomed the Appeal 'with a deep sense of the greatness and of the urgency of the issues'. It declared its willingness to enter into conversations with the Church of England on the whole question of Reunion. Its Assembly on 5 May 1921[8] gave thanks to God that Christian people were being drawn together in the unity of the Spirit and of the Body of Christ. The Assembly associated itself with the Provisional Statement which had been issued under the auspices of the Federal Council of Evangelical Free Churches.[9] They agreed to be represented on the Joint Conference which had been established to explore the issues raised by the Appeal. Unlike the Congregational Assembly which met two weeks later, they offered at this stage no critical comments on the Lambeth proposals. Both Assemblies however referred with appreciation to the crucial statement on the Lambeth Appeal which had been issued by the Federal Council of Evangelical Free Churches of England and the National Free Church Council, and associated themselves with the positions set out in that statement.[10] It is significant that the joint committee which prepared this response to Lambeth was chaired by a Congregationalist, Dr W B Selbie, and that the convener of the drafting sub-committee was the Presbyterian, Dr P Carnegie Simpson.

---

[8]   Bell, *Documents on Christian Unity 1920-24*, p. 104.
[9]   Bell, op. cit. p. 118.
[10]   ibid. pp. 120-41, May 1921.

A Crucial Response from the Free Churches Federal Council

The Federal Council recognised that it was not empowered to make a reply to the Lambeth Appeal on behalf of the Free Churches, since that could be done only by the churches to which the Appeal was addressed. The Federal Council's response had therefore a more limited purpose which was to elucidate the proposals rather than to offer direct criticism. The report welcomed and identified with the underlying concern for 'fellowship' which had inspired the Appeal. 'We believe that Christian people today are earnestly seeking more and closer Christian fellowship.' For the Free Churches sharing in Holy Communion represented 'the supreme expression of Christian fellowship'. They were convinced that 'our religious fellowship will never be expressed as Christ means it to be till we meet in this most hallowed intercourse'.

The Report identified three important elements in the Lambeth proposals which required detailed examination. The first of these was the Recognition of Churches. The Free Churches needed to be satisfied that, if they separately entered into communion with the Anglican Church, they would not lose fellowship with any Christian communions with whom they already enjoyed fellowship. It was hardly to be expected that all, or even the greater part of non-episcopal Christendom would be included in the Lambeth scheme of episcopacy, non-episcopal communions in Scotland and the United States of America offering obvious examples. Congregationalists, for example, who already enjoyed table fellowship with Baptists, Methodists, Presbyterians and others, would need to be sure that this table fellowship would continue if they accepted the Lambeth proposals, and that they would not find that some or all of these communions had rejected them. 'If we should not continue to be in fellowship with them, we should be committing schism – and a treacherous kind of schism – in the very act of union.'[11] It was also essential for the non-episcopal communions to know whether they would be recognised by the Anglican communion 'as corporate parts of the Church of Christ', and their ministries 'as ministries of Christ's Word and Sacraments'. Lambeth appeared to offer this, but it needed to be made clear beyond doubt.

The second element concerned Episcopal Ordination. Episcopacy as such presented no insuperable problem – a surprising statement given the known attitudes to episcopacy in some member churches of the Federal Council. The Report stated the view that 'no one form of church polity has been prescribed by the Lord'. The Free Churches could therefore have an open mind towards episcopal order, while resisting any form of polity which claimed to be 'an exclusive channel of grace'. The proposal however to make the episcopal ordination of ministers who had been non-episcopally ordained could not be acceptable to the Free Church. Reference was made in the Report to the Second Mansfield Conference of 1920[12] which had declared that any mutual authorisation of ministers was to be 'not re-ordination'. This declaration had no authority but as it had been signed by a representative number of Free Churchmen (as well as by many Anglicans), it might be taken as representing the Free Church view. It had followed a conference of the previous year ('The First Mansfield Conference' January 1919) which had recognised the place

---

[11]   ibid. p. 131.

[12]   The Mansfield Conferences of 1919 and 1920, held at Mansfield College, Oxford, brought together a large group of Anglican and Free Church representatives to prepare for the Lambeth Conference in 1920. See *Documents Bearing on the Problems of Christian Unity and Fellowship 1916-1920*, (London: SPCK, 1920), pp. 54-6 and 81-6.

which a reformed Episcopacy should hold in the ultimate Constitution of the Reunited Church, but had also envisaged that such a Constitution would fully conserve 'the essential values of the other historical types of Church Polity, Presbyterian, Congregational and Methodist'. The obligation therefore rested on those who urged episcopal ordination in its Anglican form as a *sine qua non* of any scheme of reunion to bring forward exceptionally cogent grounds for insisting on this if they were to win the support of the Free Churches. Greater clarity was needed on the practical intention of the phrase 'a commission through episcopal ordination' by which non-episcopally ordained ministers would be authorised to minister within the Church of England. For the Free Churches to accept it, its meaning would have to be made unambiguously clear.

The third element was the Spiritual Freedom of the Church of Christ. The Free Churches believed as a matter of principle that 'the Church must be free in matters of religious faith and moral duty to learn of and to obey the Lord, who is still living and present in her midst'. The Lambeth Appeal posed questions concerning this freedom in two particular areas, the relation of the Church to the Creeds, and the relation of the Church to the State. The first of these presented little difficulty, since the reunited Church would clearly require some common declaration of faith. They were ready to reverence the traditions of the past as expressed, for example, in the Nicene Creed, while securing the right to formulate new expressions of faith in response to the leading of the Holy Spirit. The other – the relation of Church to State – might present greater difficulty. At this stage the Free Churches were content merely to say that 'Free Churchmen cannot be asked to consent that the civil power – which, within its own sphere, is called to be the servant of God – has any authority over the spiritual affairs of the Church; or, further, to accept any position which would involve injustice or violate the rights of conscience.'

The Report concluded with a powerful identification of the Free Churches with the vision of the Lambeth Appeal. They also believed with the Archbishops and Bishops in 'a Church genuinely Catholic, loyal to all truth, and gathering into its fellowship all who profess and call themselves Christians, within whose visible unity all the treasures of faith and order, bequeathed as a heritage of the past to the present, shall be possessed in common and made serviceable to the whole Body of Christ'. From their experience they urged the value of the 'interchange of pulpits' as a means by which the various communions of the church might discover the unity in the Gospel which they already possessed. This had also led them to value 'inter-communion' as 'that supreme expression and seal of the Gospel in the Sacrament which manifests the unity of Christians with one another as well as their oneness in him.' Citing the experience of the foreign mission fields, where new life and power had been experienced as the outcome of Christian fellowship, unity must also be expressed in unity of service for the Kingdom of God at home and abroad. The Report ended with an appeal that 'our Anglican brethren' should 'welcome and promote closer spiritual fellowship among the churches, especially through the pulpit, at the Communion Table, and in the work of the Kingdom'.

The overall temper of the response by the Federal Council was thus more welcoming than that of the Congregational Union of England and Wales. This may have reflected the influence of W B Selbie, chairman of the Joint Committee, and P Carnegie Simpson, convener of the drafting sub-committee. The Council's responsibility was restricted to making comments on the Lambeth proposals; it was empowered neither to take decisions nor even to bring specific recommendations to its member churches on how they might respond to the Appeal. Their Report had long-term value in identifying the major issues which the churches would need to address, especially those concerned with ministry and ordination, if the Lambeth vision, which they claimed to share, was to be embodied in a reunited Church.

An Anglican View of the Free Church Ministry – 'Spiritual Efficacy' and 'Due Authority'

The Church of England's response to these concerns was set out in a second Memorandum issued in June 1925 on the status of the Existing Free Church Ministry. This drew a distinction between 'spiritual efficacy' and 'due authority'. The spiritual efficacy of the Free Church ministries was not in doubt, but this did not signify that they possessed due authority. They proposed therefore that these ministries should be authorised by a form of 'Ordination *sub conditione*'. What was proposed was an act of episcopal ordination which would be prefaced and governed by a condition expressed in some such words as 'If thou art not already ordained'. From the Anglican side this appeared to resolve any residual doubts as to the authorisation of existing Free Church ministries. 'It would recognise', they said, 'that there is a doubt on one side; it would not require or involve any acknowledgement of the validity of the doubt from the other side'. The person receiving conditional ordination would be recognising the existence of a doubt in the mind of the ordaining authority without necessarily accepting its validity.[13]

The Free Church members of the Joint Conference immediately responded to this ingenious proposal by indicating they thought it unlikely that it would find acceptance among the Free Churches. Their doubts were confirmed by resolutions of the Federal Council's annual assembly held in September 1925. The wording of the crucial resolution was polite but emphatic. On the question of authorisation, 'the Anglican representatives still seem inclined …to insist that Free Church ministers accept ordination – at least in the form known as *sub conditione* – at episcopal hands. The Council agreed with the earlier impression of their Free Church representatives that there was, in their view, little or no prospect of this being accepted by any non-episcopal Church. The Council agreed with this view and went on to say that 'it would deeply regret if the fortunes of the Lambeth Appeal, so far as non-episcopal Christendom is concerned, were finally bound up with a proposal so unconvincing and so unpromising as that of requiring the ordination to the ministry of Christ's Word and Sacraments in the Church of men explicitly acknowledged to be in that very ministry. The question of authorisation must be answered by some other means than ordination'. They did not mean that negotiations should be discontinued forthwith. Instead the Council declared its interest in exploring an alternative option of a mutual 'commission' which would unambiguously be not an ordination.[14]

---

[13]   G K A Bell (ed), *Documents on Christian Unity, Second Series, (1924-30)* (Oxford: 1930) p. 121.
[14]   ibid. p. 126.

The End of the Lambeth Journey

It was in the light of this Report, and following the completion of a series of official conferences which had arisen out of the Lambeth Appeal, that final responses were given to the proposals by the Congregational Union and the Presbyterian Church of England.

The Assembly of the Congregational Union in May 1927,[15] in a unanimous reply to the Lambeth proposals, confirmed its longing for closer Christian unity, though with the qualification that it did not regard the existence of separate Churches as necessarily contrary to the mind of Christ. Also, while fruitful fellowship among the Churches required some agreement on the fundamentals of the faith, they did not agree that imposed creeds or formularies were the means by which this might be secured. The most significant section of the reply concerned the ministry.

> We recognise that the ministry of any united Church must be a ministry duly authorised by the whole Church through its representatives. We agree that this authorisation should take the form of ordination – as the recognition and ratification of the call of God to the ministry, and as the commissioning of the man so called, after due preparation, to work in a particular sphere. We cannot, however, agree that episcopal ordination should be essential to the exercise of the ministry in any united Church of which we as Congregationalists are to form part. The theory that only through the laying on of a bishop's hands can a ministry be made valid runs counter to our deepest convictions. If the office of bishop is to be retained in any united Church, we agree that it should be made purely elective and representative. We wish, moreover, that it were possible to avoid the use of this historic term, which, just because it is historic, cannot fail to suggest and perpetuate ideas as to authority and the transmission of grace from which we entirely dissociate ourselves.

Congregationalists did not wish to close the door on further discussions. 'We, too,' they continued, 'long for a deeper understanding, a closer sympathy, and a wider fellowship, especially in the solemn acts of worship, between all branches of the now divided Church. We therefore plead for closer co-operation along the lines of the Lambeth Appeal and in the spirit which it breathes'. Fine words indeed, but, apart from this general plea, there was not much encouragement for those who shared the Lambeth vision for the visible unity of the whole Church.

The Presbyterian General Assembly merely resolved on 5th May 1926 to instruct its representatives on the Federal Council to draw up 'a suitable letter' recalling the welcome which it had given to the Lambeth Appeal and in general associating the Presbyterian Church with the conclusions which had been reached by the Free Church Federal Council.[16] They assured the Anglican Church of their continued desire 'to do all that shall draw the people of Christ closer together in the unity which He designs for His Church'.

The real difficulty with the Lambeth proposals was the ambiguity which had crept into discussions on the status of existing Free Church ministries. The proposal, from the Anglican side, that Free Church ministers should 'receive their commission to minister to the whole fellowship through

---

[15] ibid. pp. 113-15.
[16] G K A Bell (ed) *Documents on Christian Unity, Second Series*, pp. 107-8.

episcopal ordination' was not in harmony with the expressed belief of the Lambeth Conference that these ministries 'possess spiritual reality' and have been 'manifestly blessed and owned by the Holy Spirit as effective means of grace'. Congregationalists were ready for their ministers to participate in solemn acts of mutual recognition, but not if these could be interpreted as any form of re-ordination.

The New Ecumenical Movement – Edinburgh 1910 and Lausanne 1927

The Lambeth Appeal was itself launched in the wider context of the newly emerging modern ecumenical movement which was to dominate church relationships throughout the 20th century. While 'Lambeth' had taken as its starting point the Great War and its aftermath, other factors had also been at work. These included the Student Christian Movement, which had developed as an interdenominational movement in the later years of the previous century. Its influence world-wide upon the movement towards Christian unity was immense. A second significant factor was the expansion of the Church in the 19th century through the work of the missionary societies. As the century turned, the evangelisation of the whole world did not seem an impossible dream. It was however an anomaly that new Christians should enter into denominational allegiances, not so much by conviction of their rightness as the prior agreement of Protestant missionary societies not to compete with one another but to allocate particular regions for missionary activity to each society. The London Missionary Society, founded as an interdenominational society in 1795, determined not to favour any particular form of church order and was content to leave new converts to take their own decisions about the form of church government they were to adopt.[17] Those who framed the Constitution were not indifferent to church order and their Fundamental Principle firmly implied that church order was dependent upon the continuing guidance of the Holy Spirit. A third and closely related factor was the work of the Bible Societies with their emphasis upon interdenominational co-operation.

The starting-point of the modern ecumenical movement was the convening by John Raleigh Mott[18] of the committee which arranged the first International Missionary Conference at Edinburgh in 1910. His watchword was 'The Evangelisation of the World in our Generation'. Important offshoots of the Edinburgh Conference were the Universal Christian Conference on Life and Work (1925) which explored the application of Christianity to social, economic and political life, and the Faith and Order Movement which held its first World Conference at Lausanne in 1927.

---

[17] The Plan and Constitution of the London Missionary Society contained the declaration: 'As the union of Christians of various denominations in carrying on this great work is a most desirable object, so, to prevent, if possible, any cause of future dissension, it is declared to be a *fundamental principle of The Missionary Society* that its design is not to send Presbyterianism, Independency, Episcopacy, or any other form of Church Order and Government (about which there may be difference of opinion among serious persons), but the glorious Gospel of the blessed God, to the heathen; and that it shall be left (as it ought to be left) to the minds of the persons whom God may call into the fellowship of His Son from among them to assume for themselves such form of Church Government as to them shall appear most agreeable to the Word of God. (N Goodall, *A History of the London Missionary Society 1895-1945*, (London: OUP, 1954)

[18] John Raleigh Mott (1865-1955), founder and general secretary (1895) of the World Student Christian Federation. He was instrumental in the formation of the World Council of Churches and was elected Honorary President at the first meeting of the World Council of Churches in 1948.

In its section on the Ministry of the Church[19] the Lausanne Conference transmitted five propositions for consideration by the churches:

1. The ministry is a gift of God through Christ to his Church and is essential to the being and well-being of the Church.

2. The ministry is perpetually authorised and made effective through Christ and His Spirit.

3. The purpose of the ministry is to impart to men the saving and sanctifying benefits of Christ through pastoral service, the preaching of the Gospel, and the administration of the sacraments, to be made effective by faith.

4. The ministry is entrusted with the government and discipline of the Church, in whole or in part.

5. Men gifted for the work of ministry, called by the Spirit and accepted by the Church, are commissioned through an act of ordination by prayer and the laying on of hands to exercise the functions of this ministry.

The Report recognised differences concerning 'the nature of the ministry, …the nature of ordination and of the grace conferred thereby, the function and authority of bishops, and the nature of the apostolic succession'. The first step towards the overcoming of these difficulties was the frank recognition of their existence. It was agreed that episcopal, presbyteral and congregational systems had been accepted for centuries by great communions of the Church. It was necessary therefore that 'these several elements must all, under conditions which require further study, have an appropriate place in the order of life of a reunited Church, and that each separate communion, recalling the abundant blessing of God vouchsafed to its ministry in the past, should gladly bring to the common life of the united Church its own spiritual treasures'[20]

It followed that 'the acceptance of any special form of ordination as the regular and orderly method of introduction into the ministry of the Church for the future should not be interpreted to imply the acceptance of any one particular theory of the origin, character or function of any office in the Church, or to involve the acceptance of any adverse judgment on the validity of ordination in those branches of the Church universal that believe themselves to have retained valid and apostolic Orders under other forms of ordination, or as disowning or discrediting a past or present ministry of the Word and Sacrament'.[21]

---

[19]   H N Bate (ed) *Faith and Order, Lausanne 1927*, (London: SCM Press, 1927) pp. 467-72.
[20]   ibid. p. 469.
[21]   ibid. p. 469.

Congregationalists and Lausanne

The reply from the Congregational Union of England and Wales[22] recognised that the Lausanne Conference had been a 'venture of faith' which had been fully justified. While in some quarters disappointment had been expressed at its results, the Congregational Union took the view that the aim of the Conference had not been to 'define the conditions for the organic union of the churches'. It was a starting-point rather than a goal. The Union promised its support to the Continuation Committee in 'whatever steps it may think wise and necessary…to advance the cause of Christian Unity'.

The Five Propositions in the Final Report of the Conference did not receive the Congregational Union's unqualified support. Their convictions were expressed in the following terms:

We hold that to the Church as a Society of believers no special ministry is strictly essential, but God by His Spirit gives gifts of ministry to its members, so fitting them for different functions like organs of a body (I Cor. xii, Eph. iv.11-12); and thus the special Ministry may be regarded as a gift of God to His Church, essential, not to its existence, but to its full well-being and effective activity in the world as an organised corporate society.

We recognise a ministry, called of God as well as equipped by Him, and recognised and accepted as such by the Spirit which dwells in the Church. It is thus perpetually authorised and made effective through Christ and His Spirit.

While agreeing generally with what is said of the purpose of the ministry, we do not regard any of its functions as in essence exclusively possessed by it.

The government and discipline of the Church we regard as entrusted to the Church, for which the ministry may be, and often is, authorised to act representatively.

Men gifted for the work of the ministry, called by the Spirit, and accepted by the Church, are generally set apart among us through an act of ordination by prayer, to exercise the function of the ministry: but the accompanying practice of the laying-on of hands, though quite usual among us, is not regarded as obligatory.

Congregationalists in the 1920s were prepared to accept that a special ministry of Word and Sacrament was of value to the Church and might be received as a gift of God; they could not however accept that this ministry was essential to the Church's existence. Ordination was regarded as an appropriate way of authorising those who were accepted for the ministry, but not that it should be obligatory. For some Congregationalists the rite suggested that ministers constituted a separate, and superior, order in the Church. Yet the Congregational Union agreed with the statement in the Lausanne Final Report that 'the provision of a ministry acknowledged in every part of the Church as possessing the sanction of the whole Church, is an urgent need'. It is difficult to envisage how this need might be met without agreement on the necessity and mode of ordination.

---

[22]   The Congregational Year Book 1931, pp. 86-91

On the matter of episcopacy the Congregational Union reiterated its response to the Lambeth Appeal. While recognising that the authorisation of ministers should be by ordination, they could not agree that episcopal ordination should be essential to the exercise of the ministry in any united Church of which they were a part. 'The theory that only through the laying-on of a Bishop's hands can a ministry be made valid runs counter to our deepest convictions.' The response to Lausanne however added an important footnote:

> There are some Congregationalists who, while not regarding the presence of a Bishop at an ordination as essential, would be prepared to agree that a Bishop, as the historic symbol of visible and organised unity in the one Church universal, and as a means of fostering that ideal, should be associated with presbyters and congregation in the act of ordination in the United Church.

It would be safe to assume that these were in a minority and that to the majority of Congregationalists the idea of episcopacy remained anathema. The footnote nevertheless indicates that some among the Congregationalists were prepared to accept that, if reunion were to happen, some form of episcopacy would have a recognised place within the united Church.

Presbyterians and Lausanne

The response of the Presbyterian Church of England was brief.[23] A study of the Lausanne Reports had revealed 'an underlying spiritual unity' which, with the conspicuous exception of the Roman Church, bound nearly all the Christian Churches to one another through their union with God in Christ. Differences of doctrine and practice, mainly to do with the subjects of Ministry and Sacraments, nevertheless ran very deep. These differences 'spring ultimately from different ways of apprehending such central ideas as Faith and Grace, if not ultimately from different conceptions of God'. The concept of Grace particularly required further exploration in preparation for the next Faith and Order Conference to be held in 1937.

A more substantial Presbyterian statement was given to the Lausanne Conference by the Moderator of the Presbyterian Church of England, Dr David Fyffe.[24] In an address he presented the perspective in which Presbyterians generally envisaged the Church's ministry. Four points were emphasised. First, it was fundamental to the Presbyterian perspective that the Christian community enjoys equality in spiritual rights. 'In such a community it would be impertinent, if not ludicrous, to introduce differences of rank of order.' Any member of the Christian community who held a particular office within it should regulate his conduct on the principle that 'we are members one of another'. Secondly, 'the possession of gifts was to be considered as a stewardship'. In his parables and teaching Jesus had taught the law of stewardship as an obligation each owed to God. Thirdly, authority in the Church rested under God in 'the common mind of the brethren'. The body of believers was the trustworthy vehicle for the Spirit of God. Presbyterians believed that all believers had equal access to truth and right judgement. The discernment of God's will was the

---

23   L Hodgson (ed) *Convictions*, (London: SCM Press 1934), pp. 91-92.
24   H N Bate (ed) op.cit. pp. 274-80.

responsibility of the members of God's household. Similarly, discernment of the presence of gifts for ministry or office in the Church rested with the company of believers. 'From the people of God rises the authority of the Church and the functions of the Church are by them delegated to those thus chosen.' In the fourth place, the unity of the Church is organic to the Gospel. All members of the body of Christ belong to the same family. Thus 'the objective of the Kingdom of God must be a corporate Society in which all are included and in which the spiritual bond transcends all other differences'. While there may be many Churches, there is only one Church.

In the remainder of his address, Fyffe outlined the Presbyterian understanding of ministry in the Church. From the New Testament Presbyterians derived two classes of officials – the deacon and the presbyter/bishop – with no clearly marked line of division between them. The chief functions of the elders or bishops were teaching, preaching and government. The deacons were responsible for the material concerns of the sacred community. Ordination to the Church's ministry followed the discernment of the gifts for ministry which had been bestowed. '...the gifts come first, and the ordination afterwards; there seems to be no evidence of particular gifts being bestowed upon brethren at ordination'. Those who ministered derived their authority from the Holy Spirit operating in the community of believers. It is this community which has to be satisfied that the person who feels an inward call to ministry is a person whom God has called and chosen. Once this local community is satisfied that the person is truly fitted to lead them in the things of God, ordination to the ministry and induction to the particular charge is conducted by the Presbytery on behalf of the whole Church. 'This practice of ordination, accompanied by the laying on of hands, the Presbyterian Church retains, accepting it as an ancient practice and also in the interests of Church unity'.

Churches of Christ and Lausanne

Churches of Christ had not been immediately involved in the response to the Lambeth Appeal; they had remained outside the National Free Church Council on the grounds that they were not a denomination. But they were becoming deeply committed to the developing ecumenical movement and took an active part in the Lausanne Conference of 1927. Three of their representatives – H E Tickle, J W Black and William Robinson – attended the preparatory conference in 1920. In that year William Robinson had become the first Principal of Overdale College; through his involvement he was to move Churches of Christ from the periphery to a more central role in ecumenical affairs.

In their reply to the Lausanne Report,[25] Churches of Christ declared themselves to be in general agreement with the five propositions. They heartily welcomed the first proposition that the ministry was God's gift to the Church and essential to its being and well-being. The second proposition seemed to them ambiguous and superfluous in view of what had been already stated. They recommended the deletion in the third proposition of the phrase 'to be made effective by faith' which they dismissed as 'irrelevant and meaningless' – presumably because only faith could make effective any of the benefits of Christ. To this proposition also they wished to add 'the conduct of worship' – a significant addition based upon the importance to their tradition of

---

[25]   L Hodgson, op. cit. pp. 70-1

corporate worship. They recommended that proposition four should be re-worded to read: 'The ministry is entrusted by God, through the Church, with the government and discipline of the Church in whole or in part.' This was to emphasise that the ministry flowed from God through the outpouring of the Holy Spirit upon the whole Church. In proposition five, dealing with ordination, they recommended the insertion of the word 'fasting' before 'prayer'.

Churches of Christ also welcomed the emphasis in the Report on other ministries – such as preaching, teaching and spiritual counsel – for the development of the Church's corporate spiritual life. 'We are certain', they commented, 'that the teaching and preaching of "lay" members of the Church, under the direction of the bishops, is a valuable element in the building up of Christ's Body, the Church, and in winning men and women to his service.' Nor was this all. They took the opportunity to restate their belief that, while the office of a minister in the Church of Christ is a sacred one, it should in no way be conditioned by a minister's professional occupation. 'The distinction between bishops and deacons on the one hand, and the members of the Church on the other, is not one which relates to the method by which a man earns his living. A bishop may be wholly or partially supported by the congregation, or he may, on the other hand, be not supported at all, and in this latter case he is no less a bishop.' Churches of Christ thus put down a marker that in the united Church there should be room for both a non-professional and professional ministry in all the orders of bishop, deacons and evangelist. It is significant to note that, while the goal of a united Church proved elusive, new forms of ministry, including non-stipendiary ministry, were later to emerge in many of the churches which participated in the Lausanne Conference.

Chapter Three

Congregational Traditions

CONGREGATIONAL TRADITIONS

A Fear of Sacerdotalism

The Congregationalists' responses to the Lambeth Appeal and the Lausanne Faith and Order Conference indicate that while they placed high value on the importance of the local church, and its competence and authority to act under the guidance of the Holy Spirit, their understanding of the ministry was correspondingly weak. Their principal historian, F J Powicke, had stated, for example, that 'ordination is, in essence, a church's recognition as its pastor of a man already called to its ministry; while on the minister's part, it marks in each case a solemn dedication of himself to the service of Christ in that particular church whose pastor he has promised to be.' Ordination had no significance beyond the call to serve in a particular place, and once that service was completed, it was as if the minister were no longer an ordained person. 'We are playing into the hands of sacerdotalism', wrote Powicke, 'if we encourage young men to seek or regard ordination as a means of making them "ministers" once for all and for good.'[1] The fear of sacerdotalism was widespread and had perhaps been strengthened by Lambeth's insistence on episcopacy as a pre-requisite for church unity. Congregationalism had been influenced by the Oxford Movement (1833-45), not least in the architecture of some of its places of worship, though it had rejected the sacerdotalism of the Anglo-Catholicism which stemmed from it. Few travelled with W E Orchard along the path to a New Catholicism.[2] As the Principal of Mansfield College, Oxford, with responsibility for the training of ministers, W B Selbie warned that 'the dangerous gulf which often appears between the ministry and the laity and leads to so much misunderstanding is generally due to the segregation of theological students during their training, and to the consequent creation of a class and professional feeling in the ministry.'[3] But it was also argued that the fault lay not with ministerial training (which has often been a convenient scapegoat for the church's perceived ills) as with the Church's understanding of itself and its ministry. A T S James argued that the ministry is shaped by the church and that 'the churches get the ministry they make'.[4] If so, that was especially important in churches of the Congregational order in which the ministry was intimately bound up with the whole body of believers. This form of church polity admitted 'nothing of sacerdotal distinctions, and (was) very little troubled about the distinction of Orders'.[5] Many would have agreed with a former chairman of the Congregational Union of England and Wales that a minister is 'merely a member of the church set apart for special duty'. A typical representative of this standpoint was the Revd A Le Marchant who took a largely negative view of ordination:

[1] *Christian World*, 27 September 1917.

[2] Elaine Kaye and Ross Mackenzie, *W E Orchard: A Study in Christian Exploration*, (Oxford: 1990).

[3] W B Selbie, *The Training of the Ministry*, (*Congregational Quarterly*, 1923, Vol. 1) p. 173.

[4] A T S James, *The Work of the Ministry*, (*Congregational Quarterly*, 1927, Vol. 5) p. 153.

[5] ibid.

The Church invites a man to minister to it, but it does not thereby make him a minister of the Gospel; it accepts him as such; he is one already. He goes through an ordination service; neither does that make him one.[6]

Warming to his theme, Le Marchant was similarly dismissive of the laying on of hands in ordination as conferring any ministerial power or authority; neither did he believe that ministers themselves possessed any power to ordain.

In some instances ministers in our churches place their hands upon the head of the ordained…if they really do something, why ministers only? Why not the chapel keeper? Are their powers in this matter greater than his? And what are they? And where did they get them from?[7]

These were questions Congregationalists needed to address. It was not clear whether ministers of neighbouring churches should be associated with ordinations as a matter of courtesy at the invitation of the local church, or whether this involved deeper matters of church order. Le Marchant's personal view, which may have been widely shared, was that ordination should be understood as merely the equivalent of the reception of the apostle Paul by churches which he visited as a recognised and valued Christian leader. Ordination *per se* possessed no effectual power in equipping a minister for his office - 'He is the same one minute after it as he was one minute before.' Yet this view is not wholly consistent with his emphasis on the importance of praying for the minister that he may be more fully equipped for his ministry. 'The congregation at every service (ie conducted by a minister) should offer an "ordination prayer".' The close connection between the laying on of hands and prayer, which in the 17th century had been clearly understood, had been lost. It had been destroyed by the fear of sacerdotalism.

There were signs in some quarters of a greater willingness to engage in constructive thinking about the ministry. D E Jarvis complained that the Congregationalist emphasis upon the priesthood of all believers sometimes gave the impression that the ministry no longer matters. He quoted approvingly from Dr J D Jones,[8] minister of Richmond Hill Congregational Church, Bournemouth:

Some amongst us have loudly proclaimed that there is no difference between the minister and the layman, and have divested the ministry of all special sacredness and authority…they have repudiated anything like 'orders'. They have so talked down the ministry that some people outside, who do not know us, may be excused for wondering sometimes if we have a ministry at all.[9]

---

6   A Le Marchant, *The Church and the Ministry*, (*Congregational Quarterly*, 1927, Vol. 5) p. 301. A Le Marchant was minister at Mawdsley Street Congregational Church, Bolton.

7   ibid.

8   John Daniel Jones, CH, MA, DD (1865-1942), Minister Richmond Hill CC, Bournemouth, 1898-1932, Hon Secretary of the Congregational Union of England and Wales 1919-1923, Moderator of the International Congregational Council 1930. Described as 'the most prominent statesman in Congregationalism and no Union meeting was complete without him'. R Tudur Jones, *Congregationalism in England 1662-1962*, (London: Independent Press, 1962) p. 383.

9   Source unknown. Quoted by D E Jarvis, *Our Sacerdotalism*, (*Congregational Quarterly*, 1928, Vol. 6, p. 386).

Jarvis argued for a higher view of ordination than many of his contemporaries. 'Ordination means at least that by a deliberate and united act of the whole Body, functioning as an agent of Christ, a man is set apart to do the work of the ministry. If we say that work can be performed by anyone, how much sincere and intelligent purpose is there in our solemn ordination?'[10] Ordination is clearly the setting apart of a person to function as a minister, and confers the church's public authority and recognition. The popular view, therefore, that any act done by a minister could equally be performed by any other church member, had the effect of negating ordination. 'If, having ordained some to office, we state that anyone may discharge their duties, we make ordination a hollow, empty farce.'[11] This issue was sharply focused by a proposal in the programme for the 1931 Autumn Assembly of the Congregational Union of England and Wales to invite a non-ministerial member to preside at the celebration of the Lord's Supper during the Assembly. This was welcomed by Professor Robert Macintosh, formerly Professor at Lancashire Independent College as 'a memorable historical landmark'.[12] The same Assembly had taken the view, in its response to the report of the Lausanne Conference of 1927, that the ministry was not 'essential to the being of the church', but only to its well-being.[13]

A more positive contribution to the discussion of ministry and ordination at this time was made by the then Principal of Mansfield College. Writing on 'Congregationalism and the Great Christian Doctrines', W B Selbie[14] commented on the ministry that

> The Congregational view of the ministry has always been prophetic rather than priestly. It could hardly be otherwise seeing that they believe all Christians to be kings and priests unto God. But they have always been accustomed to set apart men called of God and duly prepared to the ministry of the Word and Sacraments. For them the essence of the ministry is not in any form of ordination, but in God's call to the individual. Given such a call – and they must always be assured of it and its reality – ordination is but the human recognition and ratification of the fact and the setting apart of the man so called to the service of a particular church.[15]

The functions of the minister were to lead worship, to preach the Word, to administer the Sacraments, to be a watcher for souls and a shepherd of the flock, to be a teacher and prophet, a man of God and of the Word, and a good steward of the Kingdom.[16]

---

[10]   D E Jarvis, op. cit.

[11]   ibid.

[12]   R Macintosh, *The Genius of Congregationalism, Essays Congregational and Catholic*, A. Peel (ed). (London: Congregational Union of England and Wales, 1931) p.123.

[13]   *The Congregational Year Book 1931*, pp. 86-91.

[14]   William Boothby Selbie (1862-1944) was a founder student at Mansfield College when the college opened in Oxford in 1886; he was Principal 1909-32.

[15]   W B Selbie, op. cit. Chapter 6, p. 146.

[16]   W B Selbie, op. cit. p. 146.

'Our God is a God of Order'

Selbie nevertheless was clearly at ease with the prevailing view of contemporary Congregationalism that the ministry, while desirable and customary, was not essential to the Church. His successor in the Principalship, Dr Nathaniel Micklem, took a stronger view. Discussing whether the sacraments might be administered by the laity, he argued that these should not be administered by lay people unless under exceptional circumstances:

> Stress is properly laid upon the universal priesthood of all believers; but the true Congregational principle seems clear that except in cases of necessity it is the minister who should celebrate the Christian sacraments; for our God is a God of order, not of anarchy. Ministers have been called out of the Church under the guidance of the Holy Spirit in virtue of the spiritual gifts entrusted to them; they are ordained to be ministers of the Word and Sacraments. As a matter of order, therefore (not of validity), laymen should not administer the Sacraments unless under exceptional circumstances the Spirit should so direct.[17]

It is possible that Selbie would have agreed with the proposal to invite a lay person to preside at the celebration of the Lord's Supper in the presence of numerous ordained ministers. It is certain that Nathaniel Micklem would have strongly disapproved. His appointment in 1932 to succeed Selbie as Principal of Mansfield College was to mark a distinct change of emphasis and direction as he began to influence a new generation of students for the ministry. In time his influence would spread widely within his denomination and contribute significantly to the nurturing of closer relationships between Congregationalists and Presbyterians which would lead to their union in the United Reformed Church. R Tudur Jones, who had studied under Micklem at Mansfield College, said of him that he 'had been more responsible than any other single person for creating a new attitude amongst Congregationalists towards their theology, their churchmanship and their public worship.'[18]

Another who would have dissented from the proposal was J S Whale. Whale had studied at Mansfield under Selbie but to a far greater extent than Selbie drew upon the traditions of Reformed theology. After a first pastorate at Bowdon Downs, Manchester, he was appointed to Mansfield in 1929 to teach church history, and four years later moved to Cambridge as President of Cheshunt College. In an article on *Ordination to the Ministry in the Churches of the Congregational Order*,[19] Whale addressed the question of how Christ, as Head of the Church, ordains his ministers. In one sense the true Church is invisible except to the eyes of God. From another aspect it is necessarily visible and institutional. According to Calvin's understanding the invisible church is made visible where the Word is preached, the Gospel sacraments are administered, and discipline is enforced. The visible church requires ministers to be appointed by Christ, as Head of the Church, and to bear his authority. The question is how this is to be achieved. 'By what human agency', asked Whale, 'is his commission to ordinands authoritatively transmitted?' Episcopal ordination provides one answer to the question. In episcopal ordination

---

17   N Micklem (ed) *Christian Worship*, (Oxford: 1936) p. 254.

18   R Tudur Jones, *Congregationalism in England 1662-1962*, (London: Independent Press, 1962) p. 450.

19   J S Whale, *Ordination to the Ministry in the Churches of the Congregational Order*, (*The Presbyter*, July 1943).

the bishop of the diocese normally ordains a number of candidates on the same occasion, who are then sent to serve in parishes within the diocese. The congregations to which they are to minister neither 'call' their ministers, nor do they take part in their ordinations. They are intimately concerned, yet their role is entirely passive.

Whale contrasted episcopal with the wholly different emphasis of Congregational ordinations. Here 'the authority of the Church of Christ inheres primarily in each local body of believers.' Each gathered Church has 'power and commandment to elect and ordain their own ministries'.[20] In the churches of the Congregational Order Christ ordains his ministers through the agency of the local church. 'The authority of the Church of Christ inheres primarily in each local body of believers, as a microcosm or miniature realisation of the whole company of the redeemed, on earth and in heaven.' Ordination to the ministry therefore appropriately takes place within the local church which, after prayer and waiting upon the guidance of the Holy Spirit, has invited the person to minister among them. The *locus* of ordination in the local church makes visible the close relationship between the local church and the person whom the members of that church receive as from Christ to be a minister of His Word and Sacraments among them. This does not mean however that ordination is a human act. Power to ordain belongs to Christ alone. Yet Christ acts through human beings. The heart of the ordination service therefore is the Ordination Prayer, in which the whole congregation invokes the gift and blessing of the Holy Spirit.

This apparently exclusive emphasis on the locally gathered church could lead to the charge that, just as episcopal ordination neglected the local congregation, Congregational ordinations ignored the Church universal. Whale was sensitive to that criticism. The 'gatheredness' of the church into local societies of believers did not express the whole truth about the Church. Unlike many of his Congregational contemporaries Whale had a lively grasp of the catholicity and universality of the Church. It was important that ordination should be seen as the act of the whole Church and that the ministry of those ordained should be universally recognised. For Congregationalists this meant that representatives of regional unions or synods should take part in ordinations, and that the provincial moderator should preside, representing not only the Province but all the churches of the Congregational Order.

In an important comment Whale noted the historic tension in Congregationalism, which had existed since its origins in the 16th century, between the Calvinist and Anabaptist strains in its tradition.[21] How this would be resolved, if at all, would determine whether the Calvinist tradition, as it found expression in Presbyterianism, or the Anabaptist or Separatist tradition, as it found partial expression in Congregationalism, would find it possible to flow together into one stream. Congregationalists had to decide which of these two strains was more important to them. Whale took the view that the essential genius of Congregationalism was Genevan. While its polity was expressed in a form of 'decentralised Calvinism', it needed to combine a high view of the local church with a lively sense of the Church Universal. Ordination services were occasions when both convictions should be emphasised.

---

[20]   *A True Confession*, Amsterdam 1596; quoted by J S Whale, ibid.

[21]   For a discussion of these, see P T Forsyth, *Faith, Freedom and the Future*, (London: Hodder and Stoughton, 1912) pp. 91-132, and J S Whale, *The Protestant Tradition*, (Cambridge: 1955) Ch. XV.

Returning to the Roots

During the decade of 1940-50 some of the younger ministers who had been influenced by Nathaniel Micklem began to contribute significantly to discussions within Congregationalism on the nature of the ministry of Word and Sacrament. Outstanding among these were John Huxtable, Daniel Jenkins, and Robert Paul.

Huxtable had trained for the ministry at Western College, Bristol, and Mansfield College, Oxford. After a first pastorate at Newton Abbot (1937-42), he moved to Palmer's Green, London, where he became a leading figure in the Church Order Group[22] which had been formed by a group of younger ministers to rediscover the historic roots of Congregationalism. John Marsh, then Chaplain to Mansfield College, edited a series of books, The Forward Books, which explored a range of issues. One of these, *The Ministry*, was written by John Huxtable.

Huxtable's starting point was that in one sense the minister is 'just another member of the church'.[23] The minister stands alongside those who have been rescued by Christ from sin and death and called to be of God's people. The minister belongs to the universal priesthood of all believers. But because he has been ordained to ministry, the minister is not 'just like any other man'.

What difference then does ordination make? Ordination has, firstly, a backward reference. It looks back to the time when the ordinand first became aware of being called. 'There was a day', says Huxtable, 'when he felt himself to be set apart to be a minister of the glorious gospel of the blessed God.'[24] That inward call had to be confirmed by the church, and in particular it had to be confirmed by the local church of which he was a member. The members of that church were initially responsible for testing the vocation to ministry, and this was one of their highest and most serious responsibilities. Their confirmation of the call to ministry of one of their members was the essential pre-requisite for ministerial training. 'The church must bear primary responsibility for the ministry.'[25] College training was important but it could not by itself 'make' a minister. The aim and purpose of training was to stir up the gift which God had given.

At the end of the period of training the ordinand would seek a call to a pastorate before he could be ordained. This call was fundamental in that it confirmed the judgement of the church which had sent the candidate forward for training. 'It is as if the second church said to the first, "Yes, you were quite right. He has been truly called to the ministry, and we have been led to call him to be our pastor."'[26] Provincial moderators might facilitate the introductions to vacant pastorates but Congregational order eschewed any notion of centralised appointments.

The appropriate locus for ordinations was therefore the local church to which the candidate had been called. It was fitting that ministers and members of neighbouring churches of the same faith and order should be present – 'for the ordination of a minister is of moment for the whole communion of the churches.' The call is given by a particular church but the wider fellowship accepts the validity of the call, and recognises the ministry which ordination brings into being.

---

22   See Elaine Kaye, *Mansfield College Oxford*, (Oxford: 1996) pp. 277-8.
23   J Huxtable, *The Ministry*, (London: Independent Press, 1943).
24   ibid.
25   ibid. p. 17.
26   ibid.

Huxtable asked whether any 'grace' is conferred through the rite of ordination and whether there is an equivalent Congregational understanding of the Anglican 'grace' of orders. It would have been highly contentious, in the circumstances of his time, to claim that grace was conferred, and Huxtable stops short of this. Primarily he understood ordination in terms of the church's recognition of God's gift to the church of the person whom God and they have called to the ministry. In ordaining members of the church to be Ministers of Word and Sacrament the church 'recognises the divine appointment of Christ's apostle'. The Church cannot by itself create ministers, for that is God's act alone. The Church 'recognises those whom God has created and ordains those whom he has set apart'.[27] It is surprising that Huxtable did not place greater emphasis on the significance of the ordination prayer. In this prayer the local church on behalf of the whole church prays that God will empower his servant with the gifts and graces of the Holy Spirit to be a minister of Word and Sacrament. In answering the Church's prayer, God confers grace through the rite of ordination. More than a recognition, ordination is an effective act. Huxtable reaches out in this direction but fails to take his argument to this conclusion.

The laying on of hands in ordination is a human ceremonial which recognises that the person has been set apart by God. It is this 'setting apart' for ministry which makes a minister different. Huxtable fundamentally rejected the view that a person is the same after ordination as before. 'It is the merest humbug', he wrote, 'to water down that difference, and the honest recognition of it is not the first step to Rome but the reverent acknowledgement of an act of God.'[28]

Daniel Jenkins re-opened a question which had been raised fifteen years earlier by G Stanley Russell, minister of the influential Grafton Square Chapel. Russell had argued from the premise that Congregationalism needed 'an adequate conception of the ministry in our churches and among ministers themselves'. Was it therefore sufficient to claim, as many then did, that a minister was merely a member of the church set apart for special duty, in which case all or any members might serve in rotation, or was there some uniquely special role given to the ministry?[29] The 1931 Assembly of the Congregational Union of England and Wales had repudiated the notion that the ministry was 'essential to the being of the church'. The relation of function and office within the Congregational understanding of the ministry remained uneasy and confused.

It was this question which Jenkins addressed in three important books.[30] The *office* of ministry derived its significance from the *functions* of ministry. Since these were crucial to the church's existence, the office was essential to the church's being. In the New Testament ministry is recognised as the gift of God to the Church. This gift of ministry is primarily bestowed through Jesus Christ since the gift of salvation and the gift of ministry are identical. Jesus incarnated God's word of salvation and was sent to be the minister of divine saving grace. The crucial text in the New Testament is in the Gospel of Mark where Jesus says of himself that 'The Son of man came not to be served but to serve, and to give his life a ransom for many.'[31] The Church's ministry is nothing less than that saving Word of God

---

27   ibid. p. 20.

28   ibid. p. 21.

29   G Stanley Russell, *Our Ministry*, *(Congregational Quarterly* 1925, Vol. III, p. 478).

30   D T Jenkins, *The Nature of Catholicity* (London: Faber and Faber, 1942) *The Gift of Ministry* (London: Faber and Faber, 1947) and *Congregationalism – A Restatement* (London: Faber and Faber, 1954). Three core chapters of *The Gift of Ministry* were included in Jenkins' later book, *The Protestant Ministry*, (London: Faber and Faber, 1958).

31   Mark 10:45.

who is embodied in Jesus Christ. 'The Word of God', says Jenkins, 'is prior to the ministry and it is only in the light of the Word that the ministry can be understood'.[32]

The antidote to the sacerdotalism which was so much feared within the Congregational Churches was the acceptance of the paradox that the Church's Lord came in the form of a servant. Ministers are to be seen as servants not lords. Like their Lord and Master they stand within the company of God's people as those who serve. Their model is the Lord who took a towel and washed his disciples' feet.[33] Yet at the same time they have an authority which belongs to their office as 'ambassadors of Christ'[34] who have been commissioned to testify to the Lord's resurrection and parousia, and to God's act and offer of reconciliation through him. Their message is not a human invention or an exercise in religious philosophy but 'the drawing out of the meaning of God's Word in Jesus Christ as the scriptures declare him'.[35]

The authority of the ministerial office does not however confer special status. The minister does not belong to a caste set apart from the rest of the church, or have any higher status or special privileges. In a striking phrase Jenkins says that the minister's representative function 'is not a special status but a miracle'. The preaching of the Word is a deed of saving grace which becomes effective in the lives of the people to whom the Word is addressed. The minister is also a recipient of the message of divine judgement, promise and hope. 'He is a member of the church, whose status before God is the same as that of other members of the church, but with a special vocation within the church and the proper authority which is necessary for the fulfilment of his vocation'.[36]

The minister's authority derives from the Word which he is ordained to proclaim. Jenkins observed that the real issue in the debate between Catholics and Protestants is 'whether the ministry depends on the Word and sacraments for its authority', as Protestants believe, or, whether, as Catholics affirm, 'the Word and the sacraments depend on a ministry which exists prior to them'.[37] The Protestant tradition affirms that the Word is prior to the ministry, but the ministry is a direct consequence of the Word. Church order and ministry are not therefore matters of indifference or convenience. The apostolic ministry, which is called into being by the Word and given by God to the Church is essential to the being of the Church. 'The apostolic ministry is essential to the church's existence because…it is through its proclamation…that the church's service of God becomes a real offering of herself in Jesus Christ and a real offering of Jesus Christ to the world'.[38] But while the apostolic ministry is essential to the Church, Jenkins does not see this as a Protestant reinvention of the traditional divide between ministers at the centre of the Church's life, and lay people on the circumference. The ministry remains always a 'function'. It is 'a means by which all members are enabled to hear the true Word of God and live the true Christian life'.[39] The ministry is always the servant of the Church's service. 'It exists in order to deliver the Church from all human arrogance and pretension and is her effort to make sure that Jesus Christ and He alone is acknowledged in her midst as Lord'.[40]

32	D T Jenkins, *The Gift of Ministry*, (London: Faber, 1947) p. 17.
33	John 13:5.
34	2 Corinthians 5:20.
35	ibid. p. 33.
36	ibid. p. 130.
37	ibid. p. 50.
38	D T Jenkins, *The Nature of Catholicity*, (London: Faber and Faber, 1942) p. 100.
39	ibid. p. 101.
40	ibid.

In his later *Congregationalism: A Restatement*,[41] Jenkins gave further consideration to the relationship between the local church and the wider church. By the 1950s, in the aftermath of World War II, ecumenical concerns were exercising increasing influence. The British Council of Churches had been formally constituted in 1942. Congregationalists were prominent in the World Council of Churches whose first assembly was held in 1948 at Amsterdam. Yet the Congregational Union of England and Wales still lacked in its structure any theology of the wider Church. Congregationalists were clear in their conviction that the mind of Christ would be made known in the local Church Meeting. But they were at a loss to explain how the wider Church might receive the guidance of the Holy Spirit. Under the pressures of ecumenical dialogue this question could no longer be ignored.

More than half a century earlier Peter Taylor Forsyth, the Congregational theologian whose contemporary relevance was being rediscovered through the reissue, in the later 1940s, of books which had been first written before the first World War, had described the local church as the outcrop of the Great Church. 'The total Church', Forsyth had written, 'was not made up by adding the local Churches together, but the local Church was made a Church by representing there and then the total Church. It was just where the total Church looked out at one point.'[42]

From Forsyth's insight into the nature of the local church, Jenkins developed an understanding of the ministry as representing the total Church to the local church through the minister's function in relation to preaching and the sacraments. 'It is these which most effectively represent the great Church in the local church, it is these which are its primary marks of catholicity, because they represent the universal Christ who is Lord of all.'[43] The minister has therefore a far greater function than to preside, as a local leader, over the locally gathered church of which he is also a member. The minister's task is to enable the local church to see itself and its missionary vocation within God's overall purpose for the Church and the world. The minister 'represents the mind of the Great Church in the local church'.[44] Moreover the minister does this 'not merely formally or symbolically, but concretely, in his preaching, in his planning and conduct of worship and in the guidance and advice he proffers in Church Meeting and in personal counsel.'[45] The ministry also has ecumenical significance in the sense that its function 'is to help the church meeting ensure that its decisions are taken with full responsibility'.[46] By 'full responsibility' Jenkins means that the local church should consciously and deliberately live and act as a responsible unit of the universal or Great Church.

This was emphatically not, for Jenkins, the re-introduction of clericalism. He is emphatic in his condemnation of the familiar phenomenon of the minister-centred congregation who dare not do anything without the minister's approval. The sign of a vigorous local church is when leadership comes from the congregation's locally appointed leaders, in Congregational churches the deacons, and, in Presbyterian churches, the elders. 'The healthiest churches are those where, on the local

---

[41] D T Jenkins, *Congregationalism – A Restatement*, (London: Faber and Faber, 1954).

[42] P T Forsyth, *The Church and the Sacraments*, (London: Independent Press,1947) p. 65 (first published in 1917 by Longmans, Green and Co).

[43] ibid. p. 77.

[44] ibid. p. 78.

[45] ibid. p. 78.

[46] ibid. p. 79.

level, leadership comes from the diaconate rather than from the ministry'.[47]   He urged that ministers should keep themselves in the background and by a self-denying ordinance limit their opportunities for exercising quasi-secular power within the Christian community.

The ministry however is not devoid of powers, but these must be understood and exercised only in terms of service. The minister is 'the servant of the Church's service, the one who helps her to know how to make a perfect offering of obedience to the will of Christ'.[48]   The powers of ministry are threefold. In the first place the minister has the right to preach the Gospel and administer the sacraments.   To deny this right to an ordained minister is in effect to deny the right of the ministry to exist. The point is obvious but that it had to be made suggests that it was not unknown for congregations to undervalue the ministry of Word and Sacraments or to deny it a central place in the church's life.

The second power is the 'power of the keys'. This is the power to declare the divine absolution from sin and to exercise the power of discipline in order to protect the Church's integrity in a sinful world. This second power, which instantly smacks of clericalism, is exercised however in the name of the Church. Jenkins is clear that this power 'fundamentally inheres in the whole Church which fulfils the apostolic office and not merely in the ministry as such'.[49] The minister holds it only derivatively from the Church. The same point had been made in the 17th century by John Owen who had said that 'it is given to the whole Church, though to be exercised only by its elders'.[50] Ministers exercise this power by virtue of their stewardship of the mysteries of Word and sacraments. More than any other it is to be exercised with humility and with the recognition that the minister speaks to the Church as one who also belongs to it. 'He does so most emphatically from within the Church, and his authoritative speaking is always an act of God's grace, to himself as much as to his fellows'.[51]

The third power is that of confirmation and ordination. Traditional Catholicism asserted that these were the prerogative of the episcopate without giving positive theological reasons why this should be so. Paradoxically Catholicism was prepared to allow even laymen to preach the Gospel and presbyters to administer the Sacraments, yet reserved the rights of confirmation and ordination to bishops. Yet because of their administrative responsibility for large dioceses bishops were rarely in a position to know whether those whom they confirmed or ordained were 'in the spirit'. They were dependent on those, mainly presbyters, who stood in some personal and pastoral relationship to the candidates and could vouch for their suitability.   In the case of both confirmation and ordination it was fitting that these should be administered by those who represented the Church Universal.   But since ministers of Word and Sacrament also represented the Church Universal, it was fitting also that they should administer confirmation and ordination. In practice this is what happened in the Protestant churches. Church members were admitted on profession of faith by the local minister of Word and Sacrament, acting representatively for the church community which received new members by decision of their Church Meeting.

---

[47]   ibid. p. 80.

[48]   D T Jenkins, *The Gift of Ministry*, (London: Faber and Faber, 1947) p. 38.

[49]   ibid. p. 46.

[50]   J Owen, *The Nature of a Gospel Church*, quoted by D T Jenkins, op. cit. p. 46.

[51]   D T Jenkins, *The Gift of Ministry* (London: Faber and Faber, 1947) p. 41.

The service of confirmation or reception of new members made it clear that, in joining a particular church, members were being received into the one, holy, catholic and apostolic church. Similarly ministers were ordained in principle to the ministry of the universal Church.

Jenkins recognised that the doctrine and practice of episcopacy bore striking testimony to the need for unity and universality in the Church. The presence of the ministry was a mark of the Church's catholicity and a symbol of its unity. It was a reminder also of the importance of the apostolic succession which was often neglected in Protestantism. 'The continuity which succession expresses is an essential part of the life of the Church and where the living bond between ourselves and the apostolic community is not apprehended and prized our very existence as the Church is threatened.'[52] The true succession, however, was not that of the ministry but of the whole fellowship of the Church. The apostolic succession is secured where the whole Church continued in the apostles' teaching and fellowship (Acts 2:42). 'It was their faithfulness to the Lord's ministry in word and deed which ultimately established them as true apostles and it is the same faithfulness which gives ministers today any title to be considered as in any sense their successors.'[53] Lineal descent from the apostles, even if it could be proved, cannot guarantee faithfulness to the apostolic testimony. 'What is required of us if we are to minister His healing touch is not therefore a correct spiritual pedigree…but that we should obey His will for His people and strive always to continue steadfastly in the apostles' doctrine and fellowship and in prayer.'[54] The fundamental responsibility of every minister of Word and Sacrament, given in ordination, is so to serve the people of Christ that they may continue in that apostolic doctrine and fellowship and so bear witness to Christ that others may be drawn into the apostolic community.

A later contribution to Congregational understanding of ordination was made by Robert S Paul, a Congregational minister also trained at Mansfield under Nathaniel Micklem. After pastorates in England and a period as Associate Director of Ecumenical Studies at Bossey, Switzerland, Paul moved to the United States of America to teach at Hartford Theological Seminary, and later at Pittsburgh. In his book, *Ministry*,[55] Paul asked the questions: 'What difference does ordination make?' and 'In what way is a minister different from any other church member?' His answer was that every church member is ordained through the sacrament of baptism. Paul here reflected the insights of the Faith and Order Conference which had taken place at Montreal in 1963. Twenty years earlier Daniel Jenkins had recognised the need for a profounder theological understanding of other kinds of ministry in the Church than that of the Word and Sacraments, and in particular the place of the congregation itself in the life of the Church. By the 1960s these were beginning to be addressed as a 'theology of the laity' began to emerge. A Report to the Montreal Conference from the Department on the Laity declared that just as Jesus' baptism by John the Baptist in the Jordan was the point at which he understood his own special commission and received the empowerment of the Holy Spirit for his mission, so in the same way 'through our baptism Christ incorporates us for participation in his ministry'.[56] The Report went on to state that 'Baptism proclaims that, as the Christian has been called out of the world, so he returns to the world as its

---

[52]   ibid. p. 51.
[53]   ibid. p. 52.
[54]   ibid. p. 54.
[55]   R S Paul, *Ministry*, (Grand Rapids, Michigan: Eerdmans, 1965).
[56]   *Laity* No 15, (1963) *Christ's Ministry and the Ministry of the Church.*

servant; for only in his union with the world's Redeemer is he free to participate creatively and fully in its common life...Baptism is the ordination into the apostolic, charismatic and sacrificial ministry of the Church.'[57] To this Paul adds that the references to 'baptism' must be understood as the whole process of Christian initiation in 'baptism-confirmation'. Infant baptism alone could not bear the weight of this interpretation. 'Baptism-confirmation' is to be understood as a general ordination to ministry in the church which has a particular reference to God's call to that individual.

If baptism-confirmation is the 'general ordination' of Christians what place then remains for 'special ordinations', for example, to the ministry of Word and Sacrament? What does this do that baptism does not? If all are ordained through baptism, yet most remain 'laymen' in the eyes of the Church, what is a minister that a layman is not?

Paul argued that ordination to the ministry has a wider reference than the general ordination of baptism. The focus of the latter is on God's call to the individual. Superficially ordination to the ministry of Word and Sacraments also appears to focus on the vocation of the person called to that ministry. To a casual observer it may appear a wholly individualistic event. In reality its point of reference is to the vocation of the whole Church. The vocation of one person 'brings before the whole company of Christ's people what its own corporate vocation is within the world'.[58] It is 'an act of the Church which brings to a focus the nature of the Church's own ministry'. As such 'it objectifies to the Church its own ministry within the world'.[59] Paul rejects the common assumption that ordination 'adds' something to the person ordained as leading directly to clericalism and a view of the ministry as a superior caste of people who are 'set over' or 'above' the Church. Instead he insists that the emphasis of the ordination of a minister should reflect his essential unity with the ministry of the whole Church, of which his ministry is a part. Ordination therefore has to be understood in terms of ecclesiology. Rather than focusing on the special calling of one person as distinct from others, its purpose is to underline the calling of the whole people of God to engage in the servant ministry of Jesus Christ. The nature of the Church as corporately sharing the ministry of Christ, the Church's Servant Lord, imparts this same quality of servanthood to ministry. Since all ministry is derived from the ministry of Jesus, then 'it can claim nothing but the right to serve'.[60]

This view of ordained ministry as focusing and representing the Church's vocation is compatible with the concept of 'special ordination'. The witness of the Scriptures is that God calls individual people to special forms of service as, for example, Noah, Abraham and Moses. The call of individuals, however, is in relation to the comprehensive calling of a people – Israel – to be 'a light to the nations' (Isaiah 49:6) and to bring God's salvation to the ends of the earth. The doctrine of election is the key to understanding the meaning of vocation. But 'election' can never be separated from 'vocation'. The message of the prophets was that Israel could only understand the meaning of her 'election' through the acceptance of her vocation to be the servant of the Lord. Israel's tragedy, and that of the Church as well, was that she too often claimed the honour of election but ignored the vocation to service which was inseparable from election.

---

[57] ibid. pp. 17,18.
[58] R S Paul, op. cit. p. 131.
[59] ibid. p. 132.
[60] ibid. p. 137.

In the same way God calls people to ordained ministry. The minister is not called by God to occupy a place of superior status but to lead the Church to discover the meaning of its own ministry. Ordination is the act of the Church by which the Church recognises what God has done. In the act of ordination the Church does not create a minister, since that has already been done by God. Ordination is an act of the Church whereby the Church recognises God's act in calling a person to be a minister in the Church and in equipping the person with the gifts needful for ministry.

The service of ordination, with its climax in the 'laying on of hands', brings together the faith of the Church in Jesus as Lord, and the personal commitment and vocation of the person to be ordained. The imposition of hands takes place within the ordination prayer. This prayer celebrates the faith of the Church, recalls the succession of ministries by which God has blessed the Church in times past, and sets the new minister within this succession. Churches in the Protestant tradition hesitate to claim that any special grace is conferred in ordination. Rather the service emphasises the grace which has already been received through the redemptive work of Christ and the empowerment of the Holy Spirit. Yet, says Robert Paul, 'within the ancient form we do recognise that the man [sic] before us has been chosen by God for the ministry of Word and Sacrament in the Church, and that God's choice and the Church's joyful acknowledgement makes him one with the company of those who have exercised like ministry in the Church through time.'[61]

The service must clearly emphasise that ordination is to ministry, understood as service, otherwise it will appear to be conferring a special aura upon an individual member of the Church. Every ordination should recall those who are present, as church members and representatives of the wider Church, to the nature of the Church's ministry. Its justification does not lie in what it does for the minister so much as in what it means for the Church. The issue is not so much whether the minister is the same after ordination as before, but whether minister and people together have been recalled to their shared vocation.

In the Congregational tradition it was rare for an ordination service to include the Lord's Supper. This would normally be celebrated soon after the ordination when pastor and people shared their first Communion. The first Communion should be a deeply significant occasion when the Church and its minister sit together at the Lord's Table and through the broken bread and poured out wine share the gift of God's grace and forgiveness in Jesus Christ. In the act of Communion they renew their promises of commitment and service to the Servant Lord who ministers to his people through the bread and wine. In the blessing they receive the promise of their Lord's abiding presence with them in the world, and go out into the world to fulfil their ministry of service. The minister's calling and the meaning of his ordination is so to preach the Word and administer the Sacraments that the whole Church which the minister represents may fulfil the Lord's command to take the Gospel of salvation to the ends of the earth.

---

[61]   ibid. p. 153.

Preparing for Union

In 1951 the Congregationalists and Presbyterians had concluded an act of covenant and had set up a Joint Advisory Council to promote co-operation between the two denominations. This followed an earlier and abortive attempt at union which had failed to gain the support of either side, and was regarded by some as a temporising measure designed to save face rather than actively promote union. For several years little happened. The Presbyterian Church of England was experiencing modest growth and was in more confident mood. They shared the quest for church unity but union with the Congregationalists was not regarded as a high priority. Other possibilities – forming a Synod of the Church of Scotland, a union of all the English Free Churches, creating a 'British' Presbyterianism covering England, Ireland, Scotland and Wales, or even a dialogue with the Church of England – appeared to offer more exciting, if unrealisable, ecumenical opportunities. In the end a possible union with the Congregationalists proved the most realistic option. A Joint Committee was appointed and held its first meeting in November 1963.

The Congregationalists had already recognised the practical difficulties of uniting two very dissimilar bodies. The English Presbyterians constituted a Church – the Presbyterian Church of England – with its ascending hierarchy of courts. Congregational Churches on the other hand were only loosely associated in the Congregational Union of England and Wales. This was a voluntary association which exercised a limited range of functions on behalf of the churches, endeavoured to represent their views, and through an annual Assembly provided a national forum for consultation. It was emphatically not a Church. Whereas the Presbyterian Church of England could speak with one voice through its General Assembly, the annual meetings of the Congregational Union of England and Wales were not empowered to speak for the local churches, then nearly 3,000 in number. Congregationalists held strongly to their belief in the independence and spiritual autonomy of the local church. They believed as Nathaniel Micklem had long ago declared that 'the Christian group, met for common action or worship in Christ's name and in His presence, has…direct access to Christ and is responsible in the last resort to Him alone.'[62] They also believed, of course, that individual Christians and particular churches owed loyalty and obligation to the Church as a whole, but this was qualified in the sense that 'neither the Church as a whole nor any official or section of it may override the conscience of the group or interfere authoritatively between the group and its sense of Divine guidance.'[63] Micklem's understanding of the Church had long changed, but his statement of the matter was still widely representative of Congregationalist views. The problem was that Congregational ecclesiology provided nothing between the local church and the Great Church where the authoritative guidance of the Holy Spirit might be freely acknowledged. In the circumstances it was inevitable that considerable power, as well as influence, was exercised by committees and officers of the Union. The system worked on a basis of trust but it was not firmly rooted in ecclesiology.

In order to bridge the gap the Congregational Union began a searching process of self-examination through a series of Commissions which were set up to explore different aspects of the life of the Congregational Churches. The first of these was asked to examine the churches' understanding

---

[62]   N Micklem, *Present-Day Faiths, Congregationalism*, (*Expository Times 1927*).
[63]   ibid.

of Oversight and Covenant. Out of the work of this Commission emerged the proposal that the Congregational Union of England and Wales should form a Covenanted Fellowship of Congregational Churches: every local church would enter nationally into a covenant with each other to express their unity, strengthen their common life, and share more fully in the Church's universal mission. The Covenant would be made visible and effective at the local level through the fellowship and co-operation of particular churches, and, at all levels of church association, in County Unions, Provinces and the National Body. The majority of the member churches of the Congregational Union accepted the proposal which resulted in the formation in 1966 of the Congregational Church in England and Wales. Arthur Macarthur, then General Secretary of the Presbyterian Church of England, later described this 'as a move in the direction of a more catholic and less rigidly independent stance… It caused some unhappiness but in the event made the decision to join the United Reformed Church much easier.'[64]

Outwardly there may have appeared little difference between the Congregational Union of England and Wales and the Congregational Church in England and Wales. Inwardly however it represented a considerable change of attitude. The nettle of oversight – *episcope* - had at last been grasped. In the Congregational Lectures (1965) John Huxtable, now Minister Secretary of the Congregational Union, also addressed the issue.[65] He challenged the widely-expressed view that only churches which had bishops were episcopal. All forms of church order were episcopal in the sense that they made provision for the exercise of oversight, shepherding and pastoral authority. Without some form of *episcope* there could be no church order. Congregationalists had always insisted that their ministers, exercising pastoral oversight in local congregations, were bishops in the scriptural and most ancient sense. They had come now to understand that *episcope* was exercised corporately as well as individually. In a local church the minister, deacons and Church Meeting sustained a church order that was manifestly episcopal in its nature. *Episcope* was also embodied for Congregationalists within the wider fellowship of churches through County Unions, Provinces and the national Union. The readiness of the majority of Congregationalists, albeit with reluctance in some parts of the denomination, to recognise that these wider associations belonged to the necessary being of the Church was an important step on the journey towards their union with the Presbyterians.

Another of the Commissions was charged to examine the Nature of the Ministry and the Meaning of Ordination. Their Report[66] started from the premise that the one and only essential ministry in the Church is that of the Lord Jesus Christ, incarnate, crucified, risen and ascended. This ministry, in which the Church shares, is essential to the life of the Church. On the basis of the New Testament evidence 'some form or forms of ministry within the Church we believe to be essential for the ordering of the Church's life as that has been given to us by God.'[67]

---

[64]   A L Macarthur, *The Background to The Formation of the United Reformed Church (Presbyterian and Congregational) in England and Wales in 1972*, (JURCHS, Vol. 4, No 1, Oct 1987) pp. 3-22.

[65]   J Huxtable, *Christian Unity – Some of the Issues*, (London: Independent Press 1966) pp. 99-100.

[66]   *The Nature of the Ministry and the Meaning of Ordination*, Report of Commission VI, (London: Independent Press, 1965).

[67]   ibid. p. 3.

The Congregational tradition emphasised the local church, but this did not mean that ministers were ordained to a local ministry alone. Ordination was to the ministry of Christ in the whole Church. In the New Testament Church the authority and commission of the apostles was world-wide. Local churches were conscious that they belonged to the Universal Church, the new Israel of God. 'Their membership was membership in the Church of Jesus Christ; and those who ministered to them in the Lord were ministers in His whole Church.'[68]

The Commission urged Congregationalists to express more clearly than they had done in the past both the *continuity* and the *unity* of the Church. While they rejected a rigid doctrine of apostolic succession, they should recognise that their form of church order provided a succession of Scripture, the sacraments of Baptism and the Lord's Supper, faith and ministry that was truly apostolic. The ministry, as part of that succession, was a witness to the Church's continuity and unity.

It followed from this understanding of ministry that the task of recognising those whom God called to the work of ministry and of setting them apart to their office was one which belonged to the whole Church. 'The responsibility for calling a man or woman to the ordained ministry does not rest only with the local church. The whole fellowship of the Church is involved for the simple reason that the ministry is not only local but is in the whole Church.'[69] Candidates for the ministry required therefore not only the approval of the local churches of which they were members, but of the County Unions and Provincial Ministerial Committees which represented the wider Church.

The service of ordination was 'an act performed by the Church in the name and by the authority of Jesus Christ as its Head'.[70] While it was normal and appropriate that the ordination should take place in the local church to which the ordinand had been called as pastor, the participation of representatives of the wider fellowship of the Church was essential to its purpose. The Report stated unambiguously that 'the consent and participation of representatives of other Congregational Churches is considered to be essential.'[71] Their participation was not just a matter of accreditation or recognition; it belonged to the nature of the act of ordination. In ordination the fellowship of Congregational churches joined with the local church in acknowledging that God had called the ordinand to the work of ministry and had equipped him or her with the gifts and abilities for the work. This wider fellowship was also responsible for appointing the ordinand to serve as a minister of Jesus Christ. Their representatives were not present as observers but as effective participants in the act of ordination.

The Commission followed the traditional practice of the Congregational churches in affirming that the central act of ordination was prayer. To this they added a strong recommendation that the laying on of hands should be included, along with prayer, in all services of ordination to the Christian ministry. The use of prayer with the laying on of hands had biblical precedent and was mentioned in accounts of the appointment of the Seven,[72] and the commissioning of Paul and

---

[68]   ibid. p. 4.
[69]   ibid. p. 9.
[70]   ibid.
[71]   ibid. p. 12.
[72]   Acts 6:1-6.

Barnabas for missionary service. The laying on of hands derived from Old Testament and Jewish practice. The records of ordination services in the Congregational tradition showed that it was exceptional in historic Congregational practice not to include the laying on of hands. In the latter half of the nineteenth and the early twentieth century it had fallen into disuse due to a fear of sacerdotalism, and had been replaced by the giving of the right hand of fellowship, which lacked New Testament precedent.[73] It was important that the laying on of hands should be restored in churches where it had been lost as a solemn act by which the representatives of the churches signified their belief that Christ had chosen and ordains His servant.

The Report of Commission VI represented the apogee within Congregationalism of the 'High Genevan' tradition which had been initiated in the third decade of the twentieth century by Nathaniel Micklem, Bernard Manning and John Whale, and brought to fruition in later decades by others including John Huxtable, John Marsh, Daniel Jenkins, Robert Paul, and H Cunliffe-Jones. Some Congregationalists, who had initially opposed their re-discovery of earlier patterns of church order, came to share their views. The deaths of C J Cadoux in 1947 and Albert Peel in 1953 removed the last significant protagonists of the Independent tradition within Congregationalism which stoutly held to the belief that there was no other authority in the Church beyond that of the local Church Meeting. It is questionable whether that strain of Congregationalism would have either sought or been able to effect a union with the Presbyterian Church of England. It is even more doubtful whether the Presbyterians would have contemplated a union with a Congregationalism which upheld what they had traditionally regarded as a defective ecclesiology. The road to union would not be easy, but it was now no longer impassable, though its cost would be high. The tradition of Independency continued to exert a powerful hold upon English Congregationalism and claimed the allegiance of a significant minority of local churches and ministers. In 1966 some of those who could not accept the change from Congregational Union to Congregational Church affiliated in the Fellowship of Evangelical Churches. At the votes taken at the 1971 Assembly of the Congregational Church in England and Wales, 597 Congregational Churches, 26% of the total number and representing 18% of church members, remained outside the new Church rather than abandon deeply held convictions. Some congregations subsequently reversed their decision. Others dissented from the new Church and constituted themselves as the Congregational Federation. While the majority of English Congregationalists hoped that union with the Presbyterians would break the 'log jam' which had for so long held back the tide of progress towards church unity, there was sadness that a consequence of the union would be fresh division and, for many, the painful severing of long-standing and cherished relationships between churches, members and ministers.

---

[73]   The single New Testament reference to 'the right hands of fellowship' (Gal.2:9,KJV) does not refer to ordination but to a recognition of equal apostleship.

Chapter Four

Presbyterian Traditions

PRESBYTERIAN TRADITIONS

Presbyterianism differed from Episcopal and Congregational polities in a number of important respects. The Episcopal form of church government made a radical distinction between clergy and laity. It also enshrined the principle of grading ministers according to their rank and office. Ordination not only distinguished ministers from lay persons, but was the means by which the lower orders of the clergy received their authority from the higher.

The Congregational form of government rested on the conviction that every congregation of believers was an autonomous body, in such a way that the local congregation was 'the Universal Church in miniature'.[1] The views of Synods or Councils representing a wider association of local congregations might be accorded respect, but did not have authority over the local company of believers. Ministers derived their authority from the local congregation and, at least in theory, were on an equal footing with members of the local church.

Presbyterians saw dangers in each of these alternative polities and claimed to offer a *via media* for which they claimed scriptural authority. To the Anglican practice of a hierarchy of orders they offered equality of ministerial status. To the diocesan episcopate they offered an alternative model of a 'parochial' episcopate which enabled church members to participate in church government as ordained elders. To Congregational claims for the independence of the local congregation, Presbyterians offered a wider emphasis on the unity of the Church manifested in ecclesiastical courts with legislative, executive and judicial powers.[2]

There was, however, another sense in which Presbyterians stood between Congregationalists and Anglicans. Congregationalists defined themselves as Dissenters from the Church of England. In the 17th century Presbyterians and Independents had failed equally in their struggles to establish national forms of church government in England in the aftermath of the Civil Wars. In 1662 they both shared in the Great Ejectment and, involuntarily, became Dissenters. Their subsequent histories diverged. While the Independents trebled their share of the total population of England between 1714 and 1851, the combined share of the Quakers, Orthodox Presbyterians and Unitarians declined in absolute terms by 50% during the same period.[3] By then most of the Presbyterian congregations which had survived had become Unitarian. The few congregations which maintained Trinitarian belief tended to look towards Scotland for support, though the Church of Scotland as a national Church was unwilling to encourage Presbyterian dissent in England. The Presbyterian revival in England during the 19th century was founded on the contacts

---

[1]   C J Cadoux, *The Congregational Way*, (Oxford: 1945) pp. 20-21.

[2]   See article on '*Presbyterianism*', Professor Archibald Main, *Expository Times*, 1927.

[3]   M R Watts, *The Dissenters, Vol II*, (Oxford: 1995) pp. 27-28.

made by immigrants from Scotland with the scattered remnants of an older English Presbyterianism.[4] In these circumstances it was inevitable that Presbyterians should think of themselves as providing a church for Scots people in England. Chadwick comments that 'it took them forty years to think of themselves as indigenous and to revalue the older English tradition.' The consequence was that Presbyterians did not think of themselves as Dissenters in the classical meaning of the word. They offered an alternative form of church government, which they believed to have scriptural authority, rather than a polity based on dissent from an episcopal norm. They spoke therefore with more confidence than the often defensive, and perhaps understandably over-touchy, Congregationalists, who for more than two centuries had suffered numerous civil and religious disabilities on account of their Dissenting convictions and practice. While the Presbyterian Church of England was demonstrably English, it also drew theological, spiritual – and numerical - strength from its close association with its prestigious sister Church north of the Border.

It followed that from 1920 onwards Presbyterian thinking on issues of ministry and church order was directed more towards Anglican claims than towards Congregationalism. To many Presbyterians, especially in the earlier years of the period under review, the views of Congregationalists often seemed careless and confused.[5] At that time union with Congregationalists would have seemed to many Presbyterians an improbable, and perhaps not especially desirable, goal.

Authority – External or Internal?

In the first three decades of the 20th century Presbyterian thinking was greatly influenced by the Principal of Westminster College, Cambridge, where ordinands of the Presbyterian Church of England were prepared for ministry. John Oman (1860-1939) was appointed Professor of Theology in 1907 and was Principal from 1922 until his retirement in 1939. In 1911 he published *Vision and Authority*, a major work subtitled 'The Throne of St Peter', which he described in the Preface as 'an enquiry into the foundations on which all Churches rest'.[6] His purpose was to explore the relationship between the authority of the Church by which all Christians are fashioned and 'the authority within', by which he meant the individual Christian's spiritual insight. Both authorities, external and internal, needed to be harmonised.

External authority appeared to be secured by claims of infallibility. The Roman Church claimed obedience to an infallible Church. Protestant churches had traditionally rooted authority in Scripture, although the decline of the belief in the verbal inspiration of Scripture had undermined its authority. Oman held that neither an infallible Church nor an infallible Bible could achieve harmony between 'external' and 'internal' authority. 'Insistence on the need of an authority without, not to agree with the authority within, but to dominate it, is at bottom a disbelief in the possibility or even the gain of freedom.'[7]

4   O Chadwick, *The Victorian Church 1829-1859*, (London: SCM Press, 1966) pp. 398-99.

5   This view was expressed in private correspondence with The Revd A L Macarthur, General Secretary, the Presbyterian Church of England, 1960-1972.

6   J Oman's *Vision and Authority* was republished in 1928 and was reprinted four times between December 1928 and June 1929.

7   ibid. p. 95.

Jesus spoke with authority but not as the scribes. 'They had authorities but no authority'.[8] Jesus on the other hand spoke with authority because he appealed to 'the primal spiritual authority in man - the spiritual vision which discerns things spiritual.'[9] People gladly gave him the title of Rabbi as a sign of their readiness to accept his authority. Jesus refused any other foundation for his teaching than the authority of the hearts and consciences of those who heard him and responded to his teaching because they recognised that God was speaking directly and immediately to them through the Person of Christ. 'When the Divine Word speaks in the heart and men are made to see that this is God's goal in all their striving, they are enabled to say with practical, transfiguring conviction, "This is the Christ".'[10] The Church was built on the foundation of Peter's dramatic confession at Caesarea Philippi and on the other apostles who shared his conviction. To them was given responsibility for transmitting Christ's teaching, but they were not given an enslaving or infallible authority. The commission to interpret and apply the teaching of Jesus did not mean that the Church would be free from human error.

Oman addressed the crucial question of who had succeeded to Peter's blessing and now possessed his power. He understood the succession to be not that of office but of 'insight and love'.[11] 'Apostolic succession by a series of officials plays a much more important part in polemics than in life. The true succession of the Church has been in those to whom, not flesh or blood, but the Father in heaven has spoken.'[12] The true succession is that of faith and depends upon the continuous presence of the Spirit. It is found in those whose lives of service and ministry correspond to the apostolic description.[13] Their authority is not conferred by rite or ceremony but 'by penitence and faith and humility'.[14]

The true Church, Oman believed, is constituted where two or three meet in Christ's name. This gathering of faithful disciples constitutes the primary fellowship of which any enlargement up to the Church Universal is only an expansion. The primary fellowship 'is already the microcosm, wherein the great and complete Church, which is in heaven as well as on earth, is mirrored. It is an atom which potentially holds the glory of a universe.'[15] The unity of the Church is also to be discerned in the primary unit of fellowship. The two who meet in Christ's name have not suppressed their differences but have found through their fellowship with Christ and one another the power which can harmonise them. This uniting bond of fellowship is consistent with freedom and is capable of expansion to embrace all in true freedom. The goal of Church unity is not uniformity but, like an architect's vision, a building which displays perfect harmony. Uniformity is the foe of union because it rests upon compromise and regulation, and is doomed to lead to further division.

Oman believed passionately that unity must be the goal and that it was imperative for mission. He held to the determinative text in John 17.21 'that the world may believe'. Christ's purpose however was not that the world should see merely the expression of unity but should experience

---

[8]   ibid. p. 107.
[9]   ibid.
[10]   ibid. p. 120.
[11]   ibid. p. 131.
[12]   ibid. p. 136.
[13]   e.g. *I Cor 4.12.*
[14]   ibid. p. 138.
[15]   ibid. p. 140.

its reality. Too much confidence in the power of outward unity to convince the unbelieving world might be a misplaced confidence in the flesh. 'Outward unity', he wrote, 'is by itself no spiritual phenomenon.'[16] The true Catholics are those 'who worship God by the Spirit of God, and need no sacerdotal aid, but glory in Christ Jesus, and have no confidence in mere largeness and visibility of organisation or earthly rank of Church dignitary or earthly splendour in priest or temple.'[17]

Oman did not answer the question how the true Church, comprising the faithful in all churches, might be recognised. This true Church clearly could not be identified with the visible Church, nor could it be achieved by amalgamating all churches into an organisation with a uniformly accepted creed and ritual. He preferred to locate the true Church in those who had 'affinity of soul'. 'To find Christ we must discriminate the fellowship of the two or three with whom we are met in Christ's name, and discriminate our own right to be reckoned of the number.'[18] No denomination, in his view, could claim to be the true Church. Yet 'no Church wholly fails to show the active presence of the true leaven.'[19] For all their faults the churches were the treasure houses of the ages and the storehouses of the Spirit. In the context of the discussions taking place in the aftermath of the Lambeth Appeal, Oman's words took on a new relevance. Lambeth was inviting the non-episcopal churches to appropriate the treasures of the past. But they could do this only by discovering the same spirit working in their hearts, not by submitting to external authority. 'The heritage of free men', he concluded, 'can only be won and held by the free, who do not subject themselves to any human guidance, but press nearer to the centre of all truth, and live more zealously the life which tests truth. To be heirs of the free – and there is no other spiritual heritage - we must be set free with the liberty of the children of God.'[20]

In *Vision and Authority* Oman faithfully followed a strictly Protestant understanding of the Church. He made a clear distinction between the religious idea of the Church, as a society which is subject to a higher order of love and freedom, and the institutional form in which it might be embodied in any given time or place. This distinction had been a prime cause of the Reformation. Wycliffe had defined the Church as the assembly of all the elect - the *congregatio omnium praedestinatorum*. This was the mystical Body of Christ, whose sole head was Christ and its sole bond of fellowship was love. The distinction commonly drawn between priest and people was false. The idea that the Church needed a visible head was both worldly and a denial of the efficacy of the guidance of the Church by her divine yet invisible Head. It was difficult to reconcile the issues of order and ministry, which had been raised by the Lambeth Appeal, with this concept of the Church. In principle all baptised Christians had the power to forgive sins. The choice of some to serve as ministers was no more than a requirement of church order.

---

[16]   ibid. p. 164.
[17]   ibid. p. 165.
[18]   ibid. p. 169.
[19]   ibid. p. 172.
[20]   ibid. p. 175.

Fundamental Principles

The task of confronting the issues of the Lambeth Appeal was taken up by P Carnegie Simpson who was Professor of Church History at Westminster College, and chairman of the drafting committee of the Joint Conference. In 1923 he published *Church Principles*[21] which he described as a note which he had prepared for the committee of six Anglicans and six Free Churchmen who were meeting at Lambeth Palace 'to explore fundamental questions relating to reunion'.

In his third chapter, dealing with 'People and Ministry', Simpson argued that the constitutive principle of the Church was to be found in the union of Christ and his People. Against Oman he asserted that 'The Church is not constituted on two principles of which the second is "order"; it is constituted solely on the creative principle of the *unio mystica*.'[22] The Church therefore is primary and comprehensive. 'All Church powers or functions are committed in the first instance to the whole body of believing people, and not to a section or order within it.' This was a radically different approach from the view that Christ had given certain essential powers and functions to the Apostles alone. 'The Church is the primary and comprehensive conception, for whatever powers and functions essential to the Church were given to the Apostles were either given also to members of the Church who were not Apostles, or else were given to the Apostles as representing the whole membership.'[23] Simpson rejected a sacerdotalism which restricts priesthood to a clerical order and argued that the whole Church shared in priesthood:

> The New Testament never even suggests priesthood as the prerogative of the ministry, but always associates it (apart from the unique priesthood of Christ) with the whole body.[24]

The whole Church constitutes the 'priesthood', yet it has (and needs) the ministry to act as 'ministerial organs of the Church's priesthood' – a phrase which Simpson borrowed from R C Moberly, who had argued that 'the priesthood of the ministry is to be established not through depreciation but through exaltation of the priesthood of the whole body.'[25] But the ministry is not primary, nor does the ministry confer a priestly nature upon the Church. In a striking phrase Simpson claimed that 'It is not ordination which makes the priest; it is redemption.'[26] Priesthood belongs to the whole Church, including of course the ministry, but the ministry does not have a priesthood different from, or additional or superior to that of the whole Church. This emphasis on the priesthood of the whole Church did not however devalue the ministry as seemed often to happen. The ministry 'was also an "organ of the whole body" in such functions as are to be exercised not by the individual but by the body collectively.'[27] It provided, for example, for the orderly celebration by the Church of the sacraments appointed and given by the Lord of the Church. In the Lord's Supper 'it is the Cup "which we bless", the Bread "which we break"; and the "we" here is the Christian fellowship observing the sacred rite together.'[28] The minister does not create the sacrament, for this is given by Christ, but exercises a 'representative' function on behalf of the whole Church.

[21]   P Carnegie Simpson, *Church Principles* (London: Hodder and Stoughton, 1923).
[22]   op. cit. p. 63.
[23]   ibid. p. 64.
[24]   ibid. p. 65.
[25]   R C Moberly, *Ministerial Priesthood*, (London: John Murray 1910) p. 254.
[26]   Simpson, op. cit. p. 66.
[27]   ibid. p. 68.
[28]   ibid.

'Representative' does not mean that the ministry is only an administrative convenience for the sake of good order. The ministry is Christ's gift:

> It is something sent or 'given' *to* the Church – as also to the world – even more than something authorised or commissioned *from* the Church. It is therefore there to please and serve not it, but Him.[29]

The minister is not the Church's delegate. Ministry is a stewardship in which the minister is directly responsible to the Church's Head. It is therefore inaccurate to describe a minister as 'the minister of such and such a congregation or church'. 'He may serve *in* that congregation or Church; but he is there the servant *of* Christ.' The minister shares the commission given by the Risen Lord to the whole Church, but has also 'a direct vocation from Christ to speak and act as His minister.'[30]

Simpson emphasised that the minister's vocation precedes the Church's commission. It seemed to him that in too many debates on the ministry, the ecclesiastical commission appeared to be given greater weight than the personal vocation. Reformed Church principles always began with the call of Christ. It was by virtue of the minister's vocation that the Church issued its commission. A minister is made solely by the call of Christ.

> What the Church does in ordination is not to constitute a man a minister and not even to confer the primary and essential qualification of ministry, but it is to recognise a ministry of Christ already in being.[31]

The Church's principal responsibility in ordination is therefore to ensure that the person to be ordained has in reality been chosen and called. The testing of the call by the Church was far more important than the ritual of the ordination ceremony.

> I regard Churches which are specially solicitous in testing vocation as having a really higher doctrine of ordination than Churches which are meticulous about method.[32]

The local congregation had an important responsibility within the process of testing vocation. This had a long history in the tradition and could be traced back to one of the Canons of Hippolytus describing the choice of a bishop:

> Let the Bishop be chosen of all the people. Let the people say, 'we choose him'. Then, when silence is restored throughout the congregation, let them all pray for him, saying, 'O God, give strength to him whom Thou hast prepared for us'.[33]

What had often become in practice a mere formality needed to be restored to a central place in the Church's practice. Order was important to the life of the Church, and should never be down-

---

29   ibid. p. 70.
30   ibid. p. 71.
31   ibid. p. 75.
32   ibid. p. 76.
33   Lindsay, *Church and Ministry in the Early Centuries*, p. 246, quoted Simpson, op. cit. p. 76.

graded to 'mere' ceremony. 'Even secondary things', said Simpson, 'have a right to exist', since, as in the laying on of hands, they helped to 'edify' and build up the Church in faith and unity and to affirm and embody first principles. Order, however, should always be secondary to the minister's vocation to ministry and the Church's testing and recognition of the call.

In a later book, *The Evangelical Church Catholic*,[34] Simpson developed some of the ideas which he had previously worked out in *Church Principles*. He noted that in church life there is a strong tendency to give order a *determinative* place, but the effect of this was to exalt order above Christ who had not prescribed a constitution for His Church but left the Church to organise its own form and order. While he regretted that 'Half a dozen words from Christ about the transmission of the ministry might have saved endless discussion and disastrous division about episcopacy and presbytery', the Church had to live with the reality that 'Christ, who has done for us what we could not do for ourselves, does not do for us what, guided by His spirit, we can do for ourselves.'[35] In the course of the Church's long history the Holy Spirit had recognised and used various types of church order, including episcopal and presbyteral. It was dishonest to hide behind such ideas as 'uncovenanted mercies' since the only covenant was that of Christ himself. Order remained important, but it should have a 'regulative' not a determinative place. The Apostle Paul was 'the most practical organiser of the Church on ordered lines' but never allowed order to take a primary place. What mattered to him was that the gifts of God should be enabled to flow freely to build up the Church as the Body of Christ.

The fundamental principle to be observed is that of Christ's Headship of the Church. 'Its monarchy is settled, if what may be called its executive is not.'[36] The Church possesses ministers because these are Christ's will and gift as Scripture makes plain as, for example, in Ephesians 4.11ff.

> Thus the Christian ministry is not merely a human arrangement, arising from the fact that, obviously, every association must have officers and agents. While, of course, this is true of the Christian association as of any other, its application here is quite secondary. The Christian minister is, secondarily, an officer of the Church, but, primarily, he is a servant of Christ.[37]

It is not sufficient to say that Christ institutes a ministry. In an immediate and direct way Christ chooses, calls and appoints those who are to be ministers in the Church. Their ministry flows from a call 'from above' rather than through succession. Simpson underlines the point he had previously made in *Church Principles*. This is that when the Church ordains, it does not 'make' a person into a minister but rather recognises the call by Christ and enables that call to be fulfilled within the Church's ministry. Ordination is not a 'creating' but an 'ordering':

> What it can do is to recognise him as one called of Christ, and, then, place him in due *ordo* in the visible Church.[38]

[34]   P Carnegie Simpson, *The Evangelical Church Catholic,* (London: Hodder and Stoughton, 1934).
[35]   op. cit. p. 138.
[36]   ibid. p. 143.
[37]   ibid. p. 147.
[38]   ibid. p. 149.

'Ordering' follows verification which is the Church's weighty responsibility. Simpson does not discuss methods of testing and verification used by the different Churches. He does, however, stress the signficance, for the Reformed tradition, that the ultimate test and verification is that given by a local congregation which calls a person to be their minister. In a significant statement he says:

> If a body of Christian people, after prayer and consideration, declare that they have found that a certain man has a message from God for their souls, and that, therefore, they desire that he be the minister of Christ's Gospel to them, then the ordaining authority has ground, more solid than it might otherwise find, for concluding that he is indeed vocated of Christ, and so his ordination, in Christ's Name, may be carried out with believing confidence.[39]

Ordination is only permissible when a candidate has received a 'call' from a congregation ratifying the 'inward call' which the candidate had earlier received from God. The congregation's role was much more significant than that of exercising what might appear as a popular democratic vote.

The congregation was not, however, the ordaining authority. In the Presbyterian tradition ordinations were the act of a presbytery who were authorised to act in the name of the Church. The Westminster Confession had stated that 'to the Catholic visible Church Christ has given the ministry.' It was necessary that the Church as a whole, and not an individual, eg a bishop, or personally selected individuals, should authorise and carry out ordinations. The ordaining authority should be seen to represent the Church for whom they act, and not to be just the personal friends and associates of the ordinand.

Simpson added some further reflections on the question of 'succession' which remained a major topic of debate. Both episcopal and presbyterian churches could point to an impressive historical succession. However it was mistaken to base claims for the validity of ministry on theories of succession which could not be historically verified. 'No human being can guarantee that the chain has been kept intact all through the centuries; and the possible errors and deceptions are incalculable.'[40]

Theories of succession misrepresented the New Testament where the functions of the ministry are given to the Church in a rich variety of ministries, and not to an *'ordo'* in the Church. The Church as a historical institution was rightly concerned to transmit the tradition which it had received, and to do this through those who were authorised by the Church, yet it was important always to remember that

> We are nearer to the living Christ than we are to the apostles; and, far surer than we can be of any clerical chain throughout the centuries, are we certain of the continuity of the Church to which the ministry was given.[41]

These issues would continue to be fiercely debated in ensuing decades.

---

[39]   ibid. p. 151.
[40]   ibid. p. 156.
[41]   ibid. p. 160.

South India and Episcopacy

The major event in the life of the 20th century Church was the inauguration in November 1947 of the Church of South India. This involved the reunion of four dioceses of the Anglican Communion with the South India Province of the Methodist Church and the South India United Church, which had united Presbyterian, Congregational and Dutch Reformed bodies in 1908. It achieved in South India – on the 'mission' field – what Lambeth had failed to achieve in Britain. The Scheme of Union brought into one church the Anglican dioceses which claimed to have maintained an unbroken succession of episcopal consecration and ordination from the undivided Church with other religious bodies whose ministerial succession lacked this continuity.

The method of reunion was based upon four principles. First, the mutual acceptance of all members of the uniting churches. Bishops of the four Anglican dioceses were accepted as Bishops in the united Church. Ordained ministers of Word and Sacrament in the uniting churches were acknowledged by the united Church and were given the status of presbyters.

In the second place, the ordination of new presbyters in the united Church would be by the laying on of hands by bishops and presbyters. The consecration of new bishops would be by the laying on of hands of at least three existing bishops, thus maintaining continuity with the historic episcopate.

Thirdly, within the united Church conscientiously held convictions would not be over-ridden, nor would forms of worship or a particular ministry be imposed on congregations to which they conscientiously objected.

The fourth declared the intention of the uniting churches that eventually every minister exercising a permanent ministry in the united Church should be episcopally ordained.

It was noteworthy that the method chosen provided for the *reunion of divided parts of the Church*. It was *not the return to the one Church of some who had been separated from it*. Furthermore, from its formation the united Church was to stand within the historic succession of episcopal ordination and consecration. The Scheme of Union enabled non-episcopal churches to enter into that succession without denying the previous ordinations of their ministers. The Basis of Union did not insist on the acceptance of episcopacy as divinely appointed, nor did it claim episcopacy as the sole guarantee of valid sacraments and a valid ministry. Concepts of 'validity' were consciously eschewed.

The formation of the Church of South India owed much to the vision, leadership and theolgical pre-eminence of the Presbyterian Lesslie Newbigin. Though born in England and trained for the ministry at Westminster College, Cambridge, Newbigin was ordained a Church of Scotland minister by the Presbytery of Edinburgh in 1936, and went immediately to India to the Church of Scotland Madras Mission. At the formation of the Church of South India in 1947 he became Bishop of Madurai and Ramnad.

Newbigin saw the Church of South India not as the creation of something new but 'the restoration of something which had been broken'.[42] It was not a 'merger' but the return to a broken unity. Thus it was important to him that the united Church should stand within the continuous succession of episcopal ordination and consecration, and that it should enable the non-episcopal churches participating in the union to enter into that succession. These were not required to accept that their existing ministries were either irregular or defective, or that a continuous historical order in any way guaranteed the Church's union with Christ and in the Father through the Spirit. A ministry carrying the unbroken authority of the whole Church might nevertheless be its appropriate expression.

The Scheme of Union rejected a proposal for 'supplemental ordination' which had lain within the Lambeth Appeal of 1920. 'Supplemental ordination' implied that those who received it had already been truly ordained, but would additionally receive, in the words of an American proposal, 'such authority for the wider exercise of his ministry as, according to God's will, may be conveyed through the action of the Church in and by which the rite is performed.'[43] This proposal, while praising the grace of willingness by Christian churches to recognise what they lacked and to seek it from others, nevertheless exposed a serious flaw. Essentially this was that it was not clear *what*, for example, would be conveyed to episcopally ordained ministers who received supplemental ordination by a Presbytery. It could not be ordination because the Presbytery already recognised Anglican orders. it might be spiritual enrichment through sharing the inheritances of the divided churches, but that kind of mutual sharing did not require ordination. The nub of the problem, in Newbigin's view, was that the non-episcopal ministries had nothing to give in return. Their orders were derived from bodies, eg Presbyteries, which in the undivided Church did not possess authority to ordain. Hence they were unable to offer any corresponding authorisation to the Anglicans.

Newbigin also argued that ordination was not a repeatable rite. If the 'supplemental ordination' proposal were accepted, every future act of reunion in the Church would require the re-ordination of the entire ministries of the uniting churches. In time this would diminish the value which the Church had always attached to ordination. Ordination is to the ministry of the Church of Christ; its sphere of authority is in principle to the one Holy Catholic Church, not to just one or another of the 'branches' of the Church. The proposal for supplemental ordination therefore confused ordination with 'acts of authorisation, induction and installation by which an ordained minister receives authority to exercise his ministry in a particular sphere. The latter may be repeated many times, but the former is unrepeatable.'[44] Presbyterian tradition made a careful distinction between ordination to the ministry of the Holy Catholic Church and induction to a particular sphere of service within the Church.

The Scheme of Union affirmed that 'The Uniting Churches believe that the ministry is a gift of God through Christ to His Church, which He has given for the perfecting of the life and service of all its members'. All members of the Church share in the heavenly High Priesthood of the risen and ascended Christ. This heavenly priesthood could not be the exclusive possession of any individual or of any one order in the Church. The Church however possesses a 'special ministry' to which those who are called by God and set apart in the Church are ordained as ministers of Word and Sacrament:

---

42   L Newbigin, *The Reunion of the Church*, (London: SCM Press, 1948) p. 108.
43   Quoted by Newbigin, op. cit. p. 110.
44   op. cit. p. 113.

> The uniting Churches believe that in ordination God, in answer to the prayers of His Church, bestows on and assures to those whom He has called and His Church has accepted for any particular form of the ministry, a commission for it and the grace appropriate to it.[45]

Newbigin recognised the importance of the variety of ministries in the Church; ordained elders, unordained deacons, stewards, wardens, lay preachers, Sunday School teachers, and evangelists all shared in the Church's ministry. He regretted that these had been excluded from discussion on the ministry. As a Presbyterian he especially deplored the inadequate treatment in the Scheme of Union of the eldership as it had been understood in the Reformed Churches. His prime concern was with critics of the Scheme in regard to the ministry. Prominent among these were those who had contributed to *The Apostolic Ministry*,[46] a volume of essays on the history and doctrine of episcopacy which had been prepared under the direction of K E Kirk, then Bishop of Oxford. Contributors to the essays were for the most part critical of the South India Scheme. Their criticisms were founded on their belief that episcopal ordination alone was the guarantee of a valid ministry, and that the proposal to recognise non-episcopally ordained presbyters surrendered something that was vital to the existence of the Church. Eucharists celebrated by such presbyters would not in their view be true celebrations of the sacrament.

Newbigin had no quarrel with episcopacy as such. He had himself accepted consecration as a Bishop of the new Church, and recognised that episcopacy had existed historically in a variety of forms. The Church of South India offered a way of reconciling and uniting congregational, episcopal and presbyterian traditions. The Presbyterian minister, surrounded by elders and sharing with them the duty of *episcope*, while alone having the right to administer the sacraments, was a modern example of the earliest form of *episcope* in the churches of the New Testament. His dispute was with the claim that the continuity of the episcopal ministry was a guarantee of the Church's existence, and that 'there was from the beginning a continuous chain of ministerial authority from the Apostles to the bishops *distinct from the unity and continuity of the Church as a whole*.'[47] The historical argument, while confidently stated in *The Apostolic Ministry*, depended on hypothetical reconstructions. If these were, as was claimed, vital matters of faith, they required certainty rather than probability. The faith of the Church had to rest upon the certainties of the Gospel – the death of Christ for sinners, Christ's resurrection and ascension to the right hand of God, Christ's gift of the Holy Spirit – rather than upon the uncertainties of historical reconstruction. There were also profound theological objections to be stated. *The Apostolic Ministry* emphasised the importance to the Church of being able to claim that her ministry, in the Bishop of Oxford's words, 'derives direct from the Lord Himself in the days of His flesh'[48] and that the successors of the apostles exercised the plenitude of Christ's power 'looking back to Christ as its source, not by way of "the Church" but by way of the apostolic line of descent.'[49] In Newbigin's view this was seriously to detach the apostolate from the Church as the Body of Christ and the dwelling-place of the Spirit. It established the ministry 'defined in purely legal terms as a body of

---

[45]   *Scheme of Union*, pp. 6-7.
[46]   K E Kirk (ed) *The Apostolic Ministry*, (London: Hodder and Stoughton, 1946).
[47]   Newbigin, op. cit. p. 152.
[48]   *The Apostolic Ministry*, p. 52.
[49]   ibid. p. 49.

men entrusted with power of attorney on behalf of Christ, looking back to Christ in the flesh as the source of their authority.'[50] It thus completely omitted the emphasis in the New Testament on the ministry as the gift to the Church of her ascended Lord. According to Presbyterian understanding, ordination is an act of the living and ascended Christ in response to the prayer of the Church. In ordination the Church acts as the hands of the living Christ. *The Apostolic Ministry* effectively treated the apostolate as an extension of the Incarnation and detached the apostolate from the Church as the Body of Christ and the dwelling-place of the Spirit. The ascension of the Church's risen Lord and the pouring out of the Holy Spirit at Pentecost were thus deprived of their central place in relation to the Church's ministry. The Bishop of Oxford claimed that 'every theory of Church order must start from (the distinction) between the gifts of God and ecclesiastical enactments.'[51] Newbigin argued that this was not supported by the New Testament. The crucial question was rather how ecclesiastical acts were to be related to the will of Christ and in what manner the authority and grace of Christ were given to His ministers in the church's acts of ordination and consecration. It was indisputable that the exercise of the apostolic ministry required a commission to represent Christ to his Church, and through the Church to the world. Contributors to *The Apostolic Ministry* claimed that this commission could only be given by way of the apostolic line of descent, since only such an apostolic succession could provide the Church with the guarantee of its claim to be the Body of Christ. The logical conclusion of this claim, in Newbigin's view, must 'issue either in a total disconnection of the doctrine of the Church from that of the Holy Spirit.'[52] Pressed to its inexorable conclusion Pentecost need not have happened.

> The constitutive fact of the Church is not now a communion with the Living Christ in the Spirit, but the existence in its midst of men who have received a commission from Christ in the days of His flesh many centuries ago.[53]

Newbigin's fundamental argument was that, while the apostles were in some sense logically prior to the Church, and the apostolic ministry existed from the beginning in the sending of the Son by the Father, the constitutive fact of the Church was a communion with the living Christ in the Spirit, not by the relation of its members to the bishop.

> The apostolic ministry is, therefore, *both* continuous with, and a part of, the continuous organic life of the body *and* at the same time the bearer of a commission from Christ to the Church.[54]

In its acts of ordination, therefore, the Church both prays for the gifts of the Spirit to be poured out in and through the living Christ upon the Church, and, acting as the Body of Christ, commissions and empowers those who are set apart for the sacred work of ministry. Ordination is an act of the whole Church, including its lay as well as its ministerial members, which has received the apostolic commission. Here was an authentically 'Presbyterian' voice speaking as a missionary bishop within the historic succession.

---

[50]   Newbigin, op. cit. p. 159.
[51]   *The Apostolic Ministry*, p. 16.
[52]   L Newbigin, *The Reunion of the Church*, p. 163.
[53]   ibid. p. 164.
[54]   ibid. p. 166.

T W Manson and Apostolic Succession

The debate on apostolic succession was carried on simultaneously by T W Manson whose book, *The Church's Ministry*,[55] also offered a Presbyterian response to the issues raised in *The Apostolic Ministry*. Manson contended that the whole Church as the Body of Christ is the continuation of the Incarnation.

> The Body of Christ is the organism which He uses to carry out his purposes in the world in the same way that He used his physical body in the days of the ministry in Galilee and Judaea.[56]

The Church's ministry is a continuation of the Messianic ministry of Jesus in such as way that the Real Presence of Christ is manifested in the Christian community. While contributors to *The Apostolic Ministry* envisaged two forms of ministry in the Church – the 'essential' ministry tracing its descent from the apostles, and the 'dependent' ministry which emerged in the early Church communities, Manson argued that there is only one 'essential' ministry, which is the perpetual and ongoing ministry of the Church's Risen and Ever-Present Lord.

> That is the ministry which the Lord Jesus Christ opened in Galilee after John the Baptist had been put in prison, the ministry which He carried on in Galilee and Judaea, the ministry which He continues to this day in and through the Church, which is His Body.[57]

All other ministries derive from that one essential ministry, depend upon it, and are functional in that they represent within the Church the ministry of Christ, who came not to be served but to serve. Every ministry in the Church is a *diakonia*. Through the gift of the Spirit, the Church shares the risen life of her Lord, yet lives and serves in the world as the Body of the humiliated Christ.

Manson argued that the apostolic ministry belongs to the whole Church, and that the apostles were organs of the Church. Inasmuch as the Twelve had a special status conferred upon them by Jesus, it was personal and inalienable, and, more importantly, could not be transmitted to another. Their successors did not succeed to the special status, but to the continuation of the apostolic ministry. 'The Church is apostolic', said Manson, 'because she is called by Christ and empowered and instructed by Christ to go and make disciples of the nations.'[58]

The outcome of the apostolic work is the establishment of local congregations which in their turn enter into the apostolic ministry. The local congregation has a twofold ministry: it is to *proclaim* the Kingdom to those who are still outside, and to *manifest* the Kingdom in its own community life. Within the community some are marked out for leadership. The New Testament indicates the presence within the early Christian communities of a rich variety of 'ministries' including prophets, evangelists, and teachers.[59] When the congregation assembled for worship at Corinth, each member was a potential contributor to the liturgy.

---

[55]   T W Manson, *The Church's Ministry* (London: Hodder and Stoughton, (1948).
[56]   op. cit. pp. 20-21.
[57]   ibid.
[58]   ibid. p. 52.
[59]   e.g. *Ephesians* 4.11, *I Corinthians* chs 12-14.

One may have a psalm, another a piece of teaching *(didache)*, another a piece of prophesying *(apocalypsis)*, another speaking with tongues *(glossa)* and another the interpretation thereof.[60]

It is clear that in the early days the ministry of the Word belonged to the whole community. At this stage also organisation was fluid. What was of primary importance was the Real Presence of Christ in His Church, the allegiance of the members to Christ, the fulfilment of the Church's apostolic and pastoral task, and the availability of the means of grace. Organisation in these early communities was subordinate to function. The life of the Church in its totality was the continuation of the messianic ministry of Jesus.

In *The Church's Ministry* Manson identified two approaches to ministry which had developed within the Church during its two thousand year history. On the one side there was the ministry conceived in terms of 'hierarchy' in which power was conferred from above; on the other the ministry was understood in terms of specific tasks undertaken in obedience to the call of God and by the appointment of a congregation of believers. There is no suggestion, for example, that the various ministries in the Corinthian Church were of apostolic appointment or commission. Ministry conceived as 'hierarchy' emphasised orders and ordination, while the alternative view of ministry emphasised 'calling' and the equipment by the Spirit of those called for the varied tasks of ministry. These two understandings often appeared incompatible and irreconcilable. But this could be the case only if one, at least, were radically false. Since both forms of ministry had manifestly been blessed by the Spirit in the course of the Church's history, Manson concluded that 'both conceptions of the ministry embody some basic truth which can be found if we will look earnestly enough for it.'[61]

In any act of ordination two factors were involved. The first was the call and appointment of the minister by Christ. 'This is the necessary and sufficient condition of ministry: necessary because every genuine ministry is Christ's gift to the Church; sufficient because Christ is the source of all authority and power.'[62] The second is the acceptance of Christ's gift by the Church and the Church's formal recognition of the person whom Christ has called. 'By accepting him the ordaining body also recognises him as belonging to the order of ministers of the Word and sacraments, than which there is no higher ministry.'[63] The ordaining body may be a bishop, a presbytery or a congregation; the historic experience of the Church was that its prayer that the one appointed should be equipped for the task had not gone unanswered.

If he has been called and equipped by Christ, all the bishops, presbyteries, and congregational meetings in the world cannot make him any more a minister than he is already.[64]

---

[60]   Manson, op. cit. p. 57.
[61]   ibid. p. 83.
[62]   ibid. p. 95.
[63]   ibid. p. 96.
[64]   ibid. p. 97. NB The Presbyterian Church of England did not at this time ordain women to the Ministry of Word and Sacrament.

It followed therefore that the Free Churches could not, without shameful disloyalty, compromise on the question of their orders. They should be prepared to accept any form of recognition by another communion provided this did not require or imply re-ordination. This was not a question of Presbyterian inflexibility but flowed from their high doctrine of the Church as the Body of Christ. Manson states this uncompromisingly when he writes

> It is because we believe in the Real Presence of Christ in His Church that we deny that any particular man or group of men is essential to an ordination. The Christ, who is for us the only and ever-present King and Head of the Church is the Maker of ministers; and He needs no Vicar to act for Him.[65]

Manson appears to imply that the composition of the ordaining body was immaterial and to lend support to an extreme view of congregational independency. He quotes approvingly from an ordination charge given by Bernard Manning, a leading Cambridge Congregationalist, at the ordination of a Congregational minister in which he had said to the members of the congregation: 'It is you who ordain. Other ministers present merely represent you'.[66] Yet for a Presbyterian this came too close to claiming for a local congregation rights which the Free Churches properly denied when they were claimed for the Papacy. To suggest, as Manning did, that other ministers present at an ordination were merely representatives of the local church was to push the autonomy of the local church beyond what might be warranted either by Scripture of the history of the Church. 'If the minister is ordained to the ministry of the universal Church, it follows inescapably that any ministers who take part do so as ministers of the universal Church, which is what they are by their own ordination.'[67] Manning's re-statement of congregational independency had the effect of reducing such ministers to mere spectators of a transaction which did not require their presence for it to be effective. This was a matter which, as Manson was aware, was exercising the minds of contemporary Congregationalists who had, for the most part, been brought up on the doctrine that the local congregation possessed all the powers of the Universal Church, and should therefore be free from any external constraint on its authority. This understanding of congregational autonomy owed much to the continuing influence of the five principles of the Congregational Polity which Dr R W Dale had set out in his *Manual of Congregational Principles*.[68] The fifth principle had stated that 'By the Will of Christ, every Society of Christians organised for Christian Worship, Instruction, and Fellowship is a Christian Church, and is Independent of External Control.' It was in reaction to such a claim that Anglicans and others asserted that Congregationalists ignored the wider life of the Church. Manson shared these concerns and offered a 'Sixth Principle' to Dale's five:

> By the will of Christ every Christian Church has an obligation to care for and be in fellowship with other Christian Churches.[69]

---

65   ibid. p. 97.

66   B L Manning, *A Layman in the Ministry*, (London: Independent Press, 1942) pp. 152-160.

67   Manson, op. cit p. 93.

68   R W Dale, *Manual of Congregational Principles*, (London: Congregational Union of England and Wales, 1884) pp. 9-89.

69   Manson, op. cit. p. 94.

In offering this additional Principle, Manson was reaching back beyond the 19th century to an earlier expression of Independency in which the importance of Councils and Synods had been recognised. His suggestion was warmly welcomed by some of his Congregationalist contemporaries, including John Huxtable, who agreed that 'Those who understand the origins of Congregationalism can testify that there is nothing here at all inconsistent with churchmanship as Congregationalists have been given to understand it, their plain failure to express this insight in their church life notwithstanding; and there are signs that they are learning in the school of experience what their fathers understood to be a truth of revealed religion.'[70]

In *The Church's Ministry* Manson was primarily responding to what he believed to be extreme and unwarranted claims for the historic episcopate as interpreted by contributors to *The Apostolic Ministry*. Dialogue between Congregationalists and Presbyterians had not yet seriously begun, but Manson provided a basis on which dialogue might begin. There were possibilities that Presbyterians and Congregationalists might overcome their differences and draw closer together.

---

[70]   J Huxtable, in a review of *The Church's Ministry*, (*The Presbyter 1948*, Vol. 6, No 4)

Chapter Five

Traditions of
Churches of Christ

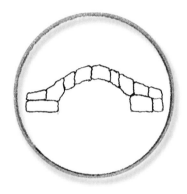

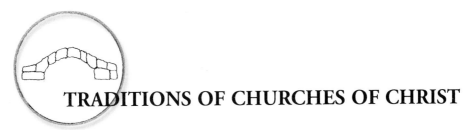

TRADITIONS OF CHURCHES OF CHRIST

A 'Bridge' Church?

The Churches of Christ, while standing within the Free Church tradition of worship and church order, maintained a certain distance from the other Free Churches in Britain. Their leading theologian of the mid-20th century, William Robinson, described the Churches of Christ as 'anti-denominational', and held that they regarded denominations as sinful.[1] They did not, for example, join the Free Church Federal Council until 1941. In the middle years of the 20th century two major church historians assessed the significance of the Free Church tradition without reference to the contribution of the Churches of Christ to that tradition.[2] This was not entirely due to the disparity of their number compared to the much larger Baptist, Congregationalist, Methodist and Presbyterian denominations. The Churches of Christ were a 'Free Church' with roots in the Reformed Church, yet by their weekly celebration of the Lord's Supper – then unheard of in the larger Free Church denominations - they appeared to represent a more 'Catholic' tradition than the predominantly preaching tradition of those denominations. In the ecumenical context of the 1930s Professor Will of Strasbourg included the Churches of Christ in a select group of what he called 'bridge churches' which were opposed on the one hand to Catholic ecclesiasticism and on the other to Protestant biblicism[3] They rejected the Apostolic Succession because of their conviction that the continuity of God's grace could not be guaranteed by what they regarded as 'mechanical legalist devices'. They believed that the authority of Christ was more than that of a hierarchy and depended upon a living and personal relationship between God and God's people. The sacred character of ordination derived from being conferred in Christ's name and on a personal plane.

Origins in Scotland – the 'Glasites' and the 'Scotch Baptists'

The liturgical traditions of the Churches of Christ may be traced back to John Glas (1695-1793), a minister of the Church of Scotland, who was deposed in 1730 for advocating 'the divine rights of the Redeemer in His Kingdom.' Glasite churches were established in Scotland and in other parts of Britain. The distinguished scientist, Michael Faraday, was a member of the Glasite Church in London. In the Glasite churches the chief Sunday service was a celebration of the Lord's Supper. The liturgy included the reading of Scripture, the preaching of the sermon, acts of praise, offertory and communion. Glas insisted that since the offering of worship was the priestly act of the whole Church, it was essential that the worship should be corporate and not be performed by a single minister on behalf of the congregation. Thus in the Glasite churches – and unusually for worship in the Reformed Churches

---

[1]   William Robinson, Principal of Overdale College from 1920-49.

[2]   E A Payne, *The Free Church Tradition in the Life of England*, (London: SCM Press, 1944), and H M Davies, *The English Free Churches*, (Oxford: 1952).

[3]   R Dunkerley (ed) *Ministry and Sacraments*, (London: SCM Press, 1937) p. 499.

– the services were led by several ministers, The President would be an ordained Presbyter, but there would also be readers, a precentor, a preacher and servers. Glas additionally introduced into the liturgy a section which he called the 'Prayers of the Church' in which any member of the congregation might offer prayer which the President would conclude with a summarising collect and the Lord's Prayer said by the whole congregation. The liturgical emphasis lay on the offering of worship by the whole Church as a corporate – or what Glas himself called a 'social' - act.

Ministry was held in high esteem in the Glasite churches. Each congregation had two orders of ministry - Presbyters and Deacons - but ministry was not related to professional status. A Presbyter might be wholly or partly supported financially by the church, or might receive no financial support.

In the 1760s another group emerged as a breakaway from the Glasite churches. These were known as the Scotch Baptists. Their leaders, Archibald McLean (1733-1812) and Robert Carmichael, had been members of the Glasite congregation in Glasgow, but withdrew from the congregation over differences of opinion over baptism. They rejected infant baptism and sought a more evangelical stance on Baptism and Holy Communion. The Scotch Baptists continued the Glasite emphasis on a plurality of elders and pastors in each congregation rather than the single pastor of the Dissenting tradition.

The 'Campbellite Baptists'

The Churches of Christ arose later through a group who were originally known as the 'Campbellite Baptists'. They took their name from their formative theologian, Alexander Campbell (1788-1866). Campbell had been brought up as an Irish Presbyterian minister. He was educated in the University of Glasgow where he came under the influence of Greville Ewing, the minister of the Independent congregation at Glasgow Tabernacle, and was especially convinced by their practice of weekly communion. In 1809 Alexander Campbell and his family emigrated to America to join his father, Thomas Campbell (1763-1854) who had emigrated two years earlier in 1807. Following a dispute with the Secession Presbyters of Charteris in Western Pennsylvania over his practice of allowing all Presbyterians to receive communion in his congregation, Thomas Campbell withdrew from the Presbyterian Church and with other like-minded friends formed the Christian Association of Washington, Pennsylvania. In a long declaration and Address (1809)[4] he enumerated a series of Fourteen Propositions for the new Association. The first of these began by emphasising the essential unity of the Church.

> The Church of Christ upon earth is essentially, intentionally, and constitutionally one, consisting of all those in every place that profess their faith in Christ…

This Proposition set out the fundamental belief of Churches of Christ in the organic unity of the Church. According to their understanding, denominations were sinful and their goal was that all Christians should be gathered into one holy, catholic and apostolic church. Campbell went on in his Second Proposition to insist that, while the Church upon earth necessarily existed in particular and distinct societies, local churches should offer recognition and acceptance to one another.

---

[4]   The text of Thomas Campbell's Declaration and Address is printed in D M Thompson (ed), *Stating the Gospel - Formulations and Declarations from the Heritage of the United Reformed Church*, (Edinburgh: 1990) pp. 118-183.

...there ought to be no schisms, no uncharitable divisions among them. They ought to receive each other as Christ Jesus hath also received them to the glory of God.

In Proposition Four Campbell stated his belief that the New Testament offered a perfect constitution for the worship, discipline and government of the Church in the same way as the Old Testament had provided a model for the worship, discipline and government of Israel. Where the New Testament was silent on matters of church order, no human authority was empowered to impose new commands or ordinances upon the Church.

Nothing ought to be received into the faith or worship of the Church, or be made a term of communion among Christians, that is not as old as the New Testament.

Campbell's abhorrence of schism in the Church is clearly indicated in Proposition Ten where he describes division among Christians as 'a horrid evil', as anti-Christian, anti-scriptural and anti-natural:

It is anti-Christian, as it destroys the visible unity of the Body of Christ, as if He were divided against Himself, excluding and excommunicating a part of Himself. It is anti-scriptural, as being strictly prohibited by His sovereign authority; a direct violation of His express command. It is anti-natural, as it excites Christians to condemn, to hate and oppose one another, who are bound by the highest and most endearing obligations to love each other as brethren...

Campbell's Propositions provided a basis for the Association. In keeping with the Scotch Baptists the Campbellites looked to the New Testament as the only sufficient basis for faith and church order. They believed that the Church should faithfully model its life on the pattern revealed in the New Testament, and that it was possible to restore that pattern. The idea of searching for the 'old paths' would later exert a profound influence upon the Churches of Christ.

Churches of Christ

The Churches of Christ in Great Britain emerged in 1842 from this ferment of ideas as they sought expression in the Glasite, Scotch Baptist, Campbellite Baptists and other disparate groups. It was a body including both Presbyterian and Congregationalist elements. Their origin in the Scotch Baptists and their rejection of infant baptism might have suggested a stronger affinity with the Baptist Churches but their polity was less 'independent' than that of the Baptist Churches.[5] William Robinson described the Churches of Christ as having 'emerged out of the Presbyterian household.'[6] Yet from their foundation they emphasised, perhaps more strongly than Congregationalists or Presbyterians, the necessity of organic unity to the Church as the Body of Christ. They had a lively sense of the authority of the Church. An American member of the 'Disciples', as the Churches of Christ were known in the United States, stated that '"The Disciples"

---

[5]   20th century discussions with the Baptist Union of Great Britain failed to lead to union. See D M Thompson, *Let Sects and Parties Fall*, (Birmingham: Berean Press, 1980) p. 190.

[6]   R Dunkerley (ed) *Ministry and Sacraments*, (London: SCM Press, 1937) p. 253.

believe the Church to be divine, and that it is as important to obey the bride as the bridegroom. Hence they do not believe that a man can be a Christian outside the Church.[7] This emphasis was important at a time when the Protestant Churches were tending to disregard the authority of the Church and to conceive the Church more in terms of a moral society than a divinely appointed institution.

Church Order, Ministry and Worship

Churches of Christ anticipated the ecumenical movement of the 20th century in their conviction that the whole Church, including themselves, was in schism, and that the churches needed to repent of their disunity before the wounds in the Body of Christ could be healed.

In contrast to the typically Protestant doctrine of the interpretation of Scripture as the Word of God, often leading to private interpretation, or a Catholic doctrine of Papal Infallibility, Churches of Christ sought a consensus of the considered and qualified opinion of the Church Catholic.

In their church order they insisted upon parity between the non-professional and the professional ministry. They were strongly opposed to the common Protestant practice of 'one-man ministry'.[8] From their Glasite roots they maintained in the local church the twofold ministry of Presbyters (Elders or Bishops) and Deacons, and in the Church national or Catholic the single order of Evangelists or Missionaries. They held that, since it is the Church which as the priestly body corporately celebrates the Eucharist, a congregation might appoint a lay person to preside. In no sense did the ministry 'validate' the celebration. William Robinson affirmed that 'as the Church is the fountainhead of orders, there would be nothing invalid in a layman celebrating the Eucharist, if the Church appointed him to do so, as the sacrifice of praise and thanksgiving is performed by the whole Church as the priestly body.'[9]

Since worship was the priestly act of the whole Church, and the Eucharist was the central act of the Church's worship, it followed that the eucharistic celebration should be the normal act of Sunday worship, and that all who were present should communicate. Churches of Christ diverged from the Presbyterian tradition, in which the eucharist was normally a quarterly celebration. They differed also from Congregational practice where, in most congregations, the Lord's Supper had become a distinct service following upon the preceding 'preaching' service and often attended by only a minority – perhaps the specially devout - of those who had been present at the earlier service.

It is clear that, while there were similarities between Churches of Christ and Congregationalists and Presbyterians, the differences were even greater. From the perspective of the 19th century, it would not have been obvious – or even likely – that these three traditions would come together into one Church. For this to happen there were many obstacles to be overcome. That it happened at all is one of the many surprises of church history.

---

[7]   Prof Lowker 1888, quoted by W Robinson, *A Church Order, Reformed and Catholic*, The Presbyter, 1944.
[8]   See D M Thompson, op. cit. p. 175.
[9]   Robinson, op. cit.

Churches of Christ join the Ecumenical Movement

Churches of Christ, as we have seen, had not been involved in the response to the Lambeth Appeal of 1920 as they did not belong to the National Free Church Council. There were those amoung them who favoured membership but fundamental differences over the nature of faith, baptism and conversion meant that there was no possibility at that time of such a proposal being accepted. But they had become deeply committed to the developing ecumenical movement through the Faith and Order Movement which emerged from the Edinburgh Missionary Conference of 1910.

Their participation in the Faith and Order Conference at Lausanne had given Churches of Christ greater confidence in both the ecumenical movement and their contribution towards it. They had been able to restate in a wider context their conviction that their church order was a conscious attempt to restore the permanent elements of the ministry of the New Testament Church. Their twofold ministry of a pastoral and teaching ministry of bishops (presbyters) and deacons in the local Churches, and a ministry of evangelists (missionaries) with a wider commission to preach the Gospel and extend the Kingdom, whether at home or abroad, was firmly rooted in the New Testament, and offered also a viable model for contemporary church order. They had welcomed the emphasis in the Conference Report on other ministries – such as preaching, teaching and spiritual counsel – for the development of the Church's corporate spiritual life. They had taken the opportunity to re-affirm their belief that, while the office of a minister in the Church of Christ is a sacred one, it should in no way be conditioned by a minister's professional occupation. They had argued for their conviction that in a united Church there should be room for both a non-professional and a professional ministry in all the orders of bishop, deacon and evangelist. They were well placed to make their contribution to the ongoing ecumenical debate concerning ministry and ordination.

Edinburgh 1937

The next milestone on the ecumenical journey was the Faith and Order Conference held at Edinburgh in 1937. In preparation for this important Conference William Robinson prepared a detailed exposition of the views of Churches of Christ on a range of issues including Infant Baptism, the Eucharist and the Ministry.[10] On the question of the Ministry, Robinson agreed on the importance of continuity but rejected the claim that the continuity of the Church could be maintained by its '*structure* or *form*'. 'There must be continuity in the structure of the Church', he said, 'but, in the first place, such continuity is guaranteed by the preaching of the Word and the administration of the Sacraments.' Churches of Christ therefore refused to accept the claims of a rigid theory of *successio apostolica* as guaranteeing a valid ministry. He hinted that Churches of Christ might be prepared to recognise that Episcopacy might possess a measure of authority and provide some guarantee of regularity, but rejected as untenable the claim that where there was not an episcopally ordained priest there is no real Sacrament.

---

[10]   R Dunkerley (ed) op. cit. pp. 253-68.

Robinson's other main concern was to restate the witness of Churches of Christ to the authority of the Church over against that of the hierarchy. Hence their emphasis on 'lay' ministry and the restoration in the Eucharist of the *Orate Fratres* which had formed an important part of the liturgy of the primitive Catholic Church.[11]

A New Look at Ministry and Ordination

Exposure to and participation in the developing ecumenical movement of the 20th century thus stimulated Churches of Christ to re-examine their traditional stance on the ministry and ordination. They came to realise that a definition of the Ministry was not as straightforward a matter as many had assumed. Under the influence of their leading scholars, and in particular of William Robinson, they became aware of the immense amount of research which had been undertaken in recent years by New Testament scholars worldwide, and to accept that their findings had to be taken into account. The external ecumenical debate necessitated internal discussion within Churches of Christ on matters concerning ministry and ordination.

The groundwork for this debate was laid by important Conference Papers on the Ministry by A C Watters in 1936 and W J Clague in 1937 and 1938. Archie Watters' paper examined the question of how Churches of Christ might meet the need for an increase in whole-time ministry while preserving – and enhancing – their tradition and practice of mutual ministry. The previous two decades had seen an increase in the number of whole-time ministers from 18 in 1914 to 31 in 1936. Most of these had been attached to one church for more than one year. Overall membership during the period had remained virtually static (1914: 15,228, 1936: 15,838) but there had been a loss of members by 'Separations' almost equivalent to the total membership, A more detailed examination of membership statistics revealed, however, that where a worker had been employed whole time, the ratio of losses had fallen dramatically. The evidence suggested that congregations with a whole-time minister benefited from a higher quality of teaching and more effective pastoral care. There were thus strong arguments, on evangelistic and pastoral grounds, for increasing whole-time ministry. But would this jeopardise the mutual ministry which was crucial to their witness? Watters recognised the danger that congregations might become listless and passive through relying too heavily upon whole-time ministers, but believed this might be avoidable. Part of the remedy, as he saw it, lay in abandoning the doctrine of Independency of Congregations 'which I believe to be unscriptural'.

> The Church Universal is composed of many individual congregations, not one of which is independent of the others in the highest conception of the Church's welfare.[12]

An individual congregation should rather subordinate its independency to the general interest of a wider group of congregations. Mutual ministry might then flourish between congregations. Watters suggested that a number of congregations in a city or district might co-operate by sharing their resources.

---

[11] These were intercessions offered by members of the congregation and summed up by the President who presented the Prayers of the Brethren in a brief collect.

[12] A C Watters, Conference Paper 1936, *How We May Increase Whole-time Ministry and, at the same time preserve Mutual Ministry in our Churches,* p. 45.

> It would then be possible in many cases to have a plurality of whole-time ministers employed in the mutual ministry of one Church, but serving in rotation the group of congregations forming the Church.[13]

Perhaps these are prophetic words for the United Reformed Church as it seeks how best to use its resources of ministry in the opening years of the 21st century.

The Conference Paper delivered by W J Clague at the annual Conferences of 1937 and 1938 was entitled: *The Principles of Church Organisation in Primitive Christianity and Their Application to Present-Day Church Life*. The Conference of 1937 was held in the same year as the World Conference on Faith and Order at Edinburgh. The Churches, with the exception of the Roman Catholic Church, had prepared for the conference a conspectus of their doctrine and practice in relation to the Ministry and the Sacraments. The Ministry was the crux of the matter since there was far more agreement among scholars of the different Churches on Baptism and the Lord's Supper than on the Ministry. Differences on Ministry derived from different conceptions of the Church. Early in his Paper Clague made the comment that

> If, for example, our conception of the Church is "Catholic" merely, the Ministry will be regarded as imposed on the Church from above, hierarchical in system, sacerdotal in function, possessing authority unquestioned because believed to have been handed down in unbroken descent from the Apostles of our Lord. If, on the other hand, our conception is "Protestant" merely, the Ministry will be regarded as from below, evolved out of the Churches' needs, subordinate to the Church and without any priestly function other than those which are the spiritual birthright of every member of Christ's Body.

Much of the Conference Paper of 1937 was given to tracing the development of the organisation of the Primitive Church. Initially the Church in Jerusalem held their general assemblies and meetings for missionary preaching in the Temple. They also met in household groups for prayer and the breaking of bread. While the *house* was the unit for purposes of worship, the *city* itself was the unit for administration and for directing the Church's mission. This pattern prevailed as the Church moved outward into the Roman world. Paul's letters, for example those to Corinth, were directed to the Church in a particular city, because the city Church, not the house church, was the primary unit for regulating the Church's affairs. These City churches regarded themselves as members of the one Body, into which they had been incorporated by Baptism. The government of this primitive Church was centred in the Apostles, but as the Church grew numerically and spread geographically into Gentile communities, church authority was exercised either directly by the Apostles who had founded them, or by apostolic delegates, such as Timothy and Titus. When the ministry of the Foundation Apostles became extinct, authority became centred in the local ministry of Bishops and Deacons. From the second century these local communities began to combine in more extensive federations. Out of informal assemblies of Bishops, Presbyters, and sometimes Deacons, there emerged the Provincial Councils. In the fourth century the Ecumenical Councils appeared, attended by Bishops representing the Church in all parts of the Roman Empire and ranking above the Provincial Councils. The final step in the

---

[13]   ibid. p. 46.

organisation of the Primitive Church was the development of the Patriarchate through the division of Christendom into five provinces based on the major cities of Rome, Constantinople, Alexandria, Antioch and Jerusalem, the Bishop of each of these cities being the Patriarch of the province.

Clague's purpose in tracing this development was to demonstrate that the Church had not developed according to a 'blueprint' which had been given by Jesus. Its Church order had evolved under the guidance of the Holy Spirit. Churches of Christ believed that their system of church organisation was in harmony with that of the Primitive Church. In the New Testament period the form of the Church's ministry in any given locality had not been uniform or stereotyped. The principle of the New Testament Church was 'not rigid uniformity or organisation but adaptation of methods to the need of the moment and the character of the work waiting to be done.'[14] It was clear that the constitutional unit was the Church of a whole city or district. Within the city or district there might be several congregations, but the basis of the Church's organisation was not Congregationalism, which Clague described as 'a theory of Church government ...of relatively recent development in Church history' and as 'the doctrine of democracy as applied to the Church.'[15] He claimed that the New Testament gave no sanction to the theory that 'each congregation can order its own affairs and is wholly independent of other parallel congregations or that the city groups of Christians were separate Churches self-sufficient in themselves.' His view was that Churches of Christ had in fact drawn too heavily upon Congregationalist ideas and that these had had a detrimental effect upon the vitality of the Churches, leading in many congregations to corporate weakness. The present need, as he saw it, was to relate city and district Churches to each other in life and service by bonds that were stronger than mere co-operation. The solution was to blend "Congregational" and "Presbyterian" principles of church government and practice. This needed to be done in such a way that the ministry of Elders and Deacons would remain necessary and vital. The 'whole-time' ministry of Evangelists should be clearly seen as bearing responsibility to the whole Body and not just to a particular local community. This was a necessary principle which had not been sufficiently recognised, and which the ordination of Evangelists should make clear. 'No local Church should be able or indeed desirous of acting independently or individually in the matter of enjoying their services. They should have a recognised status throughout the brotherhood as representing in their person and service the whole Body.'[16] Clague recognised that the designation of "Evangelist" was open to a variety of interpretations and suggested that the 'scriptural and time-honoured' designation of "Minister" should be used to describe those who were in the full-time service of the churches.

In the sequel to his Paper at the 1938 Conference, Clague pursued the theme with particular reference to present day systems of Church order. Sections of the Paper reviewed Episcopalianism, Presbyterianism, and Congregationalism and Independency, and offered valuable analyses of these traditions from the perspective of Churches of Christ. In a brief reference the Methodist Church is classified as Presbyterian in structure, comprising a hierarchy of courts of the Church, the highest court of the Methodist Conference corresponding to the Presbyterian General Assembly.

---

[14]   W J Clague, *Conference Paper 1937*, p. 41.
[15]   ibid.
[16]   ibid. 43.

In the course of their history, the Episcopalians, Presbyterians and Congregationalists had all claimed scriptural authority for their Church order, though in the case of the Presbyterians and Congregationalists these claims had now been modified:

> Leaders of Presbyterianism and Independency today would justify their respective systems of Church order less on a literalistic interpretation of the New Testament Scriptures than on grounds of adaptability to present day requirements.[17]

The same might not however be said of Anglican claims for episcopacy, and the forceful re-statement of those claims in *The Apostolic Ministry*[18] was not to appear until nearly a decade later.

The significance of Clague's Conference Paper of 1938 lay in his recognition that questions of order and ministry in the Church, which Churches of Christ had traditionally regarded as simple and clear-cut were in reality matters of great complexity requiring careful study and wise judgement. Churches of Christ needed to change their attitude on these questions if their contributions to the movement for Church Union, to which they were fully committed through their membership of the Faith and Order Movement, and not least their understanding of Conversion in relation to the sacrament of Baptism, were not to be neutralised. Their doctrine of Baptism was the only ground on which they could justify their separate existence as a religious connexion, since they held practically little else of vital importance in common with one or another body of Christian believers. In a historic statement Clague declared that the use of modern research methods in the study of the New Testament 'has shown our position on Church order and ministry to be untenable.'[19] It was therefore essential that Churches of Christ should formulate a system more in keeping with New Testament principles and modern needs. He pleaded that over the next generation Churches of Christ should move away from a congregational independency towards 'a system of city or district Church order' as he had advocated in his previous Paper. This would not be easy, and might take a generation or more to accomplish, but he believed it could become 'the instrument of order and unity throughout the whole Body'. In the matter of Church order, Churches of Christ had more to learn from Presbyterians than Congregationalists, who at that time continued to maintain their emphasis upon the autonomy of the local congregation. He deplored the evidence that too often decisions of Conferences or Assemblies were ignored by the very congregations whose members had influenced those decisions by their votes. Conferences and General Assemblies, in keeping with the Councils of the Primitive Church, needed to possess 'executive authority', not to usurp the place of Christ as the only Lawgiver in His Church, but to facilitate administrative government, spiritual leadership and evangelistic enterprise. These changes, though far-reaching, looked forward to the day when Protestant Christianity would have healed its divisions and become one organic body. While no one at that time could forecast the structure of a re-united Protestant Church, Clague was prepared to believe that it would take the form of an Episcopal Church, though shorn of its exclusive claims and freed from the doctrine of Apostolic Succession.

---

[17]   ibid. 45.

[18]   K E Kirk, *The Apostolic Ministry*, (London: Hodder and Stoughton, 1946)

[19]   *Conference Paper* 193. p. 58.

The Commission on Ordination 1942

The discussion and debate which was stimulated by these Papers provided the context for the appointment by the Annual Conference in 1936 of a Commission to consider the ordination of Evangelists and also the ordination of Elders and Deacons. This Commission reported back to Conference in 1942, their Report[20] following closely the work of a similar Commission of the American Churches which had reported to the International Convention of Churches of Christ in 1939.

The Commission examined the New Testament evidence and concluded (from I Cor 15.5) that the Twelve Apostles, as the first witnesses to the resurrection, had been the first to hold the office of missionary or evangelist. They were 'the first officers of the Church Universal', having been appointed to their office by Jesus after his resurrection.[21] The apostles were appointed to a unique office in which they could have no successors. 'In the nature of the case', said the Report, 'they could have none, for one of their chief qualifications was to have seen Jesus after his resurrection.' Their task, according to the Report, 'is the evangelisation of the world by witnessing to the facts of the Gospel, the supreme fact of which is the resurrection.'

While the apostles had no successors – Churches of Christ emphatically rejected claims of 'apostolic succession' – the Twelve appointed others to office, as is evidenced by Acts 6.1-8, where seven men of good repute, full of the Spirit and of wisdom, were appointed to undertake duties in relation to the pastoral care of widows, thus enabling the apostles to concentrate on prayer and the ministry of the Word. The seven were appointed to office by prayer and the laying on of hands. Later Paul commissioned Timothy and Titus for work in Ephesus and Crete.

The Report acknowledged a lack of clarity in the New Testament over the nature of some of these appointments to ministry. Little is known of the work of the Seven, except for Stephen and Philip, who appear to act more as evangelists than deacons; in Acts 21:8 Philip is described as an 'evangelist'. Both do the work of evangelists rather than the work of 'distribution' to which they were initially appointed.

Similarly, while the apostles had no successors, the group of the first apostles was widened to include others. Matthias was appointed to fill the place vacated by Judas (Acts 1:15-26). Paul, Barnabas, Silas and James, the Lord's brother, are all described as apostles,[22] although no account is given of their appointment and ordination. One member of the Commission actually proposed a distinction between 'Apostles of Christ' and 'Apostles of the Church', regarding Barnabas, Silas and James in the latter category.

The Commission recognised that the designation 'evangelist' was rare in the New Testament. Evangelists were included among the gifts of ministry listed in Ephesians 4:11 – 'some prophets, some evangelists, some pastors and teachers'. Timothy was directly charged to 'do the work of an evangelist' (2 Tim 4:5). 'Nevertheless', says the Report, 'though the references to Evangelists

---

20   *Churches of Christ Year Book 1942.*
21   John 20:23.
22   I Corinthians 9:1, Acts 14:14, I Thessalonians 2:6, Galatians 1:19.

as such are scanty, it is clear that the Office belongs, not to the foundation of the Church, like that of the Apostles, but to the normal life of the Church; for so long as the Church pursues its missionary task, the Office is a necessary one.' The Commission agreed with Campbell that the three perpetual offices of Bishops, Deacons and Evangelists were necessary to the Church's existence, but 'none required more varied endowments than that of Evangelist.'[23]

In considering the manner and choice of ordination, the Report tabulated instances of ordination in the New Testament, noting Campbell's comment that in the New Testament 'the community of the Church, the multitude of the faithful are the fountain of official power.'[24] This was supported by the Epistle of Clement (CE 96) where it is said that presbyters were chosen by consent of the whole Church. The Seven had been similarly chosen by the whole community. From references in the New Testament it appeared that ordinations were carried out by prayer (usually with fasting) and the laying on of hands. This was normally done by the Apostles or by presbyters, but 'there is no suggestion of sacerdotal power being in men as such nor in their office.' The Report quotes Campbell, who had said that 'Seniors or Elders always ordain', but the Commission made clear that they did so 'not in their own right or power, but as appointed by the Church. It is Christ Himself *through the Church*, who appoints, ordains and send His ministers forth. The New Testament knows nothing of "holy hands" by *jure divino*, but it does enjoin that in this matter, as in all others, "all things shall be done decently and in order".' Of equal importance to the laying on of hands were prayer and fasting.

Applying the evidence and principles of the New Testament, the Commission re-affirmed the traditional position of Churches of Christ in recognising a twofold Ministry. That of the local Church consisted of Elders (Bishops, Presbyters, or Pastors) and Deacons. The ministry of the wider Church consisted of the single order of Evangelist or Missionary.

Elders and Deacons were officers of the local Church. Their ministry was to be exercised only in the local church in which they were chosen to serve. Evangelists had a wider ministry as Officers of the whole group of Churches. Their function was to found Churches and provide them with oversight until appropriately gifted people emerged within the congregation to be appointed to the offices of Elders and Deacons. This was based upon an interpretation of New Testament texts from which they claimed that Apostles and Prophets belonged to the temporary ministry of the Church, while Evangelists, Pastors, and Teachers belonged to the Church's permanent Ministry.[25]

The Commission noted that it was customary practice in Churches of Christ for Elders and Deacons to be ordained in local Churches by fasting, prayer and the laying-on-of-hands. Ordination followed choice and election by the congregation and was to life office. In some situations ordination had been abandoned following controversy, or, in some cases, due to careless neglect. The Commission wished to urge upon Churches 'that greater care and reverence be observed in the matter of the choice of Elders and Deacons and the advisability of proceeding to Ordination when choice has been made.' They deplored the lack of uniformity as 'disconcerting' and destructive of their concern for Christian Unity. 'It ill becomes a community', they said,

---

23   A Campbell, *The Christian System*. pp. 79-84.

24   ibid. p. 84.

25   e.g. I Corinthians 12:28, Ephesians 4:11

'which makes such a strong plea for uniformity in the matter of Baptism that it should have grown so lax on the proper matter and form of Ordination.' Such laxity was not the official policy of Churches of Christ; where it existed, the fault lay in the practice of local Churches.

In their Report the members of the Commission re-affirmed the view that the question of whether ministry in the local Church was supported wholly, or in part, or not at all by the Church had nothing to do with the reality of the offices of Elder and Deacon.

> A man who earns his living apart altogether from his Ministry and receives no support whatsoever from his Ministry is just as much Elder or Deacon as a man who is wholly supported, provided he be lawfully chosen and ordained to the Office.

This was an important element in the witness of Churches of Christ and should be maintained at all costs. Rightly understood, 'it witnesses to the sacred character of the Offices, and ought to lead to greater care and more reverent procedure both in election and in Ordination, and to higher estimation of the Offices of both Elder and Deacon.'

The Report gave careful consideration to the choice and ordination of Evangelists and to the Election and Ordination of Elders and Deacons. Candidates for the office of Evangelist would normally be chosen by their local Church and be commended by the District or Divisional Committee. Candidates should be chosen on the evidence of their character and spiritual fitness rather than intellectual ability or the attractiveness of their personality. The first requirement was that candidates should exemplify the spirit of Jesus whose ministry was one of service and not of lordship. Intellectual ability and personality needed to be 'above the ordinary, with a passion for the winning of souls'.

On completion of their training, for which specific recommendations were made, Evangelists should be ordained at a solemn service at a special session of the Annual Conference. The ordination service would include the laying on of hands by appropriate persons, who might usually be the Chairman of Conference, the Principal of Overdale College, and a Presbyter of other appointed representative of the candidate's home Church. A later writer remarked upon the profound impression made by the first such service in the year following the passing of the Report of the Commission. On that occasion fourteen evangelists had been ordained 'in a session of the utmost dignity and reverence' and 'such services in annual conference continue to create the fitting spiritual atmosphere for the men who have responded to the call of the Ministry as their life's work.'[26]

In the election and ordination of Elders and Deacons the Commission stressed the importance of careful preparation. Churches needed to be aware of the 'heavenly plane' in which they were moving when they were called upon to appoint the Church's Officers. Since the members of the local Church were the instrument through whom God was acting, it was 'essential that the whole procedure should be as far removed from business and political procedure as is possible'. The election of Officers was an act of worship and not a business decision. The Commission

---

[26]   J Gray (ed), *Towards Christian Union*, (Leicester: Churches of Christ Union Committee 1960) p. 41.

recommended that, where a Church already had a body of Elders and Deacons, nominations for those offices should be made in the first place by the Elders with the opportunity for further nominations to be made by any other member of the Church. These nominations should be announced without comment in a service of Holy Communion, and be separate from other public notices. On at least two Sundays before the election took place teaching should be given on the work and scriptural qualifications of Elders and Deacons. The election should be prepared for by prayer and meditation and not by argument, 'lobbying', or discussion. 'In such teaching the sacred character of the act of election should be stressed, and in the Prayers of the Church attention should be given to prayer for right guidance in the choice, so that those nominated come to election prepared to submit themselves to the voice of the Church as to the voice of God.' Finally it was recommended that the actual election should take place in the Communion Service as an act of worship. Following the election, the whole Church should prepare for the solemn occasion of ordination through prayer and teaching on at least two Sundays. The ordination would again take place in the context of the Communion Service. Appended to the Report were draft orders of service for the ordination of Evangelists, the election of Elders and Deacons, and an order for a Communion Service in which the Election of Elders and Deacons might take place.

Commission on the Ministry 1954

The Commission on Ordination was followed by a further Commission on the Ministry. This was appointed by the Annual Conference in 1947 and reported in 1954. By now Churches of Christ were deeply involved in ecumenical discussions. In 1946 the Archbishop of Canterbury, in a notable sermon, had suggested that, as a preliminary step, the non-episcopal churches might try out episcopacy by 'taking it into their own system'.[27] In common with other churches, Churches of Christ took this suggestion as an invitation, which could not be ignored, to examine their understanding of ministry. The Archbishop's sermon compelled them to face the question whether the New Testament offered one clear and fixed form of church order which could be exactly determined and, more importantly, be precisely reproduced.

The first part of the Report, which was largely the work of William Robinson, examined theological and historical considerations. For Churches of Christ the authority of the New Testament was paramount. It was necessary, however, to distinguish between the New Testament as a set of historical documents which throw light on their own period, and the New Testament as the Word of God 'by which the church in every age is judged'. The Commission reached the conclusion that, contrary to the belief long held in Churches of Christ, the New Testament could not provide a definitive picture of the structure and form of the Church. This did not mean that 'form and structure' were 'a matter of indifference'. The Church needed structure in order to function as the Body of Christ. The ministry, which gives form and structure to the Church, is the 'gift of Christ' to His Church. The whole Church constitutes the '*LAOS*' – the People of God – but the New Testament makes a clear distinction between those who are ordained and the unordained. 'It is clear', says the Report, 'that from the first there were in all churches some who

---

[27] The Archbishop's sermon, *A Step Forward in Church Relations'* was preached before the University of Cambridge on Sunday, November 3rd, 1946. The text is printed in *Church Relations in England,* (London: SPCK 1950).

had the duty to lead, to admonish, to guard sound doctrine, to have pastoral oversight.' The ministry is not set over the Church but belongs to the nature of the Church; it is not a hierarchy, but 'there is a definite authority of office conferred by Christ'. Its authority is that of service.

In considering the forms of ministry in the New Testament, the Report disagreed with the claim that Jesus had made no arrangements for the continuance of his ministry. He had chosen the Twelve and sent them forth. His commission empowered them to continue his ministry. The foundation of his teaching had been the growth and development of the Kingdom. The New Testament thus offered clear evidence of Jesus' intention that the Church would continue his ministry. Other questions could not be answered with the same certainty. Apart from the choice of the Twelve, He gave no instructions on the form of order the Church should adopt. To the question whether the Lord's commission was given exclusively to the Twelve or to the Church as a whole, the Report suggested that it was given to both –

> Not to Apostles as over against the Church, nor to the Church as over against the Apostles, but to the Apostles with the Church.

From the evidence of the New Testament it seemed probable that the form of the Church's ministry emerged to meet needs as they arose. Rather than finding in the New Testament one clear and fixed form of ministry, as the Anglicans claimed for the threefold ministry of bishops, priests and deacons, the Commission discerned 'a movement towards a fixed form of ministry, the nature of which can only be determined by looking into the period immediately following that covered by the New Testament.'

Clearly this represented a substantial shift away from earlier – and more dogmatic – convictions. It did not mean however that any other form of church order, which might also find its justification in the New Testament, was to be regarded as binding and definitive. Nor did it mean that the form of the ministry was a matter of indifference:

> Just as the Sacraments of Baptism and the Lord's Supper are not arbitrary forms, to be abandoned or discarded according to the varying demands of different generations, but are a permanent part of the structure of the Church, *because they uniquely express the content of the Gospel;* so the Ministry is a permanent part of the structure of the Church, and if there is a particular form of the ministry which is a more fitting expression of the Gospel than any other, that is the form which should prevail.

The Commission identified seven elements which were required for the ministry to be faithful to the Gospel:

1. The ministry must possess the call and commission of Christ. It is this call and commission which are the true apostolic succession. Christ calls and commissions His ministers through the Church under the guidance of the Holy Spirit.
2. The ministry must express *'diakonia'* in order to be a faithful embodiment of Christ's ministry of service.

3. The ministry is given, according to Scripture, 'to equip God's people for work in his service, for the building up of the body of Christ.' (Ephesians 4.12). It is therefore 'to be devoted to the building up of the loving fellowship of every congregation and to be prepared to labour and suffer that the fellowship may grow.'

4. Since the primary emphasis of the New Testament is on *episcope* and pastoral oversight, this must be embodied by the ministry in every Church.

5. It must be made clear that the Body of Christ consists of the whole company of Christ's people, and that He, not the ministry, is the Church's Head. 'The ministry must be so one with the Church that the corporeity of the Church is not obscured. The whole company of the faithful is Christ's body, and He (not the ministry) is the Head. The Ministry cannot usurp this position which belongs to Christ alone.'

6. The function of the Ministry is to preach the Faithful Word of God and to preserve sound doctrine. The Ministry has also liturgical functions of ordering worship and distributing the sacraments, and disciplinary functions relating to doctrine and the Christian way of life.

7. The Ministry must express the universality and continuity of the Church. It must do this because 'the one Church (finds) its expression in the local community from place to place and from age to age'. Behind this important statement lay a profound reconsideration of the traditional doctrine of the independence of the local congregation which would have significant influence upon later discussions on church reunion.

The Commission argued that these seven elements were sufficiently safeguarded in Churches of Christ. The ministry of Evangelists equated with that of the Apostles who appeared to have a ministry wider than the purely local. But since the word 'evangelist' had now come to signify an itinerant revival preacher, the Commission recommended that designation of *Minister* should in future be used for those who, following training, were ordained by Conference to serve all the Churches as a valid Ministry of the Church universal.

Under the heading of 'Local Ministry', the Commission retained the Presbyters (who in New Testament terminology were synonymous with 'Bishops') and Deacons, who as local leaders were chosen by the congregation in which they were to serve. They considered also the implications in the evidence of the New Testament to the considerable contribution made by women to the work of the Church. It was difficult to form a clear picture, yet there was strong evidence of the ministry of the Deaconess and the Prophetess in the Apostolic Church. Less clear was the place given to Widows, or how the different types of ministry related to each other. The Commission made the interesting suggestion that the prohibition on women imposed by I Timothy 2:8-11 may have had a special application to that particular time rather than to be of universal application for every time and place.

> There is no barrier 'in theology and tradition to the extension of the Ministry of Deaconesses, even if the question of the ordination of women to the Presbyterate has to be left until a larger measure of agreement is reached.

The Report reaffirmed the historic tradition of Churches of Christ in denying the distinction between clergy and laity, while upholding the distinction between ordained and unordained members of the Church. They maintained their insistence that distinctions should not be based upon remuneration. 'Ordained Elders and Deacons', said the Report, 'have been regarded as Ministers in the fullest sense even though they have earned their living in a "secular" calling, as the majority have done.'

The Report of the Commission on the work and status of the Ministry re-positioned Churches of Christ in two significant ways in the ecumenical encounter with other Churches. One was the abandonment of their long-cherished conviction that their form of ministry alone was consistent with the practice of the New Testament:

> We also believe that the form of ministry claimed by Churches of Christ to be the form derived from the New Testament, is not the only possible form in which the essential elements of structure can be embodies; for instance an Episcopal system, shorn of its mediaeval corruptions (such as the centralisation of the Papacy and the turning of Bishops into 'Prelates) or a Presbyterian system, may equally well express these essentials.

The second lay in their willingness to reconsider the status of the local congregation within the whole economy of the Church. Too great an emphasis on the independence of the local congregation might obscure the New Testament revelation of the unity of the whole Church in Christ:

> ...the 'independence' of each congregation has been mistakenly regarded as an absolute principle. The form of Church organisation implied by the New Testament is more closely knit than that practised by Churches of Christ...we should aim to set forth the unity which was a mark of the New Testament Church and which must be a mark of the re-united Church. In working towards that aim we see the need for a much closer liaison between the Churches and the Annual Conference, and among the individuals themselves.

Churches of Christ and the Congregationalists were simultaneously making similar explorations. They were travelling on different roads and without any expectation at that time (or even desire) that their paths would converge. The seeds of reunion were however being sown.

Chapter Six

United and Reformed

UNITED AND REFORMED

The United Reformed Church came to birth on 5 October 1972 nearly ten years after the opening of conversations between the Congregational Union of England and Wales and the Presbyterian Church of England. The Uniting Assembly held in Westminster Central Hall, London, was a memorable moment in the life of the Church in Britain. Two Churches, each with its distinctive traditions yet also owning an historic affinity reaching back into the sixteenth and seventeenth centuries, voluntarily laid down their lives in order that the new Church might be born. Dr John Huxtable, who as minister-secretary of the Congregational Church in England and Wales had worked tirelessly for the union of the two churches, was appointed the first Moderator of the General Assembly. Later that day the new Church was welcomed into the ecumenical family at a service of Thanksgiving in Westminster Abbey. To a fanfare of trumpets the Archbishop of Canterbury and the Cardinal Archbishop of Westminster walked side by side in a great procession which included representatives of the British Churches, Overseas Churches and ecumenical bodies. The climax of the service was an Act of Dedication and Commitment when the two Archbishops and the Moderator of the Free Church Federal Council publicly gave thanks for the union which had been achieved, and resolved with the United Reformed Church to seek that wider unity which they affirmed to be God's will.

At its inception the United Reformed Church believed that its life would be short. The celebration in Westminster Abbey was intended to mark a first yet decisive step on a pilgrimage which others would quickly join. The intention was not to create a new denomination in perpetuity. Its Basis of Union committed the united Church to 'take, wherever possible and with all speed, further steps towards the unity of all God's people'. At the Service of Thanksgiving Dr Huxtable preached from Ephesians 4.13 –'until all of us come to the unity of the faith and of the knowledge of the Son of God'. It was a text for a grander theme than the union of two relatively small Churches. The goal was nothing less than the visible unity of all God's people in one Church.

These high hopes were not to be realised immediately, and much frustration lay ahead. But the formation of the United Reformed Church had one immediate consequence. At the Uniting Assembly of the United Reformed Church in 1972, the Churches of Christ, who had been observers in the negotiations between Congregationalists and Presbyterians, formally requested the opening of talks between Churches of Christ and the United Reformed Church with a view to uniting the two bodies. The Assembly had agreed with acclamation, and one of the first acts of the new Church was to appoint a Joint Committee to conduct negotiations and bring forward proposals for union. As the talks proceeded, it became clear that Churches of Christ, as then constituted, would not reach the legally required majorities for union to be possible. The negotiations revealed the historic tension between those who prized Christian unity and those who sought the restoration of New Testament patterns of church order. Since however a substantial majority of congregations were in favour of union, the Central Council of Churches of Christ agreed to dissolve their Association of Churches in order that local congregations might freely make their choice. In its place there was set up a Re-formed Association of Churches of Christ comprising those congregations which wished to proceed to union. This Re-formed Association and the United Reformed Church formally united in 1981 as the United Reformed Church in the United Kingdom.

The new Church which emerged in 1972 was neither a resurrected Congregational Church in England and Wales nor a resurrected Presbyterian Church of England. It was evident that both these churches had laid down their separate existences, and that the United Reformed Church was not a continuation of either of its predecessors under a new name. For those who had been Presbyterians the difference was immediately apparent. The Presbyterian Church of England had been a relatively small and intimate body. Many of their ministers had been trained at Westminster College, the Presbyterian Church of England's college in Cambridge. The ethos of the Presbyterian Church of England has been described as that of an extended family with its home at Church House in Tavistock Place. The experience of entering into a much larger body brought ambivalent feelings when, in District Councils and Synods, former Presbyterians found themselves in a minority. For some there was a sense of disorientation and, on occasion, alienation.

In some respects, however, the former Presbyterians were better prepared for life in the new Church than their former Congregationalist partners. They brought to the new Church their long experience of living and working in a conciliar church. This proved a better preparation for life in a Church – united and Reformed – than the Congregationalist experience which had almost entirely focused on the local church. Former Congregationalists were surprised at early meetings of District Councils and Synods by the reliance of the officers of these councils on the Manual as a prescriptive guide for the ordering of the Church. It was not that Congregationalists were averse to rules or discipline; local congregations normally conducted their affairs according to a constitution which church members had freely adopted. Many of the older churches had been founded on the basis of a Covenant which included rules for the ordering of their life. The Congregationalists brought to the new Church a rich tradition of local church order centred upon the Church Meeting. While they valued the diaconate and local congregations looked to their deacons for leadership and example, the diaconate had not been regarded as a 'court' of the Church or as having any authority over the members of the congregation who had elected them. Deacons meetings were not infrequently hesitant to offer advice to the Church Meeting lest they should appear to undermine the latter's authority. Congregationalism had no theology of the diaconate. Notwithstanding the recent transformation of the Congregational *Union* of England and Wales into the Congregational *Church* in England and Wales, County Unions, Provinces, and even the National Assembly had remained subordinate in importance to the local church. The United Reformed Church was to offer a steep learning curve to its former Congregationalist members.

Structure

The new Church was to be conciliar in its structure. This had been long foreshadowed in the negotiations for union. In 1965 the Assemblies of both participating churches had received from the Joint Committee a crucial document in which the negotiating committee set out its vision for the future united church.[1] It provided an outline of basic principles and an interim constitution for the united Church.

The Statement began by affirming that there is but one Church of God. It is *holy* because it is called and set apart to serve God; it is *catholic* because it is called to embrace the whole of mankind (sic); it is *apostolic* because the Church is the body which Jesus Christ founded in and through the apostles and in which he carries on his mission. God has created the Church through his redeeming act in Jesus Christ, and its life is maintained and renewed by the Holy Spirit, through whom Christ continues his ministry until all things are gathered up in him. The Gospel entrusted to the Church is a Gospel of reconciliation, but in its divided state the Church cannot fully know, experience or communicate the life of the one holy, catholic and apostolic Church. All Christians are called to repentance and a new obedience. It was in response to this call that the Congregational and Presbyterian Churches acknowledged their duty to unite, and to see this union as part of what God is doing to make his people one. Their vision for the united Church is both catholic and reformed. It would be catholic in that it would share the faith and worship of the universal Church and respond to God's call to offer the Gospel for the life and well-being of all people. It would be reformed in recognising the Word of God in the Scriptures of the Old and New Testaments to be both the creative stimulus to Christian living and the abiding standard for judging the forms and traditions of the Church's life.

The Statement of Convictions proposed *a fourfold structure* for the united Church.

1.   The Local Church

The Joint Committee recognised that the work of the Church is principally done in and through the local church, whose membership should normally include a minister or ministers, and elders/deacons. The chief responsibilities of the local church were seen to lie in the areas of worship, pastoral care, witness and service, evangelism at home and abroad, Christian education, ecumenical action, local inter-church relationships, and, significantly, 'sustaining the wider responsibilities of the whole Church'. Responsibility for implementing these concerns would be shared by the session/diaconate and the Church Meeting through which every member participates in the life and work of the church. The Church Meeting is to be more than a business meeting; it is the forum for the exercise of ministry by the whole people of God. Executive responsibility for the stewardship of the finance and property of the local church may be appropriately delegated to the session/diaconate, or to such other committees as a local church may appoint for these purposes. Implicit in the proposals, however, is that responsibility for worship, witness, mission and service cannot be delegated but must

---

[1]   *'A Statement of Convictions on which a united Church, both catholic and reformed, might be built'*,
     published by the Congregational Union of England and Wales and the Presbyterian Church of England, 1965

remain at the heart of a local church's life and concern. Responsibilities of major importance to be given to a local church would be the calling of a minister, and the election of elders/deacons and members of the church's committees.

2.   The District or Presbytery

This second tier in the fourfold structure would comprise a grouping of 25 to 40 local churches in order to exercise mutual oversight. To this Council of the Church might be assigned responsibility for the oversight of the ministry, the sustaining of calls issued by member churches, ordinations and inductions, periodic visitation of local churches, advice and guidance on property matters, the care of smaller churches, provision of a forum for concerns and appeals, and for their transmission to other councils of the Church, interviewing and commending candidates for the ministry and other full-time service of the Church at home and overseas, and the furthering of home and overseas missions. The purpose of District Council or Presbytery would be to enable member churches to experience the reality of mutual support and united action.

3.   The Provincial Synod

The Provincial Synod was envisaged as a wider grouping of about 250 churches. In conjunction with the District/Presbytery the Synod might be responsible for church extension, the recognition of ministerial students, their supervision during training and their eligibility for a call, rural churches, relationships with any theological college(s) within their area, home and overseas missions, ecumenical relationships, and with matters of discipline – including, presumably, churches, ministers and members.

4.   The General Assembly

The General Assembly was proposed as the final tier in the structure. It would need to be large enough to be truly representative of the united Church but small enough to work efficiently. Though it was not spelled out, the Joint Committee was sending a signal to the Congregational Churches that their May Meetings – a large, diffuse and inspirational assembly in which every local church had the right of representation – would not be the model for the united church. The purpose of the General Assembly would be to embody the unity of the Church and be the central organ of its life. Its task would be to oversee the total work of the Church by making decisions on recommendations and reports from its departments and committees, and on matters brought forward by Synods, Districts/Presbyteries and local churches. 'In these and other ways', said the report, 'it shall take such action as is conducive to the welfare of the Church, the propagation of the Gospel, the interests of the Church of Christ as a whole, and the well-being of the community in which the Church is placed.'

Questions would inevitably be raised, especially by Congregationalists, concerning the *powers* which would be assigned to the different councils of the Church. The Joint Committee did not specify in their report whether the various councils were to be conceived as ascending tiers of hierarchy, or as concentric circles. The latter image might be regarded as more appropriate. The Joint Committee attempted to deal with the distribution of powers within the councils in a comprehensive statement in which they affirmed that 'All these councils have consultative, legislative and executive functions and each shall be recognised as having such authority as shall enable it to minister to that sphere of the Church's life with which it is concerned.' In this statement may be discerned the ground on which battles would be fought in debates in local churches and Assemblies before the final decisions on union were taken by the two Churches. The outcome of those debates was that some Congregational Churches, and some ministers also, decided not to join the United Reformed Church because they were persuaded that their conviction that ultimate authority should lie with the local church would be fatally compromised. Others went forward in the hope that the autonomy of the local church would continue more or less unchanged. The more percipient recognised that there would be tensions but hoped that these might be creatively resolved in a new relationship of mutual commitment.

The new Church – united and reformed – was therefore to be recognisably 'presbyterian' in its structure. Those Congregationalists who ultimately rejected the proposals had some justification for their argument that the balance of power in the united Church would shift from the local congregation to the wider councils of the Church. The concerns of the Joint Committee – and those who supported their proposals - were twofold. On the one hand they sought to emphasise the critical importance of local churches as the spearhead of the Church's mission and evangelism. Within its sphere the local church was entrusted with awesome responsibilities which the wider councils of the Church could not exercise on its behalf. Their second concern was to provide a structure which would support the local churches in their mission. Every function of District/Presbytery, Provincial Synod and General Assembly was directed towards this end. The proposed structure was intended to be faithful to the Congregationalist belief in the local church as an outcrop, in a particular place, of the Great Church.

Oversight in the Church

The key issue, which the debates on the proposals for union tended to obscure, was not in reality the autonomy of the local church – or the diminished autonomy which union might bring – but the requirements of oversight – *episcope*. Central to the thinking of the Joint Committee was the conviction that 'the oversight *(episcope)* of the Church shall be the concern both of the local Church and of wider representative councils.' In the local church oversight is primarily represented through the ministry of the minister(s) and elders/deacons who corporately exercise a ministry of pastoral care. In Presbyterian congregations each elder was normally assigned a group of church members for whom they were pastorally responsible, and, more recently, this had also become the practice in some Congregational churches. A marked characteristic of most local churches was a mutuality of pastoral care in which members cared for each other and supported the minister(s) and elders in their specific ministries. Local churches generally offered a high standard of pastoral care within their fellowships; the intention was that this should continue in the united Church.

The 'wider representative councils' also had a role in providing pastoral oversight. They were intended to answer the question: 'Quis custodiet custodes?' – who cares for the carers? Ministers and elders might become dispirited and need more support than a local church could provide on its own. There might be situations in which a local church experienced serious division in its fellowship through theological or personal differences of opinion. A local church might need advice and support in taking new initiatives for mission and evangelism. In all such situations the 'wider representative councils' might offer support and make available personal, professional, or financial resources to enhance the mission of the local church. Their purpose was not to diminish the responsibilities of the local church but to supplement its resources in order to strengthen its effectiveness in the service of the Gospel. This was emphasised by the Joint Committee when it said that

> This oversight by wider councils shall be exercised in a setting of responsible action by local Churches, which may initiate new concerns and shall have recognised means of appeal against the decision of wider councils.

Oversight by Provincial Moderators

Oversight in the united Church would not only be exercised by committees or councils. The Joint Committee noted that 'some measure of corporate oversight can be exercised by persons representing the wider councils of the Church.' Congregationalists had received a significant measure of personal oversight from their system of Provincial Moderators which had been introduced in 1919. The principal reason for their appointment at that time had been to facilitate the settlement and removal of ministers within the denomination as a whole. Their influence was personal rather than structural. They attended meetings of County Unions within their areas of responsibility by invitation rather than by right. The first appointees were 'pastoral facilitators rather than authoritarian leaders'.[2] Although they were sometimes informally referred to as 'our bishops', this designation had been studiously avoided in the discussions leading up to the inauguration of the scheme. Their appointment nevertheless represented a shift of emphasis from the model of local congregational autonomy to a greater sense of denominational self-awareness. As they gained increasing esteem, they came to embody *'episcope'*, while remaining marginal to the structures of the denomination. The Joint Committee in the *Statement of Convictions* invited both churches to accept and develop the moderatorial system within the united Church. They recommended that moderators should be appointed to preside over Synods and to exercise a pastoral office towards the Churches, as well as the ministers, within their Synods. Provincial Moderators would henceforth be integrated within the structures of the Church and its wider councils. Their appointment would not however be for life, but for a fixed term of years during which they would be separated from any particular pastoral charge.

On the Presbyterian side the proposal for a separated ministry of provincial moderators aroused greater misgivings. Throughout its history the presbyterian form of church order had consistently upheld the principle of parity among ministers. Some feared that this would be jeopardised by what appeared to be the elevation of some ministers to a superior status. The intention of the Joint Committee was that any temptation to the abuse of power by a provincial moderator would be contained by the conciliar structures of the united Church. Provincial moderators would have

---

[2]   E P M Wollaston, *The First Moderators: 1919*, (*JURCHS Vol 5 No 5*, 1994)

influence, but decisions on all matters concerning ministers and churches would be taken by the appropriate councils of the Church. The fourfold conciliar structure provided built-in checks and balances by which the undue exercise of power by any officer of the Church – whether provincial moderator or committee convener – might be constrained.

Ministry

The goal of the Joint Committee was that the united Church should have a form of church order which would reflect the Gospel and enable its members to behave with freedom and responsibility. The particular ministries of the Church would take their place within its various councils which would define their responsibilities and provide oversight and support.

The whole church, as 'the people of God called and committed to His service', shares in the ministry which the Lord Jesus Christ, risen and ascended, continues through the Church. His ministry is exercised primarily through the members of His Church. The *Statement of Convictions* does not explicitly refer to the 'priesthood of all believers', perhaps because that had become too much of a party slogan, and in the past had been mis-used to drive a wedge between ordained ministers and church members. It was however explicit in affirming that *membership* in the Church of Jesus Christ, and the participation of church members in the continuing ministry of the Church's Lord, would be exercised by members through sharing in public worship, by mutual and corporate caring and responsibility, and by prayer, witness and service. The whole life of the members of the Church would be an offering to God of their daily lives at home, at work, at leisure and in service to the community. An important part of the life of the Church would be to provide strength and support for church members in exercising their ministry.

The Ministry of Word and Sacrament

The ministry of the whole people of God provided both the context, the need, and the opportunity for particular ministries. The *Statement* affirms that the Lord Jesus Christ, as Head of the Church, gives gifts for particular ministries in order that the Church may fulfil its total and universal ministry. The Joint Committee recognised that in due course the united Church might discover the need for a range of full and part-time ministries, and it would be for the Church to determine their nature. At its formation as a united Church, both parties to the union would unite in receiving and affirming the ministry of Word and Sacraments as a continuing gift of Christ to his Church. The task of this ministry is seen as preaching the Word, administering the sacraments, exercising pastoral care, leading the life of the Church and fostering its evangelism.

The Joint Committee was concerned to ensure that the ministry of Word and Sacrament should be available to every congregation. They suggested that 'where such ministers are not available, the united Church shall through its wider councils determine the proper method of meeting these needs'. Behind this lies their appreciation of the different circumstances of the negotiating churches. The Presbyterian Church of England, though numerically smaller overall, comprised for the most part larger congregations in predominantly urban areas, each congregation having its own minister. It was axiomatic that the ordained minister of Word and Sacrament should preside at celebrations of the Lord's Supper. The Congregational Union, while the larger body, had included in its membership many small congregations, often in rural areas, which did not always have a designated minister. Presidency by lay preachers at the invitation of the local church was common practice.[3] Whereas Presbyterians would forgo the sacrament if an ordained minister were not available to preside, Congregationalists had by this time forgotten their ancient tradition that the celebration by a particular church of the sacrament of the Lord's Supper required that the church be furnished with officers duly appointed for the purpose.

The Congregationalists also had in their ranks an informal order of *lay pastors*. They were accorded a degree of recognition by County Unions, and acted as *de facto* ministers to the mostly rural congregations which they served. They exercised the functions of ministers of Word and Sacrament, and in some cases were given – or assumed – the courtesy title of 'reverend'. Their status was anomalous in that they were neither trained nor formally accredited by ordination. There could be no question that they should be immediately admitted to the Roll of Ministers of the united Church. The best the Joint Committee could do in the circumstances was to suggest that lay pastors who had been recognised by the Congregational Union of England and Wales and its County Unions should continue their ministries in the united Church.

Elders and Deacons

The other recognised ministry in the local church would be that of elders /deacons who would work in association with ministers of Word and Sacrament. The offices of minister and elder/deacon were to be accepted by the united Church as gifts of Christ to the whole Church for its oversight and pastoral care. Here the Joint Committee was clearly nudging the Congregationalists in a Presbyterian direction in boldly declaring that elders, as well as ministers of Word and Sacrament, should be given 'appropriate authority in ordination, by the gift of the Holy Spirit and the action of the Church'. The Joint Committee also followed the practice of the Church of Scotland and the Presbyterian Church of England in proposing that the ordination of elders in the united Church would be for life. These recommendations provoked heated debate on the Congregational side. Many were unable to understand how an elder could be ordained yet remain a 'lay' person. For all their occasional ambivalence towards ordination in the course of their history and their suspicion of ritual, Congregationalists had always understood ordination to be the means by which a person ceased to be a layperson and became a minister. The proposal to ordain elders required a massive process of theological and ecclesiological re-education, which was only imperfectly accomplished when the union eventually took place. A large body of Congregationalists joined the united Church primarily because they were persuaded that the unity of the Church was the will of God, and also in the hope that this union would be the forerunner of a wider reunion of the divided churches. They accepted the ordained eldership as the necessary price of reunion rather than because they had been persuaded by arguments in its favour. The Joint Committee wisely forestalled controversy by suggesting that those already serving as elders or deacons in the uniting churches should not require re-commissioning.

---

[3]   The writer, for example, first presided at the Lord's Supper as a lay preacher without having been given prior warning that the service would include Holy Communion.

Congregationalists were equally hesitant about the proposal that elders should be ordained for life. Deacons in their churches were normally elected to serve for a period of years and, on completion of their term of service, were either re-elected or ceased to be deacons. It was customary by this time for deacons who had completed their agreed period of service to be ineligible for re-election for at least a fixed term of years. The Presbyterian Church of England followed the practice of the Church of Scotland in ordaining elders for life which, in effect, meant lifelong service in the Session of the congregation which had elected them. It was difficult for Congregationalists to agree that elders should serve for life. It was even more difficult for them to conceive the role in the local congregation of *ordained* but non-serving elders who, by their ordination, would seem in some way different from other members of the church. This was a concern which could only be resolved over a period of time and by the experience of sharing in the life of the united Church. The Joint Committee did not attempt to resolve it in advance, and merely stated that 'the ordination of elders/deacons for life shall not necessarily involve lifelong service on the session/diaconate'. The newly united church did not resolve this concern. It was intensified as local congregations began to introduce fixed terms of service for elders with the requirement that serving elders should 'stand down' for a period before becoming eligible for re-election. This created the anomaly, at least from the former Presbyterian perspective, of the presence in many congregations of ordained elders whose ordination appeared, at least temporarily, to be in abeyance.

This *Statement of Convictions* was the foundation document of the Scheme of Union which, after acceptance by both Churches, formed the Basis of Union on which the United Reformed Church came into existence in 1972. The uniting ceremonies, which marked the end of a long road towards union, were also a staging post for a new journey. One of the first decisions of the new Church was, in the year following the union, to set up a widely representative Commission 'to explore the forms of ministry needed in the United Reformed Church in the foreseeable future; to estimate the number of full time, fully trained ministers required; to suggest the scope and content of the training desired; and in the light of this examination to recommend a policy for the whole Church concerning the use of the existing Colleges and the available financial resources for ministerial training.' 'Forms of ministry' was understood to mean 'the total ministry of the People of God in the United Reformed Church and in particular the functions and purpose of the fully trained and ordained ministers of Word and Sacraments', while 'foreseeable future' was envisaged as the first ten to fifteen years of the new Church's life.

In its Interim Report[4] presented one year later to the General Assembly the Commission highlighted the importance of a realistic approach to the ministry of the Church in the contemporary situation. For half a century the Church had experienced a serious decline in church membership which seemed likely to continue in face of social mobility and the widespread indifference to Christianity in society. Christian hope however prohibited the acceptance of continuous decline as the future to which God was calling the Church, and ministry was still required. The ordained ministry was given by God to the Church in order that the Church might fulfil its purpose on earth of worship, fellowship, mission and service. The calling of the ordained ministry was to enable the whole membership to face the Church's task. In this task two functions of the ordained ministry were central. As a representative of the catholicity of the

---

4   United Reformed Church, *Minutes of Assembly 1974*, pp. 75-87.

Church, the minister is 'a living sign of the faith which creates the Church', and serves the people by 'interpreting the Bible and the significance in life of a Christian understanding of God'. The second function of the ordained ministry is to encourage the commitment of the people to the goals of the Church, both locally and internationally. To fulfil these functions ministers needed to be equipped by training in biblical and theological understanding and to develop skills of communication and leadership. It was to be expected that the focus of the minister's work would be primarily within the context of local congregations, though some would provide 'a Christian presence within the wider community, mainly among people alienated from the churches'.

This did not mean that the work of the ordained minister should be an isolated vocation: the Commission insisted that 'a genuine ministry of the laity is also vital', and not least because 'only the lay people of the Church can carry the presence of Christ into all parts of the life of our society'.

An important section of the Interim Report questioned the deployment of ministers in the traditional 'one church one minister' situation. The current low rate of recruitment to the ordained ministry and the steady fall in membership, together with increasing financial costs, were rendering this form of ministry non-viable as the norm. Many small congregations could not provide a minister with a challenging full-time task. The complex human problems of secularised society called for the need for specialisation in ministry and the use of special skills. Uncertainty also prevailed about the minister's public role in society when other helping professions were fast multiplying and congregations seemed less influential in their communities. All these factors pointed to the need for the Church to evolve new patterns of ministry. The Commission recommended that the United Reformed Church should move from the principle of 'one church one minister' to that of the team. Such teams would be formed by closer groupings of churches within their regions. They would also require a closer alliance of ministers and laity within their regions and the development of specialist functions. Team ministry should not be seen a something wholly new, for it already existed in local congregations in the form of the ordained minister, ordained elders, Junior church teachers and providers of music. The Commission recommended that this principle should be extended to the ministry of the Church in each District. By facilitating specialisation, a team ministry might usefully include lay specialists and ordained ministers in secular employment, of whom there was a growing number at that time. Team ministry would enable the Church's resources of people to be used realistically and to greater effect.

In making these proposals the Commission was strongly influenced by the discussions then taking place between the United Reformed Church and Churches of Christ which, as we have seen, had a more comprehensive understanding of ministry in the Church. It was probable that the successful outcome of the negotiations would introduce a concept of ministry more hospitable to the team model than that of the solo minister.

An over-riding concern in the Interim Report was the Commission's awareness that the Church had failed in recent years to provide or deploy resources that would make possible effective ministry in new towns, expanding universities and educational institutions, and in other situations where there would be no ready-made supporting congregation. The Interim Report urged the United Reformed Church to commit itself to such outreach, but in a planned way which took account of ecumenical possibilities to which it was committed by its newly adopted Basis of

Union. Ministry in such 'outreach' situations needed where possible to be linked with the life of a local congregation in such a way that the whole body of the Church might be involved. A specific proposal was that a minimum of 5% of the Church's ordained ministers (approximately 54 at that time) rising to 10% in the next decade and a half should be made available for ministry in 'frontier' situations.

The Commission presented its Final Report in the following year, 1975.[5] They re-iterated the difficulties in planning for the future at a time of marked decline in church membership and cultural change. There had been erosion of faith within the Church as well as outside. A prophetically warning note was sounded that 'Christians must not take it for granted that they will easily be able to satisfy a new hunger, even if there is some form of turning to God'. The uncertainties surrounding the Church affected ministers especially, because their work and livelihood were intimately involved. The Church therefore had a duty to its ministers 'to make it possible for them to testify effectively to the "things which cannot be shaken" in a constantly changing world.'

Comments on the Interim Report from congregations and councils indicated a lukewarm response to the proposal that the Church should move towards the norm of team ministry. On the contrary, responses had testified to the value of ministry as the full-time pastoral care of a local congregation. The Commission still wished to argue that fewer churches were now able on their own to offer a minister a satisfying full-time job either in their internal lives or as a basis for mission.

> In most churches there are fewer services, fewer flourishing organisations, fewer members to visit, and the church is in touch with a smaller segment of society.

The intellectual argument for team ministries seemed unassailable but hearts and minds had not been won. The Commission admitted that the grouping of churches sometimes led to a frustrating increase in administrative and other chores. Many ministers were acting unilaterally by spending more time outside their pastorates in teaching, welfare work, hospital or industrial chaplaincy, and were doing so out of a sense of vocation as a means of keeping open their links with the community and leading their congregations in new ways of service. While this was a positive response to the imperative of mission, the drawback was that those ministers – a growing number – who had moved to full-time service in secular situations could contribute only marginally to the Church's pastoral ministry. The Commission concluded that the Church still needed the full-time pastoral ministry and should continue to ensure that there was adequate scope for it. But it was paramount that the focus of the Church's ministry should be the world rather than the Church.

> As most people are not now within church life, Christians will find more and more that their opportunities of service are away from "home ground" in the churches.

The notion was firmly rejected that the minister should look after the Church while lay people witnessed in the outside world. Rather -

> the minister should share in leading the congregation in its corporate witness to society and experiment with his own role as a missionary in the community.

---

[5]   United Reformed Church, *Minutes of Assembly 1975*, pp. 50-69.

While the argument in favour of team ministries had not been won, this did not mean that the pattern of 'one minister one church' would indefinitely prevail. The Commission envisaged a range of potential ministries in teams, group pastorates, and ecumenical situations as well as in single pastorates. So far as these were concerned, the Commission declared in one of the strongest statements in its Report that

> a local church will have to show special justification for maintaining a single pastorate situation, and this should be based not on ministerial or financial strength, but the District Council's conviction of the strategic importance of the particular situation.

Much debate lay ahead before this principle would be – often grudgingly – accepted.

There are anticipations in the Final Report of what would later be designated as the contrast between ministries of *maintenance* and those of *mission*. The Commission sought to move the United Reformed Church in the direction of 'mission' with its emphasis on the importance of engaging in the life of society outside the Church and its explicit support of those ministers who were seeking to extend their ministries into the structures of secular society. It was also apparent that such new forms of ministry would require a re-thinking of the minister's role as preacher and teacher. No longer would it suffice to expound the Bible or Christian doctrine as if their application were obvious. Ministerial training would need to change its emphasis from the *systematic* exposition of what Christians believe to the *contextual* exploration of what the Christian Faith meant in a particular situation. Experience of other work situations or previous training in a discipline other than theology should be positively encouraged to provide ministers with a broader background and a greater ability to interpret a situation. Ministerial training should foster competence in theological exploration and equip ministers to engage in creative exchange between people of different kinds of experience, including those who were not committed Christians. The minister was not to be a virtuoso performer, or the sole repository of authority and wisdom, but should rather empower the members of the congregation to make their distinctive contributions to the understanding and *praxis* of the Christian faith. Their contributions in certain respects would be more significant than those of the ordained minister.

These proposals were put forward within the framework of the Basis of Union on which the United Reformed Church had come into existence, and the convictions about ministry which it enshrined. These were, briefly, that the essential ministry in the Church is that which 'The Lord Jesus Christ continues…in and through the Church'. Any authentic Christian ministry must make manifest the love of God for the world which Jesus expressed in his life and ministry.

The Church must clearly understand that the ministry is therefore 'not the work of an order set apart in the Church' but belongs to the whole people of God. The term 'ministry' - understood in such terms as 'discipleship' or 'Christian service' – should be claimed for the contribution of every member, individually and corporately, and should not be regarded as the preserve of either a succession of the ordained or a professional class. The Reformed conviction that all Christians are 'ministers' and share in the priesthood of the whole Church had often had to struggle, even in Protestantism, against a 'mystique' of the ministry as a class apart. The Report stated emphatically that 'all Christians should realise their responsibility for ministry, and that ministers traditionally so called should know that their proper place is within the total ministry of the Church.'

This conviction however was held in creative tension with the equally strong and historic assertion that the Church required particular ministries for its total ministry to be fulfilled. The Basis of Union testified to this belief in declaring that 'The Lord Jesus Christ...calls some of his servants to exercise (particular ministries) in offices duly recognised within His Church.' Fundamental to these in the Basis of Union are the offices of minister and elder. These are set apart by ordination which both *confers an authority* which others are not given, and at the same time put those who are so ordained *under authority* in a way that other church members are not.

Unification with Churches of Christ

This Commission on the Ministry in the newly united Church did its work in the context of the negotiations for unification which had already opened between the United Reformed Church and Churches of Christ. If these could be brought to a successful conclusion, the way might then be open to radically different patterns of ministry from those which had become customary in the former Presbyterian and Congregational Churches.

The Joint Committee which had been formed in 1972 worked quickly and produced its first Report for the 1974 Assembly of the United Reformed Church.[6] The Report was in two parts, the first dealing with Baptism and the second with the Ministry of Word and Sacrament in a Church uniting the United Reformed Church and Churches of Christ. Ministry in the latter claimed to be based upon apostolic authority and practice, and its ethos was hostile to the concept of the ministry as a 'profession'. From the Pauline epistles Churches of Christ derived a local ministry of ordained elders and deacons and a universal ministry of itinerant evangelists who were mainly concerned with the establishment of new congregations and building up existing congregations. In time, as evangelists tended to remain in one congregation for longer periods, they came to resemble the ministry of Word and Sacrament in the United Reformed Church. But because there were many fewer evangelists than congregations, the pattern of 'one minister one church' was not as strongly developed as in the Congregational and Presbyterian traditions.

Eldership in Churches of Christ differed also from eldership in the Presbyterian tradition since elders' responsibilities included presidency at the Lord's Table as a recognised and constant function. It was rare for a full-time evangelist to preach and preside at the same service. Thus in Churches of Christ there was no necessary doctrinal relationship between ordination and presidency. One of the Churches of Christ representatives on the Joint Committee explained that 'they are ordained not so that they might preside, but because both God and the Church called them to be responsible for the Church's life.'

In both negotiating Churches local customs varied in the matter of presidency. While in the United Reformed Church this was more formally regulated by the District Council, there was nevertheless considerable variation between District Councils in the interpretation of the degree and character of 'pastoral necessity' on the basis of which recognition might be given – or withheld.

---

[6]   United Reformed Church Reports to Assembly: *Joint Committee on negotiations between Churches of Christ and the United Reformed Church*, Report for 1974.

The Joint Committee took the view that every local church should have the fullest opportunity to celebrate the Holy Communion and hoped that union might lead to an extension of the practice of weekly celebration. The president at the Lord's Supper should be chosen by the Church for that office and be set apart. In this context the 'Church' was understood in more than a local sense. It was also more important that the president should be pastorally related to the congregation than that a 'qualified' minister should be constantly brought in from outside the local fellowship. This latter proviso was not intended to debar an 'outside' minister, but rather to ensure that local – and unordained – pastors from the former Congregational Church should not be regularly displaced. This concern also had important implications for the future of the ministry to be provided for the united Church.

Proposals for Ministry

One of the issues which the Joint Committee could not ignore in framing its proposals was the possibility that the forms of ministry which the United Reformed Church had inherited might not remain viable for an indefinite period. The number of ordained ministers was decreasing. Fewer candidates were coming forward for ordination. Older candidates who brought the benefit of wider experience could not look forward to the length of ministry of many in the past. Radical questions were being asked about the 'inward-turned' character of many congregations, and the apparent 'domestication' of ministry when the world needed to be penetrated for Christ.

The Committee's proposals sought to take account of such future uncertainties. They proposed that the united Church should move towards two basic forms of the ministry of Word and Sacrament. One - described as the 'general ministry' – would be a continuation of the ministry as known within the United Reformed Church and, in Churches of Christ, the ministry of evangelists. These 'general ministers' would be full-time, fully trained, and stipendiary. They would be called to a ministry of leadership, teaching and training in relation to a number of congregations. In all probability their number would be fewer than in the past. While 'general ministers' might exercise wider or 'sector' functions, it was important that they should not become detached from local churches.

The second form of ministry - that described as 'local presbyters' - would include those ordained to a ministry of Word and Sacrament while remaining employed in secular life. It was envisaged that in time every church would have such 'local presbyters'. The Committee hoped that this ministry would offer a challenging and life-time vocation, and not least to younger church members. The proposals offered to non-ordained United Reformed Church local pastors the opportunity to become ordained members of the local presbyterate. Some of those who were presently serving as elders in Churches of Christ might also become local presbyters.

The eldership, as exercised in the United Reformed Church, would continue after unification 'as an office of counsel and pastoral care'. Churches of Christ elders who did not become local presbyters would become elders in the new Church.

Most of the responses to the Joint Committee's proposals on the ministry focused predictably on the local presbyterate. For some the name felt alien, but, more seriously for former Congregationalists, touched the still raw nerve of the distinction which had once prevailed between List A ministers and unordained ministers on List B with its perceived stress on status rather than function.

A major concern on the United Reformed Church side was whether suitable recruits would be found for the local presbyterate. A counter suggestion had come forward that the proposal for the local presbyterate be abandoned and wider authorisation be given to elders to preside at the Lord's Table. The Committee however was unable to recommend that all elders should be regarded as ministers of Word and Sacrament, as was the case in Churches of Christ. The majority of United Reformed Church elders did not feel that this was the ministry to which they were called, and there were fears that church members might be reluctant to become elders if this would be expected of them. Nor did it seem appropriate that all Churches of Christ elders should be authorised to preside on the grounds of 'pastoral necessity' since this was more than could be honestly read into the phrase. On the United Reformed Church side there was a strong sense that the right to preside rested with those who were called to a ministry of full-time pastoral care and preaching of the Word. More thought needed to be given to the possibility of a multiple ministry within a local congregation where the varied tasks of ministry in preaching, presiding and pastoral care would be shared between several people.

The Joint Committee was however sufficiently encouraged by the responses to their 1974 Report to re-affirm their belief in a twofold pattern of ministry of General Ministers and Local Presbyters, while recognising that different names might finally be adopted. At the point of union Churches of Christ elders would have the opportunity to become local presbyters. Since they had already been ordained to a ministry of Word and Sacrament, no further ordination or additional training would be required of them, although some might voluntarily undergo further training in order to fulfil the particular duties of the local presbyterate in the united Church. After union had taken place, only those elders who were ordained to the local presbyterate would preside at the Lord's Table, except where District Council authorisation was given on grounds of 'pastoral necessity'.

The 1975 Report responded to concerns over the place of lay preachers in the united Church. In some quarters there were fears that the Committee wished this ministry to disappear, but this was not their intention. The issue of lay preachers highlighted a significant difference between the negotiating churches. United Reformed Church lay preachers were entirely responsible for the conduct of worship in the churches at which they preached, and on occasion were authorised by the District Council to preside at the Lord's Supper. In Churches of Christ, where the main Sunday service was a Communion service, the sermon might be preached by a lay preacher, but the worship service would normally be led by an elder. The Committee's thinking on ministry had concentrated on presidency rather than preaching, but this did not imply any under-valuing of the ministry of lay preachers which would continue in the united Church. However any United Reformed Church lay preachers who became local presbyters under the proposals for union would have to recognise that their new ministry included pastoral responsibility in a local church.

The Joint Committee published its Final Report in 1976.[7] In the light of comments on its earlier proposals, it was now proposed that the two forms of ministry in the united Church should be known by the titles of *minister* (as then in use) and *auxiliary minister*. The designation of 'non-stipendiary minister' was rejected as too cumbersome for ordinary usage. 'Ministers' would be full-time and stipendiary. 'Auxiliary ministers' would be ordained to a ministry of Word and Sacrament 'while remaining employed in secular life'.

The doubts which had been expressed within the United Reformed Church on whether church members with full-time jobs would come forward for the auxiliary ministry and also whether such part-time ministers, because of the restrictions imposed by their secular employment, could offer more than occasional ministry were dismissed as reflecting too great a dependence on denominational traditions and inherited patterns of ministry. The experience of Churches of Christ provided sufficient evidence that not only the retired and self-employed might be expected to offer themselves for the auxiliary ministry.

The concern that the auxiliary ministry would be an inferior form of ministry, approximating to the discredited List B category of ministers in the former Congregational Union was not, in the Committee's view, based on a comparison of like with like. 'List B' ministers had been unordained, full-time and in sole pastoral charge, whereas auxiliary ministers would be ordained, part-time and normally without sole pastoral charge.

Transitional arrangements were proposed to permit those in Churches of Christ who were authorised to preside at Baptismal and Communion services to continue to do so while the auxiliary ministry was being developed. These arrangements would ensure the provision of presidents for weekly celebrations of Holy Communion.

No single pattern was proposed for the duties of an auxiliary minister since in every case a minister's availability would determine the nature of the ministry to be offered to the Church. Some would be restricted to leading services of worship at weekends while those with more flexible timetables would be able to officiate at weekday services, including funerals and weddings. The Committee wished to uphold the witness of Churches of Christ that

> a plurality of ministers has been a matter of principle in Churches of Christ and not merely an expedient to overcome a shortage of full-time ministers.[8]

Fundamental to the proposal was the Committee's conviction that auxiliary ministers were not to be regarded as 'assistants to full-time ministers'. 'Ministers' and 'auxiliary ministers' both shared one ministry. The only difference was that 'the minister will be available to the church full-time while the auxiliary minister will only be available as other commitments allow.'[9] The *auxilium* or 'help' given by the auxiliary minister would not be that of an assistant to a superior minister but would be offered to the whole Church.

[7] *Proposals for Unification* (Joint Committee for Negotiations between Churches of Christ and the United Reformed Church, 1976).

[8] ibid. p. 12.

[9] ibid. p. 14.

Responses to the earlier Reports had indicated some scepticism about whether candidates would come forward for the auxiliary ministry. The Committee faced this by addressing the question 'Who would become auxiliary ministers?' They were hopeful that the auxiliary ministry would brought into existence from a number of sources. These would include ordained elders in Churches of Christ who should be given the opportunity to become auxiliary ministers at the time of union. They would be inducted to their new ministry under the oversight of the District Council but would not be re-ordained.

New entrants to the auxiliary ministry were envisaged from both uniting Churches. A Working Party was already considering how to implement this proposal and the Committee hoped there would not be too long a delay between union and the ordination of new auxiliary ministers.

It was also hoped that some lay preachers would offer themselves for the auxiliary ministry. A proviso in their case would be that they should undertake pastoral responsibility in a local church. They would be ordained after further preparation or training if this was required by the Synod in accordance with the general rules for the training of auxiliary ministers.

In the case of registered local pastors, the Committee did not propose that these should automatically become auxiliary ministers because of the different circumstances in which they were working. Those who were part-time and non-stipendiary were already exercising a ministry similar to that envisaged for the auxiliary ministry, and it would be appropriate for them to enter that ministry. Others who were giving fuller service approximated more to the full-time ministry, and their future required further exploration. The promise was given that the act of unification would not adversely affect the existing rights of registered local pastors and that they would not be disturbed in their present ministries.

The major proposal in the Report that the united Church should have a twofold ministry of 'ministers' and 'auxiliary ministers' was, as far as local congregations were concerned, an offer rather than a requirement. In a significant qualifying statement the Committee declared that 'No congregation will be required to have auxiliary ministers and not every congregation will see the need for such.'[10] This was tantamount to saying to the United Reformed Church (with its Congregational/Presbyterian traditions of 'sole' ministry) that United Reformed Church congregations need not take too seriously the conviction and practice in Churches of Christ of the plurality of ministers. Union with Churches of Christ need not fundamentally change the ethos of the United Reformed Church. The Committee had set much store on retaining the values of both traditions of ministry, but provided an escape route for those, especially in the United Reformed Church, who did not wish to move from their existing patterns.

In the event the failure of the Proposals for Unification to reach the required majorities in Churches of Christ signalled the end of the Committee's work. Their Report to the United Reformed Church Assembly 1978 concluded however that, in spite of the disappointment at the outcome of the negotiations, 'we remain convinced that our work has led to a significant growth in understanding of the ministry and sacraments of the Church.' Internal discussions within

---

[10]   *Proposals for Unification*, p. 14.

Churches of Christ soon led to the formation of the Re-formed Association of Churches of Christ, comprising the constituent elements of the former Churches of Christ who favoured unification with the United Reformed Church. The Re-formed Association of Churches of Christ and the United Reformed Church formally achieved unification at a Unifying Assembly held at Birmingham on the twenty-sixth of September 1981 in accordance with the Proposals for Unification. The Basis of Union was amended in paragraph 7(21) to make provision for the introduction of auxiliary ministers. These would be 'under the same oversight but continuing in other occupations, earning their livelihood within them, and sharing in all the circumstances of a "secular calling".' Full-time ministers whose place and form of service became dependent on an agency not under the discipline of the General Assembly, would become auxiliary ministers unless the General Assembly agreed to continue their recognition as full-time ministers.

The newly united Church was thus committed to making real the proposals for a twofold ministry of Word and Sacrament to include 'ministers' and 'auxiliary ministers'.

Developing Auxiliary or Non-Stipendiary Ministry

Significant work on the development of the auxiliary ministry had been undertaken prior to unification. The United Reformed Church Assembly in 1978, faced with the failure of the plan for unification, had resolved to establish the auxiliary ministry, and a Working Party which had been set up to bring forward proposals had reported in 1979.[11]

The Working Party argued that the principle of auxiliary ministry was rooted in New Testament evidence and practice. It was clear from the New Testament that ministry in the apostolic church was not tied to a stipendiary system. The apostle Paul had firmly asserted the right of the preacher of the Gospel to be financially supported by the Church, while refusing to exercise that right for himself.[12] Historically also the rapid expansion of the Church in missionary situations had relied upon a non-stipendiary ministry. In practical terms also the full-time stipendiary ministry could not on its own provide for the United Reformed Church a ministry of Word, Sacraments and pastoral care to all its smaller congregations, many of which were nevertheless potential centres of growth.

An important consideration was that in the missionary situation, in which the Church found itself, a non-stipendiary form of ministry was uniquely placed to penetrate 'unevangelised areas' in the life of contemporary society where there was at present little or no relevant Christian witness. 'A ministry of those already working in these areas could open the way for the birth and growth of Christian congregations within them, developing a style of life, worship, teaching and ministry appropriate to their needs.'[13]

---

[11]   United Reformed Church, *Reports to Assembly 1979*
[12]   *I Corinthians 9:12-15*
[13]   United Reformed Church, *Reports to Assembly 1979*, p. 47.

Non-stipendiary ministry might also be the means for awakening talents for various aspects of ministry which were lying dormant because traditional patterns of church life provided no recognised place for their fulfilment. The Working Party hoped that these dormant talents might be awakened and brought into use.

The experience of sister Churches, notably the Church of England which had been developing non-stipendiary ministry for several years, provided a basis for encouraging the United Reformed Church to believe that the Spirit might be leading the Church in this direction.

The report of the Working Party defined an auxiliary minister as

> one who is ordained to the ministry of Word and Sacraments but continues in a secular occupation, using his gifts both within that occupation and within the life and worship of the Church. He will exercise his ministry in association with a local church and a stipendiary minister.[14]

Auxiliary ministers would be under the oversight of their District Council, who would be responsible for their ordination and induction to a particular sphere of ministry. In the first instance their term of service in their sphere should be no more than five years.

Various situations for ministry were envisaged. An auxiliary minister might undertake the pastoral care of a small congregation. A large church might have an auxiliary minister as an assistant minister, perhaps specialising in one area of its work. The auxiliary ministry should operate in outreach situations such as in hospital chaplaincy, community development, or in industry, government or one of the professions. For such ministers 'their main ministry would not be in the local church but in the community where they were working and living.'[15] The Working Party did not dwell on the particularities of team ministry but left an impression that a principal focus of the training of auxiliary ministries should be to prepare candidates to participate in team ministries. It was beyond the Working Party's brief to suggest how stipendiary ministers should be similarly equipped.

It is clear that the goal of the Working Party's proposals was to equip the Church with a more flexible form of ministry than that which it had inherited from the past through its parent traditions. The Church now required different patterns of ministry to meet the missionary challenge of its contemporary situation. Yet at the same time the two forms of ministry – ministers and auxiliary ministers – needed a sense of common identity and purpose. This would be emphasised by identical selection procedures for both forms of ministry. Stipendiary and auxiliary candidates would need the approval of their local church, District Council, national Assessment Conference, and Provincial Ministerial Committee. Their call to ministry would also be expected to follow a similar pattern. The selection procedures for all candidates would seek evidence of an inward conviction and call to ministry. That sense of inward call would be tested by the wider Church to ensure that it was from God.

---

[14] ibid. p. 48. The Working Party noted that the auxiliary ministry would be open to men and women and that the pronouns used in their report were intended to include both.

[15] ibid.

Ordained ministry in the United Reformed Church in 1981, following unification with Churches of Christ, was thus significantly different from that of 1972. The initial union of Congregationalists and Presbyterians had, for the most part, preserved the closely similar patterns of the parent Churches in which ministry was primarily understood as full-time service within local congregations or groups of churches. The increasing number of ministers working in secular employment as a means of engaging more directly with the world outside the Church were often regarded as having defected from the ministry. The introduction of the auxiliary ministry gave positive recognition to the potential of ministry in secular situations. Auxiliary ministers working in such situations were to be provided with support and oversight (*episcope*) by District Councils. It was intended that they would also provide *auxilium* to local churches in their mission.

The introduction of the auxiliary ministry also provided opportunities for many who had taken early retirement – often involuntarily in the economic circumstances of the 1980s – to respond to the call to ministry and offer service to the church as ordained ministers. The link between ordained ministry and stipendiary provision by the Church was broken. In principle auxiliary and stipendiary ministers were held in parity of esteem, though their functions within the Church might differ.

A cynical observer of this development might be forgiven for thinking that it would have happened in any case. Low recruitment to full-time ministry and the Church's growing inability to pay adequate stipends were symptoms of the need for a new approach. It was not coincidental that other Churches, episcopal and non-episcopal, were simultaneously introducing their own forms of non-stipendiary ministry. This would inevitably have happened in the United Reformed Church even if unification with Churches of Christ had not been achieved. The important difference for the United Reformed Church was that, as a condition of union, Churches of Christ brought to the new Church their deep belief in a plurality of ministries. This belief and their long experience of its practice were embodied in the new Church. Time would tell whether these high expectations would be fulfilled.

Chapter Seven

Ordination Services

ORDINATION SERVICES

Ritual action – or liturgy – is the means by which the Church articulates its beliefs and affirms its nature as a community of God's People. The church traditions which we have explored shared a distaste for sacerdotalism and cherished their freedom from what they saw as the constraints of imposed liturgies. Two of the traditions – the Congregational and Presbyterian – were shaped by the response to the Restoration Settlement of 1660-2 (culminating in the Act of Uniformity of 1662) when more than two thousand ministers, lecturers and fellows, were deprived of their posts.[1] The imposition by the Act of the liturgy of the Book of Common Prayer was not the only question at issue, but it contributed significantly to the rejection of sacerdotalism and hierarchy in the Dissenting churches. Henceforth words like 'ritual' and 'liturgy' tended to disappear from the Dissenting vocabulary. But this did not – and could not – mean the abandonment of ritual action. Ritual was manifest in the apparent simplicity of the presidency of the ordained minister of Word and Sacrament at the worship of the gathered community, and not least at celebrations of the Lord's Supper. The nature and form of sacred ritual reflected relationships within the worshipping community. Was the ordained minister set over the community as one possessed of authority, and, if so, what was the nature of that authority? Or was the ritual act of presidency a sign that the ministry existed for the sake of the Church and that the minister stood within the community of the faithful as one who served? These questions remain of contemporary importance. There is clearly a case - and a need – for ritual or liturgical leadership in the Church. The liturgy in use defines the responsibilities of the participants. Where worship is led exclusively by the minister, apart from the congregation singing hymns and putting money in the offertory plate, the congregation is effectively relegated to passive participation. Good liturgy confers a sense of worth and purpose upon its participants. Inappropriate liturgy can rob members of the worshipping community of their dignity as saints in the household of God.

Worship services by which a man or woman is ordained to the ministry of Word and sacrament are, for the most part, only occasional events in the life of most worshipping communities. Yet they have a pivotal role in defining the nature of the community and its beliefs concerning the ministry which, through the liturgy, it receives as God's gift to the Church. In this section we examine some of the ordination liturgies which were in use by Congregationalists, Presbyterians and Churches of Christ in the period under review.

---

[1]   M R Watts, *The Dissenters*, (Oxford: 1978) p. 219.

1.   Congregational Ordination Services

A Manual for Ministers (1936)

This Manual was first published at a time when written orders of service still aroused widespread suspicion in the Congregational community. In the previous century R W Dale had accepted, in response to pleas for at least the partial use of a set Liturgy which would include opportunity for extempore prayer, that there was nothing in Congregational principles that was inconsistent with the use of such a Liturgy in public worship.[2] Yet the tradition of hostility remained to what the early Congregationalists had described as 'stinted and set forms of prayer'. Dale upheld the view that Liturgies were 'out of harmony with the genius of Congregationalism.'[3] His influence continued well into the 20th century but by the 1930s had begun to wane. In a Foreword to the *Manual*, Dr Sidney M Berry, then General Secretary of the Congregational Union of England and Wales, noted the tendency in some Congregational Churches to make more use of 'liturgical material' and that this had led to greater orderliness and reverence in worship. *A Manual for Ministers* offered for the first time a range of 'semi-official' liturgies for a range of services including the sacraments of Baptism and the Lord's Supper and – a sign of the growing importance of the observance of the Christian Year – worship material for the major Christian Festivals. It was reprinted twice, in 1946 and 1948, and was in use for more than a quarter of a century.

The service for the Ordination of a Minister[4] was recognisably 'Genevan' in its content as may be seen from the following outline:

1.   Scripture Sentences

2.   Statement by the Presiding Minister regarding the Church and the Ministry

3.   Statements by a representative of the local church and the ordinand

4.   Questions to the ordinand

5.   A question to the local church

6.   The Declaration of ordination by the presiding minister

7.   The Giving of the Right Hand of Fellowship *or* the Laying on of Hands

8.   The Ordination Prayer

9.   The Charge to the Minister and the Church

10.   The Blessing of the congregation by the newly ordained minister.

---

[2]   R W Dale, *Manual of Congregational Principles*, (London: Congregational Union of England and Wales, 1884).

[3]   op. cit. p. 164

[4]   *A Manual for Ministers*, (London: Independent Press, 1936) pp. 132-39

The Ordaining Authority

Ordination took place within the local church which had called the ordinand to be their pastor. In accordance with Congregational tradition the local church was competent to act in this, as in every other matter concerning the life of the Church. The local church was thus the ordaining authority. The rubrics for the service however emphasise the necessity for the presence of representatives of the County Union[5] as a sign of the concurrence and approval of the wider church. It was similarly urged that a representative of the denomination, usually the Provincial Moderator, should be invited to preside since the minister ordained at the service would thereby be recognised as an accredited minister of the denomination.

Questions to the Ordinand and Church

Following a statement of the circumstances of the call by a representative of the church and a statement by the ordinand of his faith and experience, six Questions were put to the ordinand. Each was preceded by a scriptural quotation which shaped the form of the question. The Questions were:

1. Do you take this (Matthew 28:19,20) as your commission, with solemn purpose to unfold to men the teaching of Jesus Christ?
2. Will you be constant in public and private prayers, devout and reverent in the conduct of the services of the house of God? (I Timothy 2:1)
3. Will you diligently read and study God's holy Word as contained in the Scriptures? (2 Timothy 3:16,17)
4. Will you seek to fulfil this high calling with wisdom, diligence and love? (I Peter 5:2,3)
5. Will you care for the lambs of the flock, tending and leading them in the spirit of the Good Shepherd? (John 21:15b)
6. Will you thus do the work of an evangelist, and prepare the way of the Lord? (2 Timothy 4:1,2)

None of these questions required any subscription to orthodox belief in Jesus as the Son of God, the Holy Trinity, the Resurrection, or Eternal Life. This startling omission is more understandable given the ethos of the Congregational Union in 1936 when Congregationalists were suspicious of credal formulations. Nathaniel Micklem had remarked ironically in the same year that among Congregationalists it was 'a principle that neither Church member nor minister shall be required to subscribe to any particular formulae of the faith as a test of orthodoxy.'[6] While Congregationalists had maintained substantially orthodox beliefs, not least when much of Presbyterianism in the eighteenth century had lapsed into Unitarianism, they were certainly vulnerable to the charge of failing to safeguard sound doctrine and belief among their members and ministers.

An equally surprising omission from the questions put to the ordinand was any reference to the minister's responsibility for administering the sacraments of Baptism and the Lord's Supper.

---

[5]   County Unions were, as their name implies, district associations of Congregational Churches. They often acted as Trustees for church property and manses, but exercised no authority over their member churches.
[6]   N Micklem, *What is the Faith?* (London: Hodder and Stoughton, 1936) p. 14.

One question was put to the people:

'Do you, the people of this church, acknowledge and receive this, our brother, as your minister; do you promise to esteem him for his work's sake, and to encourage him in his labours; and do you engage to maintain and comfort him in his ministry? In token of your acceptance of these obligations will you now, as an assembly of God's people, stand in silent prayer'.

This question also lacks any common affirmation of faith. The people promise to receive, esteem, encourage, maintain and comfort their minister, but there is no sense that, as members of the priesthood of all believers, they share with their minister a priestly ministry of worship and service. Nor are they allowed any verbal response but mutely stand in silent prayer.

The Mode of Ordination

The order reflects uncertainty as to the means by which the ordination is made effective. Following the questions to the ordinand and the church, the Presiding Minister makes a statement – while the ordinand kneels with the ministers taking part in the service and 'some representative of the church' standing around him – in which the ordinand is declared 'to be ordained to the ministry of the Church of Christ, and received as pastor of this congregation'. The Declaration is followed by the giving of the right hand of fellowship to the newly ordained minister by the Presiding Minister and representatives of the County Union and the church *or* by the laying on of hands. These are offered as alternatives but with an implied preference for the right hand of fellowship.

The Ordination Prayer which follows omits any invocation of the Holy Spirit in relation to the act of ordination. The prayer takes the form of thanksgiving for the calling of the newly ordained minister and supplications for his ministry.[7] These include the pouring out of 'the spirit of wisdom and understanding, the spirit of counsel and might, the spirit of knowledge and of the fear of the Lord'[8] but there is no specific reference to the Holy Spirit.

In summary, the compilers of the order of service for the ordination of a minister in *A Manual for Ministers* aimed to bring some order and dignity to the act of setting apart those who were called and chosen to what the liturgy referred to as 'this holy office'. The fact that it was felt necessary to state in the introductory rubric that 'the Ordination should form part of a strictly religious service, and not of a public meeting' suggests that this had not been universal practice among Congregationalists. To this extent the liturgy represented a major advance. It certainly achieved its purpose of providing a service for the ordination of a man or woman to ministry among Congregationalists. It is less clear from this service that its intention was to ordain to a ministry of Word and Sacrament within the one holy, catholic and apostolic Church.

---

[7]   The ordinand is referred to throughout as 'he' and 'him', although Congregationalists had ordained their first woman minister in 1917.

[8]   Isaiah 11:2,3.

A Book of Services and Prayers (1959)[9]

A Book of Services and Prayers was compiled by a Committee appointed by the Congregational Union of England and Wales. It thus enjoyed a more official status than *A Manual for Ministers*, although its Preface included a disclaimer – almost obligatory among Congregationalists – that it was designed or intended as a book of common prayer. Part I provided a range of services for morning and evening worship, orders of service for the sacraments of Baptism and the Lord's Supper, and services for special occasions including the ordination and induction of ministers. Part II provided prayers for the Christian Year and a wide range of prayers for social and national occasions, many of them classic prayers of the Church.

The order of service for the ordination of a minister[10] provided a much richer liturgy than that of *A Manual for Ministers*, as may be seen in its outline:

1. Scripture Sentences
2. Prayer of Invocation
3. The Reading of Scripture (Old and New Testaments)
4. Statement by the Presiding Minister concerning the Church and the Ministry
5. Statements by a representative of the Church and by the Ordinand
6. Questions to the Ordinand
7. Question to the Church
8. The Ordination Prayer and the Laying on of Hands
9. Declaration of Ordination
10. The Presentation of a Bible to the newly-ordained minister
11. The Giving of the Right Hand of Fellowship
12. The Charge to the Minister and the Church
13. Benediction (pronounced by the newly-ordained minister)

The Ordaining Authority

As in the earlier *Manual* the ordaining authority is the local Church, which for Congregationalists could not be otherwise. The introductory statement by the Presiding Minister states that the local church, which has called the ordinand to its pastorate, 'has invited us to come together that we with them may ordain him into the office of the ministry'. The invitees are not defined but may be taken to include representatives of other nearby Congregational Churches and the Provincial Moderator who presides by the invitation of the local Church as a representative of the wider Church.

The Statement concerning the Church and its Ministry goes far beyond what would have been acceptable 30 years earlier. Here we read that

---

[9] *A Book of Services and Prayers* (London: Independent Press Ltd 1959).
[10] op. cit. pp. 90-97.

It is the office and duty of ministers soundly to deliver to the people the Word of God, instructing and admonishing them and preaching conversion to God, through Jesus Christ our Lord and Saviour; to lead the prayers of the Church; to administer the Sacraments; to care for those committed to their charge, maintaining the church in good discipline as faithful shepherds of the flock, to the end that the Church may grow in grace and in the knowledge and love of God, and shine forth as a light in the world.

While the local Church is the ordaining authority, it acts on behalf of the whole Church. Through this Statement by the Presiding Minister the wider Church offers guidance to the local Church on how it may discharge its responsibilities to the whole Church.

Questions to the Ordinand and the Church

Four Questions are put to the Ordinand.

1. Do you believe in one God, Father, Son and Holy Spirit, and do you confess anew the Lord Jesus Christ as your Saviour and Lord?
2. Are you persuaded that the Scriptures of the Old and New Testaments contain all doctrine required for eternal salvation through faith in Jesus Christ?
3. Do you believe in your heart that you are truly called by God to the pastoral charge of this church and congregation?
4. Do you promise to execute your charge with all fidelity, to preach the Word of God, to administer the Sacraments, to fulfil the pastoral office, and to live a godly life, adorning the doctrine of God our Saviour?

These questions require the ordinand to confess the faith of the Church and to preach the Word - Jesus Christ - revealed through the Scriptures as the source of salvation. Whereas *A Manual for Minister* had emphasised the *teaching* of Jesus, the emphasis here lies on the *person* of Jesus and his saving work. The bedrock of ministry lies in preaching the Word, administering the sacraments of the Gospel, and providing pastoral care.

One question was put to the local Church:

Do you, the members of this church, worshipping at…acknowledge and receive…as a minister in the Church of Christ and as Pastor of this church and congregation, embracing the Word of God which he is to deliver, and accepting him as one who is to watch for your souls and give account to God? And do you promise to encourage him and share in his labours, to maintain and strengthen him in his ministry, and give him all due honour, loyalty and support? If you so take him as your minister, as an assembly of Christ's people, will you stand in silent prayer.

This question is richer in its content than its predecessor in the *Manual* and offers a profounder understanding of ministry as rooted in the Word of God. It unfortunately perpetuates the assumption that ministers are normally male. The Church members – the *laos* – continue to occupy a subordinate role in the life of the church. While they are asked to promise to 'share in his labours', the means by which they are to do this are not specified. The emphasis continues to lie on encouraging their minister and giving him their support.

The Mode of Ordination

In this order of service it is stated that ordination is by prayer and the laying on of hands by ministers and church representatives. The words of the prayer are not prescribed, although a suggested outline is given. This includes 'Prayer for the continued gifts of the Holy Spirit', but provides no specific invocation of the Holy Spirit at the point of the imposition of hands. The clear intention is the act of ordination takes place within the Ordination Prayer.

The Ordination Prayer is followed by a declaration by the Presiding Minister that 'we declare you to be ordained to the Ministry of the Gospel in the Church of Christ, and to be appointed Pastor of this church and congregation.' Ordination has thus both a local and a universal reference. Implicit in this statement is the belief that the minister has been ordained to a ministry within the whole Church and also that this would exclude any requirement for re-ordination for the exercise of a ministry within a wider Church than those of the Congregational faith and order.

The Declaration of Ordination was followed by the giving and receiving of a Bible and the giving of the Right Hand of Fellowship by representatives of the church to which the Minister had been ordained and by representatives of the wider fellowship of the churches.

The service for the ordination of ministers in the *Book of Services and Prayers* was thus significantly different from the earlier service in *A Manual for Ministers*. They could be read as services for two quite different denominations. The later book thus mirrored the changes in English Congregationalism which we noted in Chapter 3. In particular however it drew heavily upon an Ordination Service in an unofficial publication – *A Book of Public Worship* – which had been compiled in 1948 for the use of Congregationalists[11] by four leading members of the denomination who had been members of the Church Order Group.[12] The Statement concerning the Church and the Ministry, the Questions to the Ordinand, and the Declaration of Ordination were all derived from *A Book of Public Worship*. The principal difference lay in the Ordination Prayer where, in *A Book of Public Worship*, a definite link was made between the act of ordination through prayer and the laying on of hands. To this extent *A Book of Services and Prayers* represented the apogee of the Genevan liturgical tradition within English Congregationalism.

---

[11]   *A Book of Public Worship*, compiled for the use of Congregationalists by John Huxtable, John Marsh, Romilly Micklem and James Todd, (Oxford: 1948) pp. 199-204.

[12]   See Chapter 3, p. 46 and Elaine Kaye, *Mansfield College Oxford*, (Oxford: 1996) pp. 227-28.

II. Ordination Services in the Presbyterian Church of England

The first service book of the Presbyterian Church of England was authorised in 1898 as the *Directory for Public Worship*. A new Directory, authorised by the General Assembly in 1921, served the Church until 1948 when a third book – renamed the *Presbyterian Service Book* – was prepared in collaboration with the Presbyterian Church of Wales. The Church's final service book, prior to union in with the Congregational Church in England and Wales, was published in 1968. These three books in succession provided liturgical material for the Christian festivals and other special occasions as well as orders of service for use in the courts of the Church.

The service for the ordination and induction of ministers in the service books of 1921, 1948 and 1968 followed a common pattern. A person who had been present at an ordination in 1921, and at another nearly half a century later, would have noticed little difference between the two occasions. Between 1921 and 1968 there was a marked consistency of word and action. This is not to suggest that the Presbyterian Church of England had been resistant to change. The regular publication of new service books was an indication that the Church was aware of the need for new approaches to public worship. Theology and liturgy had to keep in step. New insights into the missionary nature of the Church and the ministry of the laity required changing forms of liturgical expression. But services of ordination and induction were also important events in which the Church both re-affirmed its faithfulness to its historic traditions and, with its eye firmly focused on the future, incorporated into its ministry those who would take the Church forward into new paths of service.

The basis outline of the service for the ordination and induction of a minister was set out in the *1921 Directory for Public Worship*.[13]

1. The Constitution of Presbytery
2. Call to Worship and Prayer of Invocation
3. Praise (Psalm or Hymn)
4. Reading from the Scriptures of the Old and New Testaments
5. Statement by the Moderator (introducing the Clerk who narrates the call)
6. Declaration of the Church's attitude towards her Standards
7. Questions to the Ordinand
8. The Ordination Prayer (including prescribed words and the Laying on of Hands)
9. Declaration of Ordination and Induction and the giving of the Right Hand of Fellowship by the Moderator
10. The Right Hand of Fellowship given by the other members of Presbytery
11. The Charge to the Minister and Congregation
12. Doxology or Apostolic Benediction

The services of 1948 and 1968 added an optional recital of either the Apostles' or Nicene Creeds after the scripture readings. Prayers of Intercession were offered. The candidate for ordination was then presented to the Moderator by a minister appointed by Presbytery. Questions to the congregation followed those to the ordinand. While the basic structure remained unchanged the liturgy had a richer content.

---

[13]   *Directory for Public Worship*, (London: Publications Committee of the Presbyterian Church of England, 1921).

The Ordaining Authority

The ordination of a minister in the Presbyterian Church of England took place in the congregation in which the minister was to serve. The duty of the session clerk in the service was to narrate the steps which had been taken by the Presbytery to fill the vacant pastorate in the congregation. The ordaining authority was the Presbytery, not, as in Congregational practice, the local congregation. The Moderator of Presbytery presided by virtue of office not by invitation of the local congregation. The formal constitution of Presbytery before the service ('beforehand in a place adjoining the church') created the ordaining authority.

The service books of 1948 and 1968 emphasised the importance of good order in the arrangements for the service. It was recommended that ordinands should wear a cassock, and that ministers at inductions should wear their customary robes. The order in which members of Presbytery entered the church was laid down as Elders, the Ordinand or Minister to be inducted, the Ministers in order of their ordination (the seniors having seats nearest to the officiating Ministers), and lastly the officiating Ministers. These rubrics did not imply hierarchy or any dilution of the Presbyterian insistence on the parity of ministers. Their concern was to maintain good order and to esteem Presbytery as a responsible and honoured court of the Church.

Questions to the Ordinand

The Questions to the Ordinand followed the public declaration of the Church's attitude towards her Standards. In the *Directory for Public Worship* (1921) this took the following form:

The Presbyterian Church of England acknowledges as her Supreme Standard of Faith and Duty the scriptures of the Old and New Testaments, and as her Subordinate Standards the Westminster Confession of Faith, and the Larger and Shorter Catechisms.

The Church recognises liberty of opinion on such points in her Subordinate Standards as do not enter into the substance of the Faith, while she retains full authority in any case which may arise to determine what falls within this description, and to guard against any abuse of this liberty to the injury of her unity and peace.

The Church further claims the right, as duty may require, to interpret, alter, add to, or modify her Subordinate Standards and Formulas, under the promised guidance of the Holy Spirit, and under a sense of direct responsibility to her ever-living Head.

The statement of doctrine known as the "Twenty-four Articles of the Faith",[14] and the statement of polity known as the "Appendix to the Articles", though not Standards of the Church, represent generally her teaching and practice, and are subject to the same principles of interpretation as her Subordinate Standards.

---

14   This statement had been approved in 1890 'as a statement of the fundamental doctrines held and taught by this Church'.

The Presbyterian Service Book (1948)[15] replicated this declaration with the omission of the final paragraph. Further modifications were introduced into the *Presbyterian Service Book* of 1968[16] in the light of 'A Statement of the Christian Faith 1956' approved by the General Assembly 'as a declaration for this present time of the scriptural and historic faith'.[17] Thus its final form, prior to union with the Congregational Church in England and Wales, was as follows:

This Church acknowledges the Word of God in the Scriptures of the Old and New Testaments as the supreme standard and authority for faith and conduct.

This Church confesses the catholic faith in God, the Holy Trinity, Father, Son and Holy Spirit, to which faith witness is borne by the ancient creeds of the universal Church.

This Church acknowledges as her Subordinate Standards the Westminster Confession of Faith, and the Larger and Shorter Catechisms, in which her fathers set forth the Christian Faith.

This Church in 1956 accepted a "Statement of the Christian Faith" as a declaration for this present time of the scriptural and historic faith, and authorised its use in the teaching of that faith.

This Church claims the right to interpret, add to, modify, or supersede her subordinate standards, formulas, and statements, in accordance with the Scriptures, under the promised guidance of the Holy Spirit, and under a sense of direct responsibility to Jesus Christ, her ever-living Head.

This Church, being within the one holy, catholic, and apostolic Church, receives and exercises therein the ministry of the Word and Sacraments which Christ has given to his Church. With other Churches of the Reformed tradition she maintains the Presbyterian form of church order, believing it to be founded upon and agreeable to the Word of God.

This Church declares that the Lord Jesus Christ, the only King and Head of the Church, has appointed therein a government distinct from civil government and in things spiritual not subordinate thereto and that civil authorities are subject to the rule of God and ought to respect the rights of conscience and of religious belief.

This Church recognises liberty of opinion on matters which do not enter into the substance of the faith, while she retains full authority in any case which may arise to determine what falls within this description, and to guard against any abuse of this liberty to the injury of her unity and peace.

Questions to the Ordinand

Questions were then put to the ordinand on the basis of this declaration. In the *Directory* (1921) and the *Service Book* (1948) there were eight questions.

I.   Do you believe the Word of God contained in the Scriptures of the Old and New Testaments to be the Supreme Standard of Faith and Duty?

II. Do you accept the Westminster Confession of Faith and the Larger and Shorter Catechisms as the Subordinate Standards of this Church, believing the substance of the Christian Faith therein contained; and do you consent that by these Standards, constitutionally interpreted by the Courts of the Church, your relation to this Church shall be determined?

---

15   *The Presbyterian Service Book* (London: Publications Committee of the Presbyterian Church of England, 1948).
16   *The Presbyterian Service Book* (London: Publications Committee of the Presbyterian Church of England, 1968).
17   For the text of this Statement see D M Thompson (ed), *Stating the Gospel*, (Edinburgh, T and T Clark Ltd, 1990) pp. 184-97.

III. Are you persuaded that the Lord Jesus Christ, the only King and Head of this Church, has therein appointed a government distinct from civil government, and in things spiritual not subordinate thereto; and that rulers, while bound to render obedience to Christ in their own province, ought not to constrain men's religious belief or invade the rights of conscience?

IV. Do you acknowledge the Presbyterian form of government to be founded on, and agreeable to, the Word of God; do you promise, as a Minister of this Church, to be subject to its government, and to take the part entrusted to you in the administration of its affairs; and while cherishing brotherly love towards all the faithful followers of Christ, do you engage to seek the purity, peace and increase of this Church?

And now you are called upon to undertake the following solemn engagements as a servant of the Lord Jesus Christ, and a Minister or His Gospel:

V. Do you own and confess anew the Lord Jesus Christ as your Saviour and Lord?

VI. Do you sincerely believe, and will you faithfully proclaim, the Gospel of the love and grace of God, wherein He freely offers to all men forgiveness and eternal life, and calls them into the fellowship and service of His Kingdom, through Jesus Christ, His only begotten Son, Who died for our sins, rose again from the dead, and is alive for evermore?

VII. Are zeal for the glory of God, love to the Lord Jesus Christ, and a desire to save souls, and not worldly designs or interests, as far as you know your own heart, your great motives and chief inducements to enter into the office of the Holy Ministry?

VIII. Do you engage in the strength and grace of Jesus Christ, our Lord and Master, to live a holy and circumspect life, faithfully to discharge the duties of the ministry among this people, and zealously to maintain the truth of the Gospel, whatever trouble or persecution may arise?

In the *Presbyterian Service Book (1968)*, and following the approval of the Statement of the Christian Faith 1956, these eight questions were reduced to six. Questions 1 – 4 were no longer needed as their content was included in the new public Declaration of the Church's doctrine and practice. Two new questions took their place:

1. Do you assent to this Declaration of the doctrine and practice of the Presbyterian Church of England; do you undertake to exercise your ministry conformably to it; and do you consent that, in accordance with this Declaration, constitutionally interpreted by the Courts of this Church, your relation to this Church shall be determined?

2. Do you believe in one God, Father, Son and Holy Spirit, and do you own and confess anew the Lord Jesus Christ as your Saviour and Lord?

Questions 3, 4 and 6 followed the form of Questions 6,7 and 8 in the earlier books. Question 5 was a modification of the former Question 4 by the deletion of its first clause ('Do you acknowledge the Presbyterian form of government to be founded on, and agreeable to, the Word of God') since this was now covered by the candidate's assent to the public Declaration.

These questions are markedly 'credal' in tone and emphasis. Presbytery, as the ordaining authority, has to be satisfied that the candidate for ordination genuinely and sincerely holds to the faith of the one, holy, catholic and apostolic church. The Church recognises (though does not define) liberty of opinion insofar as this does not detract from the substance of the faith; the Church retains authority over what liberty of opinion may be permitted in any given instance, and to ensure that the exercise of such liberty shall not injure the Church's unity and peace.

Questions to the Congregation

The Directory (1921) did not invite any participation or promise of support by members of the local congregation. This was rectified in the services books of 1948 and 1968 which added two questions to be put to the congregation by the Moderator. In a preamble the Moderator reminded the members and adherents of the Congregation that the occasion of ordination and induction was one for renewed dedication and for mutual pledges on the part of the Minister and of the Congregation. In the 1948 Service Book the two questions were:

1. Do you, as members of this Congregation own and confess the Lord Jesus Christ as your Saviour and Lord, and as the Head of this Church?
2. Do you, in accepting the Minister whom you have called, promise in Christian fellowship to share with him the work of Christ in this Congregation, and to give him your support and encouragement in the Lord?

The 1968 Service Book added 'adherents' to members of the Congregation in Question 1, but modified Question 2 to read:

> Do you, the members and adherents of this congregation, in accepting
> the minister whom you have called promise *him* all due respect,
> encouragement and obedience in the Lord?

It is difficult not to feel that (although the italicised *him* implicitly recognised at last the ministry of women) the form of this question showed a weaker grasp of the place of the congregation in ministry than in the *Presbyterian Service Book* (1948) where the congregation had at least promised to share in the work of Christ in the Congregation. The later book omitted this promise and restricted the role of the congregation to the respect and obedience which the Congregation owed to their minister. It is surprising that a Church which placed high value on the ministry of the ordained Eldership did not, in its services of ordination and induction, make a connection between the ministry of Elders and the ministry of Word and Sacrament, and provide for the public recognition of the ministry of the whole Congregation.

In both service books the Congregation was invited to signify their assent by standing in the presence of the Presbytery. No spoken response was suggested.

The Mode of Ordination

The three service books of 1921, 1948 and 1968 make it clear that ordination to the ministry of Word and Sacrament is conditional upon the ordinand's response to the solemn questions. The rubrics require that the act of ordination should immediately follow the answering of the questions to the satisfaction of Presbytery. The act of ordination is by prayer offered by the Moderator and the laying on of hands by other appointed Presbyters . The rubrics prescribe the form of words to be used in the ordination prayer at the moment of ordination. In the *Directory* (1921) and *Presbyterian Service Book* (1948) the prescribed words were:

> Bestow upon him thy Holy Spirit, as we now, in the name of the Lord Jesus Christ (here the Moderator shall lay his hands upon the head of the Ordinand, and the other Presbyters also laying on their right hands) ordain him with the laying on of hands, to be a Minister of the Church of God, and commit unto him authority to minister the Word and Sacraments

The *Presbyterian Service Book* (1968) prescribed a slightly modified form of words: - 'with the laying on of hands, TO THE OFFICE OF THE HOLY MINISTRY IN THY CHURCH, AND COMMIT UNTO *HIM* AUTHORITY TO MINISTER THY WORD AND SACRAMENTS AND TO BE A PASTOR TO THY PEOPLE' - in order to include reference to the minister's pastoral role.

The Ordination Prayer was followed by a statement by the Moderator to the newly-ordained minister declaring him to be ordained to the office of the holy Ministry and inducting him to the office of Minister of the Congregation. The right hand of fellowship was given to the newly-ordained minister by the Moderator, and then by other members of Presbytery.

The successive services of ordination used in the Presbyterian Church of England between 1920 and 1980 differ in an important respect from those in the Congregational Churches during the same period. In the latter, ordination was the means by which a person became a minister to a local congregation, and through that ministry received ministerial recognition within the larger community of the Congregational Churches. In the Presbyterian Church of England, although ordination required the call of a local congregation, the act of ordination in the first instance admitted a person to the ministry of the whole Church, and consequently, albeit concurrently, included induction to ministry in a local congregation. This difference reflected the different perspectives of the two traditions. Congregationalists had a high sense of the importance of the local Church and a correspondingly weaker vision of the Church Universal. Presbyterians did not in any sense undervalue the importance of the local congregation, but had a deeper sense of being part of the one, holy, catholic and apostolic Church. The pronouncing of the Benediction at the end of the ordination service by the newly-ordained minister in the Congregational service and the Moderator of Presbytery in the Presbyterian service was perhaps a sign of that difference.

III. Ordination Services in Churches of Christ

Churches of Christ, unlike Congregationalists and Presbyterians, did not produce printed directories for worship or service books. This did not mean that the form of ordination was unimportant. As we have already seen, they followed Alexander Campbell's insistence that the fount of official power in the Church lay with the community of the Church – the multitude of the faithful. Those who ordained were not possessed of sacerdotal power either in themselves or in their office. They acted on behalf of Christ who, as the Church's Lord, himself appointed, ordained and sent forth his ministers.

Appendix B to the 'Report on Ordination' which was approved by the Annual Conference of Churches of Christ in 1942[18] suggested that a service for the Ordination of Evangelists should have the following order:

1.   Introductory Statement

Beloved brethren, we are assembled in the presence of God this day to set apart to the office of Evangelist or Missionary those who, after examination, have been called to serve God and the Church in this holy office, and who desire to be ordained thereto. These we name before you, that, together with us, you may make prayer for them in your hearts that they may be given grace to perform the office whereunto they are called, giving God praise. These we name before you: (Here the names shall be read out)
If there be any who know just cause or impediment why we should not proceed to Ordination, let them now declare it.

2.   Prayer of Invocation
3.   Scripture Lesson: Ephesians iv. 1-16; or II Corinthians iv; or John xiii. 1-17
4.   The Charge – to the congregation and to the candidates
5.   The Questions and Answers
6.   The Prayer for Grace followed by The Silence (in which the congregation pray silently for those to be ordained)
7.   Ordination Hymn (during the first verse those to be ordained kneel in their appointed places)
8.   Ordination Prayer
9.   The Laying on of Hands
10. The Giving of the Symbol
11. The Benediction

The Ordaining Authority

The Report which was approved by the 1942 Conference recommended that all candidates for Ordination as Evangelists (Missionaries) be ordained at a solemn service which would be a special session of the Annual Conference. It would be separate from any business session of the Conference, and be conducted as an act of worship by the Chairman of Conference. Conference was thus the ordaining authority and would act on behalf of the whole Church – 'the multitude of the faithful' – and of Christ as the Church's Head and Lord.

---

[18]   *Churches of Christ Year Book, 1942*

Questions to the Ordinands

The suggested order of service contained five questions to be put to the ordinands and their answers:

i)   Do you think in your heart that you be truly called according to the will of our Lord Jesus Christ and of His Church to fulfil the office of Evangelist? A. I do.
ii)   Do you believe that Holy Scripture contains sufficiently all doctrine required of necessity for eternal salvation through faith in Jesus Christ? A. I do believe this.
iii) Will you then be faithful to minister the Doctrine, Ordinances, and Discipline of Christ as the Lord hath commanded? A. I will so do by the help of the Lord.
iv)   Will you be diligent in prayer, in the reading of Holy Scripture, and in such studies as help to the knowledge of the same? Will you be diligent to fashion both yourself and your family according to the Doctrine of Christ, and to make both yourself and them as much as in you lies, wholesome examples and patterns of the flock of Christ? A. I will, the Lord being my helper.
v)   Will you maintain and set forward quietness, peace, and love among all Christian people and especially amongst those who shall be committed to your charge and your service? A. I will, by the grace of God.

An omission from these Questions is any reference to the specific nature of the work of an Evangelist in Church of Christ. The context of the service as a special session of the Annual Conference may have rendered this unnecessary for those who would be present at the ordination. Even so, there might have been value in reminding the congregation – in their role as representatives of the whole Church – of the particular responsibilities of Evangelists within the total ministry of Churches of Christ.

Members of Conference, while being encouraged to pray for those to be ordained, were not invited to promise their encouragement and support for the Evangelists in their ministry. There was a significant difference between ordination to the ministry of the Evangelist in the wider fellowship of Churches of Christ and induction to the particular pastorate, to which the ordinand had been called, in Congregational and Presbyterian patterns of ministry.

The Mode of Ordination

Ordination was by prayer followed by the Laying on of Hands. The Ordination Prayer began with thanksgiving for the gift of redemption through Jesus Christ; for the gifts of ministry (Apostles, Prophets, Evangelists, Teachers and Pastors) through whose labours and ministry the risen and ascended Lord called the Church into being 'to set forth the eternal praise of Thy holy name'; and for those now called to the office and ministry of Evangelist. The Prayer continued with a petition for grace, that God will 'seal with Thy life-giving Spirit that which we do at this time', and that through their ministrations 'many may be won for Thy Kingdom and the saints built up in their most Holy Faith'.

After the Ordination Prayer, while the congregation either stood or knelt, the Chairman of Conference laid hands upon each ordinand in turn, saying:

'N…as you have been duly chosen to serve in the Ministry of the Church of Christ, we confirm that choice, and solemnly ordain you to the Office of Evangelist in the Church of our Lord Jesus Christ which He purchased with His own blood'.

Other ministrants shared in The Laying on of Hands. The Report of the Commission on Ordination recommended that those taking part in the laying on of hands should usually be the Chairman of Conference, the Principal of Overdale College, and one Presbyter or other appointed representative from the candidate's home church.

The Giving of the Symbol was the presentation of a Bible to each newly-ordained Evangelist accompanied by the admonition: 'Be thou faithful in preaching the Word of God and in ministering the Holy Ordinances.' The ministry of the Evangelist was both a ministry of Word and Sacrament, although in Churches of Christ that ministry would be shared by others who had been ordained, also with the laying on of hands, to be Elders and Deacons.

This service continued in use with only minor changes of linguistic style, until the unification of Churches of Christ with the United Reformed Church. Its form was simple, yet dignified and ordered as befitted its importance. Its clear intention was that Churches of Christ should be seen to conform to the witness of the New Testament and the ancient traditions of the Church. Alexander Campbell had declared of the Church that 'All its officers, whether for its services at home or abroad, when fully proved, are to be formally and solemnly set apart by the imposition of the hands of the presbytery or eldership of the Church.'[19] The service for the ordination of Evangelists was intended to fulfil that requirement.

IV. Ordination Services in the United Reformed Church

The formation of the United Reformed Church in 1972 created the need for new liturgies which would both honour the Church's inherited traditions and provide appropriate forms of worship for the new Church. This task was entrusted by the General Assembly to its Doctrine and Worship Committee. Orders of service for various occasions were circulated in draft form for use and comment. These were published in 1980 as *A Book of Services*.[20] The Preface stated that the orders of services were not intended to diminish the freedom in worship which had been cherished by Congregationalists and Presbyterians in their separate traditions. It was however expected that some of the services, for example ordination and induction, would be normative for such occasions since they contained the accepted faith and practice of the new Church.

A Book of Services had a relatively short life. This was due in part to the unification in 1981 of the United Reformed Church with the Re-formed Association of Churches of Christ in Great Britain and Ireland. This union required the enlarged Church to incorporate into its worship and liturgies the distinctive traditions of Churches of Christ. The years following the formation of the United Reformed Church had also brought new insights into the language of worship, and in particular the

---

[19]   Alexander Campbell, *The Christian System*, p. 82.
[20]   *A Book of Services* (Edinburgh: St Andrew Press, 1980)

importance of using inclusive language. These considerations, and the ongoing cross-fertilisation between the three participating traditions, led the General Assembly in 1985 to request a revision of the service book. A new book was prepared and published in 1989 as *Service Book*.[21]

In both service books the orders of service for the Ordination and Induction of Ministers followed an almost identical pattern.

Constitution of the District Council

The Approach to God

Call to Worship
Prayers of Adoration and Confession

The Ministry of the Word

Scripture Readings
Sermon

The Act of Ordination

Presentation of the Ordinand
Statement concerning the call
Ordinand's personal statement (optional)
Statement of the Nature and Faith of the United Reformed Church
Affirmations by the Ordinand
Affirmations by the 'people of the place'
Ordination Prayer/Laying on of Hands
Declaration of Ordination
Presentation of a Bible
The Right Hand of Fellowship

Prayers of Intercession

Dismissal (the President)

The later book encouraged more congregational participation in the opening prayers, It also included an affirmation to be made by members of the District Council.

---

[21] *Service Book* (Oxford: 1989)

The Ordaining Authority

The Basis of Union of the United Reformed Church stated that it was one of the functions of The District Council '…with the Moderator of Synod, or his deputy presiding, to conduct, in fellowship with the local church, any ordinations and/or inductions within the district.' The rubrics for the ordination service conclude that since 'presiding' and 'conducting' are to be understood as equivalent, the Moderator of Synod should act on these occasions as the chief representative of the District Council, of which the Moderator was a member. If for any reason the Moderator of Synod was unable to preside, presidency should be undertaken by the District Chairman.[22]

The District Council was responsible for making the arrangements for the service. Although ordination services were held in the place of worship of the people who had called the ordinand to the pastorate, each such service was to be a duly constituted and minuted meeting of the District Council. Members of the District Council, ministerial and lay, should gather beforehand, together with those taking part[23] in the service, for the District Council to be formally constituted. An alternative procedure, which became widely adopted, was for the District Chairman to constitute the District Council in the presence of the congregation and then invite the Moderator to preside.

The Statement of the Nature, Faith and Order of the United Reformed Church

The wording of this Statement was prescribed as Schedule D in the Basis of Union[24] which required that it should be read aloud at ordination and induction services. The formal language of the Statement, while strange to former Congregationalists, included elements of the Presbyterian declaration of the Church's attitude towards her standards.

Affirmations by the Ordinand

The affirmations to be made by ministers at ordinations and inductions immediately followed the Statement and were in response to it. The form of the affirmations was prescribed in Schedule C in the Basis of Union.[25]

Affirmations by the People

A *Book of Services (1980)* provided two questions to be put to the 'people of the place'.

1. Do you recognise the calling of AB to be a Christian minister and receive *him* as from God to serve among you here? People: We do.

---

[22]   The office of 'District Chairman' was later changed to 'District President' in order to provide a more inclusive designation.

[23]   For the form of Schedule D in 1981, see D M Thompson, *Stating the Gospel*, (Edinburgh: 1990) pp. 262-264. This included an authorised alternative form of the Statement for liturgical use.

[24]   United Reformed Church Basis of Union, paragraph 7(26)

[25]   ibid. For the form of Schedule C in 1981, see D M Thompson, op. cit. p. 260-61.

2.   Do you promise to pray for AB and for each other, to share with *him* in seeking and doing the will of God, and to give *him* due honour, consideration and encouragement, building one another up in faith, hope and love? People: We do.

Service Book (1989) strengthened these by adding a new question I in which the congregation were invited to re-affirm their faith: Do you confess again your faith in one God, Father, Son and Holy Spirit?

Question 2 modified the former Question I by asking: 'Do you receive AB..., as from God, to serve among you here and with you in the world?' This did greater justice to the statement in the Basis of Union paragraph 7(13) that 'the United Reformed Church believes that, in the ministry of the Word, through preaching and the study of the Scriptures, God makes known in each age his saving love, his will for his people and his purpose for the world'.[26] The acceptance by the congregation of their minister to serve with them in the world introduced a new emphasis on mission.

In the 1989 *Service Book*, members of the District Council were invited to welcome and receive the newly-ordained or inducted minister into their membership in response to this question:

'Do you welcome AB ... into membership of the District Council, promising to sustain *him/her* in *his/her* service?' This question implicitly recognised that the first function of the District Council was to exercise oversight of the ministry.

The Mode of Ordination

The Basis of Union stated that 'The United Reformed Church recognises that Christ gives himself to his Church through Word and Sacraments and through the total caring oversight by which his people grow in faith and love, the exercise of which oversight is the special concern of elders and ministers.' Authority to exercise ministry within the Church is conferred by the Church, who sets apart those who have been appointed with prayer that they shall be given all needful gifts...'which solemn setting apart shall in the case of ministers and elders be termed ordination'.[27]

The Basis of Union did not prescribe the laying on of hands as a requirement of ordination, though this forms part of the act of ordination in both service books, and continued the normative practice of the three traditions. The 1989 version of the service invokes the Holy Spirit in the Ordination Prayer concurrently with the laying on of hands:

> FILL YOUR SERVANT AB...WITH YOUR HOLY SPIRIT, AS IN YOUR NAME AND IN OBEDIENCE TO YOUR WILL WE ORDAIN *HIM/HER* TO BE A MINISTER IN YOUR CHURCH

---

[26]   ibid. p. 251.
[27]   ibid. p. 254.

The intention of the act is to ordain to the ministry of the whole Church. This is clear from the Declaration of Ordination which states that the minister has been ordained 'to the ministry of the Word and Sacraments in the Church of Jesus Christ'. The United Reformed Church, as part of the one, holy, catholic and apostolic Church acts in ordination on behalf of the whole Church. In the act of induction to a particular pastorate which is consequent upon, though concurrent with, the act of ordination, the United Reformed Church acts within the more limited area of its jurisdiction and responsibility.

In its liturgy for ordination services to the ministry of Word and Sacrament the United Reformed Church sought to include elements from its inherited traditions. At first glance the Presbyterian influence might seem the strongest. The ordaining authority is the District Council which in the new Church exercises many of the functions of the former Presbyteries. Yet the Congregational tradition, as we have seen, had historically recognised the importance of the presence at ordination of representatives of neighbouring churches. 'Presence' was not merely attendance out of courtesy or curiosity, but a sign of approval and acceptance. The requirement that the ordinand should have received a call to a local pastorate as a *sine qua non* of ordination honoured Congregational as well as Presbyterian practice. The rather cautious rubric, in the service books of 1980 and 1989, that the minister-elect might make a personal statement of faith and calling, which had been normative in the Congregational tradition, quickly became a constitutive element in ordination services. Presidency by the Moderator of Synod, at the invitation of the District Council within which the ordination was taking place, focussed the identity of the United Reformed Church and, by extension, reflected its vision of the catholicity, unity, and apostolic nature of the whole Church.

Both service books reflected the consensus that the appropriate mode of ordination in the United Reformed Church was by prayer and the laying on of hands, though there might be varied interpretations of the rite of imposition of hands. For some it might be little more than a symbolic gesture. Others would see it as a real conferring of authority to minister in Christ's name. Most would agree that those who were appointed to lay hands possessed no personal power or authority, but acted in the name of the District Council as the ordaining authority. The act of touching was charged with biblical symbolism and precedent.[28] The rite was not conceived as a magical transference of power, but was it, at least in some sense, sacramental?[29] The 'authority' conferred by the laying on of hands was not the power to rule, but the royal authority of the Church's Lord who had said to his disciples 'I am among you like a servant'.[30]

It may be questioned whether the ordination liturgies in the service books of 1980 and 1989 sufficiently recognised the priesthood of the whole Church – or, as often described, the ministry of the whole people of God. They tended to reinforce the image of the church as a community in which the ordained minister to the non-ordained. Nearly a century earlier P T Forsyth had

---

[28]   e.g. Jacob laying hands in blessing on the sons of Joseph, Genesis 48:8-22; the seraphim touching the lips of Isaiah in his vision, Isaiah 6:7; the Risen Jesus blessing his disciples 'with uplifted hands' and commissioning them to be his witnesses, Luke 24:51; the commissioning of Paul and Barnabas, Acts 13:1-3, and the Seven, Acts 6:1-7; references to ordination by the laying on of hands in I Tim. 4:14 and II Tim. 1:6.

[29]   L H Countryman, *The Language of Ordination* (Philadelphia: Trinity Press International, 1992) p. 69 and passim.

[30]   Luke 22.27 (REB).

urged that '…the minister's first duty is to his Church. He must make it a Church that acts on the world – through him indeed, but also otherwise. He is to act at its head, and not in its stead.'[31] The New Testament upholds the importance of 'ministry' but understands the purpose of ministry as enabling members of the whole community to exercise their corporate and personal ministries. The United Reformed Church might need to consider whether there was an imbalance which future ordination liturgies should redress.

The United Reformed Church claimed in its ordination liturgies to be acting with the authority of Christ and also that it was ordaining to the ministry of the whole Church. In reality the authority conferred by its ordinations was proportionate to their acceptance within the wider Church.[32] Significant parts of the Church still withheld the recognition which would allow United Reformed Church ministers to preside at their celebrations of the Eucharist on equal terms. Although the language of disapproval had been modified and terms such as 'invalid' and 'illegitimate' were no longer common usage, the ministry of those who had not been episcopally ordained within the apostolic succession continued to be regarded as 'defective' or 'irregular'. The Church had been unable, despite strenuous efforts, to fulfil the vision of the Lambeth Appeal of 1920. An unfinished task of making visible that "universal fellowship 'in full and free activity'" would be handed to the Church of the 21st century.

---

[31]   P T Forsyth, *Positive Preaching and the Modern Mind* (London: 1907, Independent Press, Fourth Impression, 1953) p. 52.
[32]   For a discussion of these issues, see A T and R P C Hanson, *The Identity of the Church*, (London: SCM Press, 1987) pp. 154-56.

Chapter Eight

New Hopes for Unity

NEW HOPES FOR UNITY?

The prayer of Jesus – 'May they all be one'[1] – caught the imagination of 20th century Christians. It inspired and sustained the observance of the Octave of Christian Unity which annually united in prayer Christians of many diverse traditions whose hope of the visible unity of the Church was, in human terms, an apparently impossible dream. Gradually the realisation dawned that prayer and action could not be separated. Jesus had not only prayed that his disciples should be one, but by his death had achieved reconciliation. The Church's prayer for unity meant following Christ's way of suffering and death. The call to Christian unity was not an invitation to embark upon a process of rationalising resources – much though that might be needed in an age of declining membership and influence. It was to reveal to the world a convincing demonstration of the Church as the Body of Christ and a sign of reconciliation and peace for the whole inhabited world.

The hope of unity persisted through long decades with many setbacks. Promising initiatives failed to make progress. At the Faith and Order Conference held at Nottingham in 1964, it was proposed that the churches should covenant for unity by Easter Day 1980. The proposal was effusively received but enthusiasm waned in face of the difficulties of the enterprise and the irrationality of its deadline. Attempts by the Church of England and the Methodist Church to unite in 1972 ended in acrimonious failure. The lesser union of Congregationalists and Presbyterians in the same year was a modest sign of a possible turning of the tide. Three years later a new initiative took place in Wales where the Anglican Church in Wales, the Presbyterian Church in Wales, the Methodist Church and the United Reformed Church entered into a solemn covenant for union with the goal of forming one visibly united Church out of the four Covenanting Churches. In 1973 the General Assembly of the United Reformed Church, stimulated by its recent union and the commitment of its Basis of Union to seek the visible unity of the Church, issued an invitation to all Christian Churches in England to engage in ecumenical dialogue – what came to be described as 'Talks About Talks' – to discover whether a path to wider Christian unity might be found. Church representatives at initial discussions between a wide spectrum of churches[2] were daunted by the immensity and difficulty of the task and could see no clear way forward. Early hesitations were overcome when an unofficial conference at Oxford in January 1974 encouraged the taking of a new initiative by suggesting the creation of a Commission with full-time staff to provide a framework for the talks.

The United Reformed Church quickly adopted the suggestion and at its 1974 General Assembly, under the heading 'Talks About Talks', affirmed its belief that the visible unity of all Christian people was the will of God, and that the churches in England should commit themselves to that

---

[1]   John 17:21.

[2]   These included Anglicans, Methodists, Baptists, United Reformed Church, Roman Catholic, Orthodox, Lutherans, the Congregational Federation, Independent Methodists and the Countess of Huntingdon's Connexion.

end. It formally urged the churches to appoint a Commission, as suggested by the Oxford Conference, to forward commitment to unity and to assess the implications of existing ecumenical co-operation at local, regional, national and international levels. The expectation was that out of these discussions there would emerge a plan for union between those churches which were able to make this commitment, while also exploring other forms of visible unity. The United Reformed Church's initiative was followed by those churches which shared the vision and the Churches Unity Commission was established.[3] Dr John Huxtable, who had been one of the architects of the United Reformed Church and its first moderator of Assembly, was appointed as the Commission's Executive Officer. At an early stage the Roman Catholic representatives, while sympathetic to the aims of the Commission, indicated that they could not envisage a local union in one country preceding union at world level. The Baptists and one or two of the smaller denominations also stated that their position favoured unity but not organic union.

The Ten Propositions[4]

The Churches Unity Commission immediately recognised that no existing 'model' of a united Church[5] could be instantly adopted for the English Churches. A different way had to be found. Perhaps emulating the precedent of the Statement of Convictions which had been prepared by the Congregational Union of England and Wales and the Presbyterian Church of England to facilitate their discussions, the first task of the Commission was to enumerate those convictions which might provide a way forward to visible union. These became known as *The Ten Propositions:*

1. We reaffirm our belief that the visible unity in life and mission of all Christ's people is the will of God.
2. We therefore declare our willingness to join in a covenant actively to seek that visible unity.
3. We believe that this search requires action both locally and nationally.
4. We agree to recognise, as from an accepted date, the communicant members in good standing of the other Covenanting Churches as true members of the Body of Christ and welcome them to Holy Communion without condition.
5. We agree that, as from an accepted date, initiation in the Covenanting Churches shall be by mutually acceptable rites.
6. We agree to recognise, as from an accepted date, the ordained ministries of the other Covenanting Churches, as true ministries of word and sacrament in the Holy Catholic Church, and we agree that all subsequent ordinations to the ministries of the Covenanting Churches shall be according to a Common Ordinal which will properly incorporate the episcopal, presbyteral and lay roles in ordination.

---

[3]   The Commission was made up of representatives appointed by the following Churches: the Baptist Union, Churches of Christ, the Church of England, the Congregational Federation, the Methodist Church, the Moravian Church, the Roman Catholic Church, and the United Reformed Church. Consultant observers were appointed from the British Council of Churches, the Free Church Federal Council, and the Board for Mission and Unity of the General Synod of the Church of England.

[4]   Published in Churches Unity Commission: *The Ten Propositions* (Methodist Conference Office 1976), also in John Huxtable, *A New Hope for Christian Unity*, (London: Collins, 1977), and *Towards Visible Unity, Proposals for a Covenant*, (Churches Council for Covenanting, 1980).

[5]   e.g. the Church of South India.

7. We agree within the fellowship of the Covenanting Churches to respect the rights of conscience, and to continue to accord to all our members, such freedom of thought and action as is consistent with the visible unity of the Church.
8. We agree to continue to give every possible encouragement to local ecumenical projects and to develop the methods of decision making in common.
9. We agree to explore such further steps as will be necessary to make more clearly visible the unity of all Christ's people.
10. We agree to remain in close fellowship and consultation with all the Churches represented on the Churches' Unity Commission.

The basic proposal was that the participating churches which accepted the goal of 'the visible unity in life and mission of all Christ's people in the will of God' should declare their willingness to join in a Covenant to seek that unity, both locally and nationally. Communicant members in good standing of the other Covenanting Churches should be mutually accepted as true members of the Body of Christ and would be welcomed unconditionally to the Lord's Table in all the Covenanting Churches.

The crucial proposition relating to issues of ministry and ordination was Proposition 6 which offered mutual recognition to the existing ordained ministries of the other Covenanting Churches as true ministries of Word and Sacrament, and provided for future recognition of new ministries by means of a Common Ordinal which would incorporate the episcopal, presbyteral and lay roles in ordination. If this Proposition were accepted, the historic problem which had haunted the British Churches since 1920 and the Lambeth Quadrilateral would be solved. The question was whether it could be accepted so as to cover those whose ordinations had been conducted other than episcopally. A closely related, and deeply controversial issue, was whether those women ministers in good standing of some of the Covenanting Churches would be recognised by those which refused to ordain women. Looming on the horizon was the even more difficult question of the eligibility of such women ministers to become bishops.

The Ten Propositions were published in January 1976 with the request that the Churches should give their provisional responses during that year and their definitive responses in 1977. In the event this proved too restricted a time-table and the life of the Commission was extended for a further year. 1978 would have to be the year for decision.

The United Reformed Church responded promptly in 1977 with a resolution from General Assembly in which 'the United Reformed Church welcomes wholeheartedly the promise of further steps held out in the report of the Commission'. Proposition 6 was accepted. It was understood that 'episcopal' referred, as the Churches Unity Commission had stated, 'not to a general exercise of oversight *(episcope)* but to the role of ministers specially set apart to a wide, crucial, and peculiarly responsible form of ministry distinguishable from the presbyteral ministry and from corporate and conciliar forms of oversight, though not exercised in separation from these'.

Thus the United Reformed Church declared its readiness to accept bishops within the structures of a united Church and as a key participant in ordinations.

> We recognise that any advance towards visible church unity in England that is to include the Church of England, the Roman Catholic Church and the Orthodox Churches must honour the convictions of those Churches concerning the ministry of bishops and must find a basis for harmony between those convictions and the doctrine of the Church as held among us.[6]

The doctrine referred to in that paragraph included of course the conviction that the episcopal, presbyteral and lay roles *were* already represented in the United Reformed Church practice of ordination. Some might argue that they were better represented in United Reformed Church than in Church of England practice. The episcopal role in particular was fulfilled in a conciliar manner by the District Council as the ordaining authority and by the presidency of the moderator of Synod by invitation of the District Council. Nevertheless the Assembly agreed to accept a new form of episcopacy. Would local churches, District Councils and Synods agree?

The fundamental question for the Commission was how bishops would be created for the non-episcopal covenanting churches. Two ways forward were envisaged. The first – 'Method A' – proposed that on entering the Covenant the non-episcopal participating churches should agree to introduce into their polity a distinct ministry of bishops, in addition to their ministries of Word and Sacrament. The initial ordination of United Reformed Church bishops - chosen by the United Reformed Church - would include 'appropriate representatives of the Covenanting Churches' who would 'associate themselves by word and action with such entry of new servants into the episcopal succession'.

According to this 'Method A' the United Reformed Church and other non-episcopal churches would be welcoming the episcopal ministry as a visible expression of the continuity, unity and universality of the Church of God through space and time. It invited the United Reformed Church to recognise an inheritance which it had not traditionally cherished. It would establish a central role for bishops in ordinations to the presbyteral ministry of word and sacrament. But it was also an invitation to look forward and to be open to what the Spirit might be saying to the churches about their future. The Commission urged the non-episcopal churches to consider whether the focusing of some episcopal functions in a distinct office might now be an act of Christian obedience.[7]

In the second – 'Method B' – the Covenanting Churches would retain their separate lives while sharing in a new and committed relationship with each other, which would include the mutual recognition of existing ministries. Every future minister would be visibly commissioned by all the churches to a ministry fully recognised throughout these churches. Ordinations would include episcopal, presbyteral and lay roles. Through common ordinations the ministry of bishops would thus be extended to all the covenanting churches. 'Method B' recognised that the situation after covenanting would be different from that which would follow an act of organic union. The separate Churches would continue to function, each with their own ministries. Episcopal ordinations would not create a situation whereby authority was conferred to minister within the other Covenanting Churches. It would hopefully lead to the development of ecumenical loyalties

---

[6]   United Reformed Church, *Record of Assembly 1977*, pp. 53-58.
[7]   J Huxtable, *A New Hope for Christian Unity*, (London: Collins, 1977) p. 111.

and responsibilities, while enabling participating churches to retain their present patterns of ministry, whether these included bishops or not. It would not however meet the desire of the General Synod of the Church of England meeting in November 1976 that 'all the Covenanting Churches should become episcopally ordered in continuity with the historic episcopate'.[8]

The debate in local churches, District Councils and Synods inevitably focused on the question of episcopacy. Some emphatically rejected Proposition 6 in its entirety. Their view was represented, for example, by the Revd W J Brown who argued that history had produced a World Church which included both episcopal and non-episcopal denominations, and that the *bene esse* of the Church did not need one more than the other. Rather than become an episcopal church, the United Reformed Church's best contribution to the well-being of the whole Church was to be an exemplary non-episcopalian church.[9]

There was widespread concern that the involvement of bishops in ordinations, which would be enshrined in the proposed Common Ordinal, would imply that no ordination would be valid without the imposition of episcopal hands. Norman Goodall[10], one of the United Reformed Church's senior ministers, pleaded that the United Reformed Church should seek deliverance - and be willing to be delivered from – 'the bogeys which attach to the word "bishop"'. He hoped for the emergence of a new style of episcopacy in which bishops would stand in a new relation to the *episcope* of the whole Church. For the United Reformed Church to refuse to share in the reforming of an historic office would be to miss a great opportunity.[11]

From the perspective of a local United Reformed Church pastorate which was soon to form part of a Local Ecumenical Parish, Donald Norwood took a similar view, pointing out that the proposals of the Churches Unity Commission 'provided an opportunity for Reformed churchmen with their long experience of church meetings, church councils and mutual consultation, "authority respected but not unquestioned", to influence a new style of episcopacy which might emerge from the proposals'.[12] To preserve the Reformed principle of ministerial parity, bishops under the new dispensation should be seen at all times as 'first among equals' in their relationships with ministers and church members.

Not all were as sanguine. Daniel Jenkins, challenging the view that United Reformed Church Moderators were already bishops in all but name, feared that the reunion of episcopal and non-episcopal traditions which was the final goal of the proposals, might not be possible without sacrifice of principle:

---

8   ibid. p. 114.
9   *REFORM*, January 1978. W J Brown was United Reformed Church minister at Lewisham, Catford and Bellingham.
10   Norman Goodall, 1896-1985, had been Secretary of the International Missionary Council and an Associate General Secretary of the World Council of Churches.
11   *REFORM*, March 1978.
12   *REFORM*, December 1977. D W Norwood was United Reformed Church minister at Summertown, Oxford.

Doctrines of episcopacy vary but there can be little doubt that the 'historic episcopate' as understood by most Anglicans threatens the Reformed principle of the parity of all ministers and implies an attitude to tradition which we have usually rejected. Moderators have never been given the juridical or disciplinary powers nor the teaching authority nor the kind of right to ordain and confirm which bishops have.[13]

As the time drew near for decision, bishop Lesslie Newbigin, moderator of General Assembly, drew upon his previous experience as an architect and bishop of the Church of South India to encourage acceptance of the proposals. *Contra* Jenkins he believed that the essential work of United Reformed Church provincial moderators *was* episcopal in that they provided at the level of district or region the same quality of caring and personal leadership which local ministers and elders exercised at the congregational level. He agreed that the word 'bishop' had become contaminated for members of the United Reformed Church by its association with the mediaeval image of the 'Lord bishop', an image which many Anglicans also felt to be in need of expulsion. His experience of the Church of South India had convinced him that the true idea could be disentangled from its corruption. The acceptance by the United Reformed Church of the 'historic episcopate' would not require agreement with the so-called 'pipeline' theory of the episcopate by which divine grace seemed to be transmitted in an almost physical way by episcopal ordination. To a Protestant understanding of the Church this was both false and unbiblical. Yet the 'historic succession' nevertheless bore significant meaning in pointing to God's intention for the Church:

> If it is His will that the Church everywhere shall be one fellowship, then this unity will be expressed through the centuries by the fact that ordinations of ministers will always be done in such a way as to carry the assent of the whole universal fellowship.[14]

Unity, and therefore historic continuity, was part of God's will for the Church. A re-united Church should be one which honours and cherishes that historic continuity. *The Ten Propositions* provided a new opportunity for the Churches to move forward to unity on the basis of mutual acceptance.

The United Reformed Church made its definitive response at its General Assembly in 1978. The digest of responses from local churches, District Councils and Synods revealed a high percentage of 'Yes' returns to either Methods A or B, Synods voting 83% in favour and District Councils 71%. Local churches were more divided with 57% in favour and 39% against. When asked to express a preference for either 'Method A' or 'Method B', 'Method A' received minority support from Synods (33%), Districts (36%), Churches (32%), and Elders Meetings (16%). 'Method B' received a significantly greater measure of support from Synods (83%), Districts (67%), and Elders (48%), while 52% of local churches were against the proposal.[15]

The World Church and Mission Department noted that while the responses from churches strongly supported the United Reformed Church's resolve to seek the unity of all God's people, the focus on episcopacy in Proposition 6 had presented the churches with great difficulties, which appeared to owe as much to the political and social history (of England) as to any theological understanding of

---

13   *REFORM*, July/August 1978.
14   Bishop Lesslie Newbigin, *Why Bother About Bishops?*, *REFORM*, December 1978.
15   Responses were received from 12 Synods, 42 Districts, 403 churches and 25 Elders Meetings.

the Church. A clearer statement was needed from those who urged the value of a *personal* rather than a corporate *episcope* in the on-going life and mission of the Church as to why such ministry was required at this stage of the progress towards unity. Yet *The Ten Propositions* offered a unique opportunity to grasp the rich prizes of mutual recognition of members, mutual recognition of ministry and burgeoning projects in local co-operation and sharing.

The Assembly therefore agreed to affirm Proposition 6 in its basic intention of enabling the mutual recognition of ministries, the use of a Common Ordinal, and the bringing together of bishops, presbyters and laity in acts of ordination. This approval was given on the basis of two understandings. The first was that recognition should be equally accorded to men and women ministers. The second was that when the Covenanting Churches in future received into their ministries ministers of other churches who were eligible for accreditation under their existing disciplines, such ministers should be recognised under the Covenant without any special action by the other Covenanting churches.

The Assembly also judged that it would be premature at that stage to accept either 'Method A' or 'Method B' in Proposition 6 as the means of receiving the ministry of bishops. This was referred to the Churches' Unity Commission for continued exploration. The Commission was asked to provide a more specific vision of what a personal episcopate, constitutionally related to conciliar structures, might contribute to the life of the Church, how parallel episcopates might regularly act together in ordinations, and how the roles of presbyters and laity in ordinations might be as fully shared among the Covenanting Churches as the role of bishops. Whichever method was adopted, it was essential that changes in structure and order should be seen in relation to the Churches' priorities for mission.[16]

Proposals for a Covenant

By 1978 the Churches' Unity Commission had fulfilled its remit. *The Ten Propositions* had mapped out a possible route towards a limited but significant goal. Would the Churches follow the Commission's lead? It was clear that nothing could be taken for granted. The Roman Catholic Church had already signalled that it would not be able to covenant at this time, though it welcomed the intention of Proposition 10 'to remain in close fellowship with all the Churches represented in the Churches' Unity Commission'. Other bodies, including the Baptist Union and the Congregational Federation, had earlier indicated their commitment to visible unity rather than organic union. The final decision of the Church of England would be crucial, since the reality of the Covenant would depend on its committed participation. Looking ahead to an uncertain future, while the Churches were debating their responses to the Propositions, the Commission's Executive Officer said: 'We must realise that what we are asked to take is but an initial step on what may well be a long journey; but in one sense the first step is the most important, since without it there can be no more.'[17] Five Churches – Churches of Christ, the Church of England, the Methodist Church, the Moravian Church and the United Reformed Church indicated their readiness to go forward.

---

16   United Reformed Church, *Reports to Assembly 1978*, pp. 50-53.
17   J Huxtable, op. cit. p. 86.

The task of providing a means by which the Churches should enter into the covenant envisaged in Proposition 2 was now entrusted to a new body - the Churches Council for Covenanting – which was appointed in 1978 under the chairmanship of bishop Kenneth Woollcombe.[18] Their task was to produce the text of a Covenant by which the participating Churches would recognise and accept one another's members and ministries. *The Ten Propositions* had articulated the churches' intentions. It was now necessary to draft a Covenant capable of achieving those intentions. It would need to be what bishop Woollcombe described as 'performative and creative'. The Covenant would be 'a further step in fellowship towards that full and visible unity which Christ wills for his Church'.[19] Nothing less would suffice than the unambiguous incorporation of the ministries of all the churches (lay and ordained) in a new relationship within the historic ministry of the Church both Catholic and Reformed.

The new Council lost no time in building on the foundations which had been laid by its predecessor and in 1980, barely two years after its appointment, published its proposals in *Towards Visible Unity, Proposals for a Covenant*. The year possessed a double significance. It was exactly sixty years since the Lambeth Conference of 1920 had issued its *Appeal to All Christian People*. It was also the target year which the 1964 Faith and Order Conference had set for visible union.

The Making of the Covenant

At the heart of the Proposals lay a national Act of Worship, envisaged as being held in a large hall or an open-air stadium, which would bring the Covenant into effect and establish the covenanting Churches in a new relationship to one another. The Preamble to the service stated:

> By our Covenant together each of our Churches will be bound to the others by solemn promise, sealed by the sharing of the body and blood of our Lord Jesus Christ. We shall recognise one another as Christian Churches in membership and ministry and commit ourselves to grow together in counsel and in action. We shall seek a deepening unity with one another in faith and praise, in witness and service.[20]

The Promises made within the Act of Worship, and preceding an Act of Reconciliation, committed the Covenanting churches to welcome each other's communicant members 'without question' at their eucharists; to recognise and accept each other's ministries 'as true ministries of word and sacrament in the holy catholic Church'; to share a Common Ordinal 'in which bishops, presbyters and laity fulfil their proper service', and to conduct all future ordinations in common. The Covenanting churches bound themselves to 'develop methods of decision making in common, to act together for witness and service, to aid one another in Christian growth, and to honour the authority of shared decisions'. Provision was made for respecting the rights of conscience and to allow all members 'such freedom of thought and action as we jointly agree to be consistent with the visible unity of the Church'.

---

18   Bishop Woollcombe was a former bishop of Oxford, later an Assistant Bishop in London. United Reformed Church representatives on the Council were The Revds G J Cook, M H Cressey, A L Macarthur (General Secretary of the United Reformed Church), Bishop L. Newbigin, Mrs Sylvia Parkinson, and The Revd B Thorogood (General Secretary Council for World Mission and General Secretary-designate of the United Reformed Church).

19   *Towards Visible Unity: Proposals for a Covenant, 1980*, p. 5.

20   ibid. p. 11.

In the Act of Reconciliation, which would create the Covenant, representative groups of lay people and ministers from each of the Covenanting Churches were invited to join in a prayer of invocation with the words:

> Send down on us your Holy Spirit as we give one another the sign of reconciliation; unite us in love in the confession of our faith, through Christ, who is our peace.

This invocation would be followed by representative groups sharing the right hand of fellowship as a sign of mutual reconciliation and acceptance. Then all present were to declare:

> This is the Covenant which we make.
> We declare it before God.
> We are one in Christ.
> We go forward in the Spirit.

The making of the Covenant would then be celebrated with everyone present singing the Doxology.

The ordination of bishops

In the next stage of the service the Covenanting Churches would for the first time act together in the Ordination of Bishops. Representatives of each Church would bring forward their Bishops-elect for ordination. The presiding bishops would be those already in episcopal orders whom the Covenanting Churches had appointed to lead the ordination of bishops. Ordination to episcopal ministry was to be by the laying on of hands by the presiding bishops and by other bishops present, in the context of an ordination prayer of thanksgiving and invocation.

It was proposed that the ordination of new bishops, according to the procedure outlined above, should be followed by a blessing of comparable episcopal ministries. These would be ministers in some of the Covenanting Churches who were already exercising oversight – for example, United Reformed Church provincial moderators. These would seek God's blessing in uniting and fulfilling their ministries within the wider fellowship which the Covenant would inaugurate. The proposal to incorporate non-episcopal ministries of oversight within the episcopal ministries of the Covenanting Churches by means of invoked blessing rather than by ordination to episcopal office was controversial. In due course it would prove a major stumbling-block in the acceptance of the Covenant Proposals.

The ordination of presbyters

The service would then continue with the ordination of candidates from the participating churches to the office of presbyter. The bishops presiding over this part of the service would include a bishop nominated by each Covenanting Church. Ordination would be by prayer with the laying on of hands. Existing presbyteral ministers would then be invited to seek God's blessing in fulfilling their calling within the wider fellowship of the Covenanting Churches. The core of the prayer of invocation, to be offered by the bishops and other ministers exercising comparable oversight, was in the words:

> Fill with your Holy Spirit these your servants whom you have called to minister in your name; bring them together in the service of your Son, the great High Priest, and in the service of his priestly people, as true and faithful shepherds of your flock...

The wording of this part of the service established beyond doubt that reconciliation and mutual recognition had been accomplished but without episcopal re-ordination of existing ministers of previously non-episcopal Covenanting Churches.

The blessing of diaconal and other authorised ministries

The final stage was the blessing of Diaconal and other authorised ministries which had existed prior to the making of the Covenant. Particular reference was made to 'all who serve you as deacons, deaconesses, or elders'. Prayer was to be offered 'for those who minister in communities of prayer, for those called and authorised to preach, to teach the faith, to care for children, or to be stewards of your Church's resources'. A genuine attempt was made to recognise the plurality of ministries within the Church.

The meaning of Ordination

Since the reconciliation of ordained ministries lay at the heart of the making of the Covenant, the Council for Covenanting felt it necessary to set out its understanding of ministry in the Church and the ordained ministry in particular. Ministry, they believed, was entrusted to the whole Church which is called 'to proclaim and prefigure the kingdom of God by announcing the gospel to the world and by being built up as the body of Christ'.[21] In his lifetime Jesus had assigned particular responsibilities to chosen disciples, and in particular to the foundational ministry of the Twelve. The ministry of the apostles comprised a 'special relationship' with the historical and risen Christ and a personal commission from him to the Church and the world. In the course of time the presbyterate emerged to combine a variety of roles and ministries, discerned in the New Testament, that had been distinct in the early years of the Church. Their responsibilities included the pastoral care of Christian communities, the administration of baptism, and presidency at the Eucharist. As the Church grew and spread, the sometimes overlapping ministries of presbyters or bishops became more clearly distinguishable as responsibility for the wider work of the Church came to be exercised by bishops, synods, archbishops and patriarchs. Out of these varied experiences of ministry it became clear that the ordained ministry was an essential element in the ordering of the Church's life for its mission to the world.

> The ordained minister is a representative figure portraying to the Christian community Christ's Lordship and care of his people, and Christ's gathering of all his people into his own eternal worship of the Father.[22]

---

[21]   *Towards Visible Unity.* 5.2.1.1.

[22]   ibid. 5.2.2.4.

Within the ordained ministry the specific responsibility of bishops is 'to foster the unity and continuity of the Church through space and time in the apostolic faith, holiness and mission'.[23] Oversight *(episcope)* is exercised by both bishops and presbyters through pastoral oversight of the Church and proclamation of the Gospel by word and sacrament.

Ordination therefore denotes 'entry into the apostolic and God-given ministry'.[24] The act has a threefold nature. Recognising that the initiative in ordination lies with God, ordination is, first, an invocation to God to bestow the power of the Holy Spirit upon the new minister. 'Invocation of the Spirit implies an absolute dependence upon God for the outcome of the Church's prayer.'[25]

Secondly, it is a sign of the granting of this prayer by the Lord who gives the gift of ministry. The Church ordains in the confidence that God will answer the Church's prayer.

Thirdly, ordination is an acknowledgement by the Church that it has discerned in the candidate the gifts of the Spirit and will commit itself to using and nurturing those God-given gifts. In the same way the ordinand 'offers his gifts to the Church and commits himself to the burden and opportunity of new authority and responsibility'.[26]

Ordination is thus 'an act of the whole community of the Church Universal in its continuity with the apostolic Church and an act of the fellowship of the covenanting Churches.'[27] The various acts of ordination assigned particular responsibilities to bishops and presbyters. Bishops were to lay hands on new bishops; bishops and presbyters were to act together in the ordination of presbyters. However the whole community would act in ordination through its corporate prayer.

A Time for Decision

The Covenant Service was essentially forward looking to the ministries which would follow from the making of the Covenant. Its intention was to enable the Covenanting Churches 'to recognise and accept the ministries of all the Covenanting Churches as true ministries of the Gospel within the one holy, catholic and apostolic Church, and corporately offer these ministries to God that he may renew them, and may give to each whatever spiritual gifts are needed for the wider service which is thenceforth authorised.'[28] These ministries would comprise all those men and women who were currently serving as ordained ministers of Word and Sacrament in the Covenanting Church. It was essential to the making of the Covenant that the ministries of all the churches should be seen to have the authority of all the Covenanting Churches.

Would this be possible? *REFORM*, the monthly Journal of the United Reformed Church, noted in an editorial that the proposals published in *Towards Visible Unity* had been accepted by all the United Reformed Church representatives on the Churches Council for Covenanting, including

---

23   ibid. 5.2.2.5.
24   ibid. 5.2.3.1.
25   ibid. 5.2.2.3 (b).
26   ibid. 5.2.3.3 (c).
27   ibid. 5.2.2.4.
28   ibid. 5.4.1.

'such a sturdy independent as Graham Cook'[29]. Their influence on the proposals was immediately apparent. The United Reformed Church would embrace personal episcopacy, though by neither of the two methods which had been offered in *The Ten Propositions*. They had come to realise that the acceptance of episcopacy was the only way in which the Churches in England could be reconciled and eventually united. Their assent to episcopacy did not mean that the United Reformed Church was being asked to betray the Reformed tradition by accepting the doctrine of the Apostolic Succession. In an interview with the Editor of *REFORM*, the General Secretary stated that 'we cannot accept that bishops are essential to being a Christian Church...but I have reached the point where I believe that bishops are essential for the achievement of Church unity in England.'[30] The Reformed conscience could take heart from John Calvin who had not objected in principle to bishops provided they were seen primarily as chairmen of presbyteral gatherings. There was also growing hope that many Anglicans were searching for new styles of episcopacy and that cross-fertilisation with Reformed churches might speed their emergence.

As the Proposals were discussed within the United Reformed Church in local church meetings, elders' meetings, district councils and synods, a variety of concerns began to surface. There were fears that, as a relatively small and young denomination, which had not yet had sufficient time to establish its distinctive identity, the United Reformed Church might be both broken and swallowed up by closer association with the much larger Church of England. There were major fears that the adoption of the episcopate as a distinct order of ministry would threaten a deeply held conviction of the parity of ministers. The inclusion of the word 'ruler' in the proposed ordination prayer caused particular alarm since it appeared to endorse an Anglican model of episcopacy which many in the United Reformed Church questioned. In its place they wished to affirm an alternative Reformed understanding of episcopacy in which bishops would be closely related to the Councils of the Church. They also sought a fresh evaluation of the tasks assigned to bishops, and to question whether the continuation of the traditional style of episcopal ministry would be appropriate for the new relationships between the Churches within the proposed Covenant.

Other concerns related to what was felt to be an inadequate role for the laity in ordination services. The inclusion of Elders – almost as an afterthought - in the Blessing of Diaconal and Other Authorised Ministries gave insufficient recognition to the ministry of Elders in Reformed church order. There was disagreement in the United Reformed Church on whether important issues of church order and ministry should be dealt with after the Covenant had been made rather than in the process of its creation. Most important of all was the concern that provision for reservation on grounds of conscience[31] by which bishops and other ministers or members should not be required to act in conflict with their personal convictions, should not be used by Anglicans to maintain discrimination against women ministers.[32]

---

29 The Revd Graham Cook, then United Reformed Church minister in the South Leeds team, later to become moderator of Mersey Synod.
30 The Revd Bernard Thorogood, *REFORM*, November 1980.
31 *Towards Visible Unity*, chapter 7, pp. 64-65.
32 For these concerns, see United Reformed Church, *Reports to Assembly 1982*, pp. 49-50.

The depth of concern surfaced in a letter to *REFORM*[33] from fifteen United Reformed Church ministers who declared their view that the acceptance of episcopacy by the United Reformed Church as a precondition for unity would not contribute to the well-being and intellectual integrity of a United Church and could lead to further divisions. The response to their letter led to the formation of The Alternative Response Group which attracted support from a wide spectrum of ministers, members and local churches.[34]

The Group emphasised their commitment to the ecumenical movement and their concern that the momentum of the discussions which had led to the Ten Propositions should not be lost. They supported the idea of a covenant which would bring the churches into new and committed relationships, from which a scheme of union would emerge. What they resisted was the assumption that such a covenant had of necessity to be based on a prior acceptance of the 'historic episcopate' as the basis for the way forward. While it was incontrovertible that episcopacy belonged to the past history of the Church, it was not axiomatic that it should be part of the future.

These concerns were explored in a series of papers - *An Alternative Response* - issued by the Group in June 1981. Dr Geoffrey Nuttall argued that episcopal succession from the Apostles could not be historically demonstrated, and that through the centuries episcopacy had in fact 'encouraged clerical authoritarianism and arrogance'.[35] Dr John Sutcliffe pleaded for a 'conciliar approach' to oversight in the Church which, 'with its emphasis on commitment, participation and communal responsibility may be more appropriate for an educated populace living in a democratic state'. The fulltime ministry needed to help the gathered company to be a true church, and not to inhibit it by arrogating their ministry to itself.[36]

Professor Buick Knox feared that the new episcopates created by the Covenant would be as likely to harden divisions as to end them, and that to have parallel Anglican, Methodist, and United Reformed episcopates, not to mention the episcopate of the Roman Catholic Church, would not be a witness to unity. The effectiveness of conciliar oversight would be 'very shadowy' when a bishop had to be brought in to ensure the episcopal element in ordination services.[37]

Kate Compston questioned why the United Reformed Church had not made the issue of the full recognition and ordination of women a 'non-negotiable' factor in the Covenant in the same way as the Anglicans had insisted on the non-negotiable factor of episcopacy.[38]

In a closely-argued paper – *Covenant or Capitulation?* – Dr Daniel Jenkins strongly supported the idea of a Covenant but argued that it should be simpler and more modest than that suggested in the proposals. The public ceremonies for the making of the Covenant were too elaborate and

---

[33] *REFORM*, March 1981.

[34] The Alternative Response Group was chaired by the Revd T C Micklem, minister at St Columba's, Oxford; the secretary was the Revd D H Hilton, minister at Princes Street, Norwich. Between March 1981 and October 1981 over 200 ministers indicated their support.

[35] The Revd Dr G F Nuttall, Lecturer in Church History, New College, London (1945-77).

[36] The Revd Dr J M Sutcliffe, General Secretary of the Christian Education Movement (1974-85).

[37] The Revd Dr R Buick Knox, Professor of Church History, Westminster College, Cambridge (1968-85).

[38] Revd K M Compston, then United Reformed Church minister, Bury Road, Gosport.

inappropriate to the limited nature of the commitment. What was required, he suggested, was a covenant which would enable the churches to grow together without self-contradiction and the betrayal of vital elements in their heritage. The proposed Covenant with its precipitate emphasis on resolving the dilemma over the 'historic episcopate' threatened to divide the churches as much as to unite them. 'The case for the indispensability of the "historic episcopate" in its English form in England has simply not been made out, and it is mere fantasy to suppose that the Free Churches can produce a version of it which will be radically and challengingly different'. He made the constructive suggestion that, as a modest step forward, the Church of England should appoint one of its own bishops to serve the other covenanting Churches. This bishop's role (as a bishop 'in partibus hereticorum') would be to interpret the non-episcopal churches to the Church of England and, from his inside knowledge of both sides, show how his office uniquely 'maintains' and 'furthers' unity.

> In itself, this would not mean that we had 'taken episcopacy into our system', but it would, at least, give us a clearer idea of what it might mean to do so and it might help us to see what the difficulties in our present form of ministry are, which possession of the "historic episcopate" might be able to make up.

In an article in *REFORM* Caryl Micklem questioned how much flexibility and variety in patterns of episcopal oversight would be allowed by proposals in which all bishops of the Covenanting Churches would be invested with a juridical function. A further concern, which the Churches Council for Covenanting had not addressed, was the extent to which the Church of England would be able to share in the process of joint decision-making while it remained the Established Church and, as such, 'not master (or mistress) in its own house'.[39]

An Anglican commentator, questioning whether the concept of a Covenant was not itself outmoded, discerned in United Reformed Church objections 'an upsurge of independency' and a 'dislike of a scheme designed to accomplish essentially Catholic ends and remove Catholic scruples'.[40]

Anxiety about the Proposals extended also to the Church of England. After the Council's Report had been finalised, three of the Church of England representatives declared that they could not, on grounds of conscience, give their consent to its findings.[41] Their reasons were set out in a *Memorandum of Dissent* which at their request was attached to the final Report.[42] The dissenting members identified themselves unequivocally with the vision and concern which had led to the proposal for a Covenant. They were committed to the cause of Christian unity. They agreed that the proposed process of growing together by incorporating ministers into the historic threefold ministry, together with inter-communion between all members in good standing, and the development of common decision-making, offered the most hopeful and realistic way forward. Yet in their view the Proposals were seriously flawed.

---

[39]   Revd T C Micklem, *Anxious Thoughts on Proposals for a Covenant, REFORM*, July/August 1981.
[40]   Revd J L Houlden, *The Gospel and the Covenant*, (*THEOLOGY*, Vol LXXXV, May 1982, No 705).
[41]   The Rt Revd G S Leonard (Bishop of Truro), Canon P H Boulton, and Mr O W H Clark.
[42]   *Towards Visible Unity*, pp. 82-96.

The first area of difficulty and disagreement concerned episcopacy. Under pressure, especially from the United Reformed Church, the Council for Covenanting had abandoned 'Method A' as the means, preferred by the Church of England, by which the historic episcopate would be accepted by the non-episcopal Covenanting Churches. Its difficulty for the United Reformed Church was that it appeared to involve a total change to personal episcopacy at the point of covenanting, and in consequence to downgrade the churchmanship of the Reformed tradition. The United Reformed Church had indicated a slight preference for 'Method B' but faced strong Anglican objections to using Anglican bishops as ordaining authorities but at the cost of separating them from their pastoral functions. This divergence of view caused great difficulty to the Council.[43]

The Proposals embodied in *Towards Visible Unity* were a delicately-balanced compromise, which after the making of the Covenant would allow certain 'other ministers who exercise comparable oversight' to continue to exercise their ministries in their pre-covenanting form.[44] Thereafter all ministers newly appointed to episcopal office would be ordained as bishops in joint services conducted by the proper authorities of all the Covenanting Churches.[45]

This attempt to overcome objections to both Methods 'A' and 'B' had been powerfully advocated by bishop Lesslie Newbigin, one of the United Reformed Church representatives on the Council.[46] He believed passionately in the conviction of the 1927 Faith and Order Conference that any united church of the future would have to include in its order congregational, synodical and episcopal elements. He accepted the validity of the Anglican objection to 'Method B', but recognised that 'Method A' had no chance of acceptance by the United Reformed Church. In addition his personal view was that ' Method A', by creating parallel episcopates for the participating churches, involved using the historic episcopate to legitimise disunity rather than as a sign and means of unity. It would merely add the Church of England to what he described as the 'barren co-existence' of the still disunited Free Churches. In putting forward his compromise proposal he argued that the act of covenanting by which the churches would recognise one another's ministries and sacraments should look more to the future than the past. The Covenanting Churches should neither affirm nor deny anything about the sufficiency of their ministries up to the point of covenanting. In a paper to the Churches Council for Covenanting he stated his belief that the historic episcopate was part of God's will for the Church. Yet to make its acceptance a precondition for mutual recognition, as in 'Method A' would be a departure from grace. What was required instead was that the Covenanting Churches should 'welcome one another, as Christ has welcomed (us) to the glory of God' (Romans 15.7 RSV) and not 'for disputes and opinions' (Romans 14.1 RSV). The explicit act of acceptance and reconciliation in the making of the Covenant would confer whatever might need to be conferred. It would commit the churches to a process of growing mutual commitment and responsibility. 'It must create a situation', he urged, 'in which growing mutual responsibility is not just a possible option but a built-in element of the whole action.'[47]

43   The United Reformed Church and the Covenant, Essays on the Covenant, British Council of Churches.
44   *Towards Visible Unity*, 5.4.4.3.
45   ibid. 5.4.4.2.
46   Bishop Lesslie Newbigin had been ordained Bishop in the Church of South India and after retirement continued his ministry within the United Reformed Church. See Chapter 4 above.
47   Churches Council for Covenanting/39. See also Bishop K Woollcombe, P Capper, *The Failure of the English Covenant* (London: Churches Council for Covenanting, 1982) p. 10.

Newbigin's compromise envisaged a growing convergence of episcopal ministries rather than the establishment of parallel episcopates. On the one hand it invited the United Reformed Church to accept the historic episcopate and to 'grow' their bishops from within the new situation which the Covenant would create. His suggestion implicitly recognised that the ministries of *episcope* exercised by Anglican bishops and United Reformed provincial moderators were not identical. On the other hand it invited the Church of England to accept for a limited period of years the existing United Reformed Church provincial moderators as already exercising episcopal ministries for which further ordination would not be appropriate. The ministry of provincial moderators would be recognised as a distinct office, but it would not be new and would acquire no new powers and no different way of functioning. Their recognition would not change the structure of the United Reformed Church or alter the way in which authority was exercised and decisions made.[48]

Newbigin's approach became the keystone of the Covenant. He had been greatly influenced by a letter from Fr. John Coventry SJ, the Roman Catholic observer within the Churches Council for Covenanting, to Principal Martin Cressey in which he made the crucial suggestion that in the act of covenanting the participating churches 'were defining their attitudes to each other from that point on into the future'.[49] Newbigin took up this suggestion adding his own distinctive theological interpretation that 'what we ought to ask is that we accept one another as sinners who have not fulfilled God's intention for his Church, on the basis of the fact that God in His mercy has accepted us; and that then (unlike those who say "let us continue in sin that grace may abound") we set about together to order our common life more fully in accord with God's intention. He argued that his proposal 'would produce within a few years a ministry acceptable by all as carrying the assent and authority of all the covenanting Churches.'[50]

The dissenting members recognised that the proposed Blessing of Episcopal Ministries had been offered in order to safeguard the conscience of the United Reformed Church and its view of episcopacy. They accepted that the provision was intended to cover a period of short duration, not exceeding seven years after the making of the Covenant, since any serving United Reformed Church Moderators who were subsequently re-appointed for a further period of service would then be ordained as bishops in joint services using the Common Ordinal. Until then they would share in ordinations in collegiality with ordained bishops. However it was unacceptable for the dissenting members in principle to recognise and accept a personal episcopal ministry of oversight by those who had not been ordained as bishops within the historic episcopate. 'It seems to us also', they said, 'that to allow an arrangement of this kind (even if it is applicable to only a very few senior ministers) is to tolerate a wholly functional view of episcopacy.'[51] To the argument that a temporary anomaly should be accepted in order to overcome what the Archbishop of Canterbury had described as 'the great and disastrous and overwhelming anomaly of disunity within the Body of Christ'[52], their reply was that the essential nature of episcopacy 'cannot be trimmed here and there to make it more palatable to those who may be persuaded to accept it in practice but not to receive it as an integral part of God's purpose for and gift to His Church'.[53] If the Church of England were to depart from this principle in order to enter into new relationships with non-episcopal churches, a further barrier would be erected to closer association with other parts of the Church Catholic.

---

48 This point was made in a letter from Bishop Lesslie Newbigin to the Revd D H Hilton, 30 October 1981.

49 Quoted in CCC/39 – A Suggestion. See also G Wainwright, *Lesslie Newbigin - a Theological Life*, (Oxford: 2000) pp. 121-23.

50 Churches Council for Covenanting/39.

51 *Towards Visible Unity*, Memorandum of Dissent, paragraph 12.

52 Archbishop Coggan, op. cit. Memorandum of Dissent, paragraph 15.

53 ibid.

Even more important was their view that the proposal struck a fatal blow at the heart of the service for the making of the Covenant. The service provided for the recognition, acceptance and welcome of the ministries of the Covenanting Churches 'as true ministries of Word and Sacrament in the Holy Catholic Church' prior to the joint action of the Churches in ordination. The Covenant itself subsumed the variety of existing ministries into a new and deeper understanding of the ministry of Christ's Church. It conferred on them anything that needed to be conferred without specifying whether or not anything was needed. This and the subsequent joint acting of the Covenanting Churches in ordination created 'an effectual act of recognition and acceptance'.[54] The non-ordination of existing United Reformed Church Moderators seemed to be a public affirmation on their part that in their case nothing needed to be conferred or confessed. Nothing more was required than commissioning for wider service within a new relationship of churches. While the thrust of the Service was forward-looking in anticipation of what God would do through the churches in their newly committed relationship, failure to incorporate non-episcopal ministries of oversight into the historic episcopate meant that the churches would be looking back to their past rather than to what they might become.

The second major issue in the Proposals which presented grave difficulty was the requirement that the Covenanting Churches should 'recognise and accept the ministries of all the Covenanting Churches as true ministers of the Gospel within the one, holy, catholic and apostolic Church'.[55] This paragraph as it stood was acceptable since recognition did not equate particular ministries. These ministries were then defined, in the next paragraph, as comprising 'all those men and women in the covenanting Churches currently held by each of these Churches to be ordained to the ministry of the word and sacraments.' There followed a rider that 'the ministries of all those Churches must be so ordered that they are seen to have the authority not of one Church only but of all the Covenanting Churches'. These two paragraphs were unacceptable to the dissenting members without the inclusion, which they had been unable to secure in the Council's negotiations, of a specific application of the rights of conscience provided in Chapter 7 of the Proposals.[56] The crux of the issue was that, at the point of covenanting, *all* ministers newly appointed to episcopal office were to be ordained bishop in *joint* services conducted by the proper authorities of *all* the Covenanting Churches. A Covenanting Church would thus have the right to bring forward a woman minister for episcopal ordination. In such an event, what would be the position of the episcopal representative at such a service? Even if he declined to ordain a woman candidate or refused to participate in a service where a woman was presented for episcopal ordination, he would subsequently be required to work in episcopal collegiality with her. Yet the General Synod of the Church of England, in its definitive response to The Ten Propositions, had agreed that the discussions with other Churches which would follow their acceptance should 'in no way prejudge the admissibility and acceptability of women to the ordained ministry of the Church of England'.[57] The Lambeth Conference of 1978 had further recommended that no decision to consecrate a woman to the episcopate should be taken without widespread consultation and 'overwhelming support' in the member Church or in the diocese concerned.[58]

---

[54]   ibid. paragraph 25.
[55]   *Towards Visible Unity.* 5.4.1.
[56]   op. cit. pp. 64-65.
[57]   General Synod, 10th July 1978.
[58]   Quoted in *Towards Visible Unity*, p. 91.

A similar problem would arise in the more likely event of women being presented for presbyteral ordination. In this instance also the covenant proposals required that all such ordinations should take place at services in which all the Covenanting Churches should be represented and participate in the ordination prayer with the laying on of hands. No undertaking had been given in the Proposals that, pending a decision on the issue of the ordination of women, no action should be taken which would 'injure the developing unity of the covenanting churches and of those Churches which are not yet able to join the Covenant now envisaged'.[59] The dissenting members emphasised that they were not seeking either to pre-judge the matter or to pre-empt the responsibility of the proper Church of England authority. Their objections to the Proposals were that they assumed, without question or qualification, that the Church of England would take a decision in favour of ordination to the episcopal and presbyteral ministry of duly ordained or recognised and accepted women ministers. This was an assumption which they were unable to support.

All was to be in vain. The United Reformed Church (which from 1981 included Churches of Christ) declared its support for the Proposals at its Assembly at Bristol in May 1982. Principal Martin Cressey moved a resolution to accept the Proposals. 434 members voted in favour, 196 were against, and three members abstained. A majority of 66.88% was constitutionally sufficient to qualify for acceptance under the Basis of Union, but was not a ringing endorsement of the Proposals[60]. A minority of 31% opposing the Proposals was an indication of significant dissent.[61]

The Methodist Conference, meeting in Plymouth on 28 June 1982, voted decisively in favour of the proposals by a 79.8% majority, 425 members voting in favour and 107 against.

The General Synod of the Church of England met in July 1982 in the knowledge that two of their partners in the Churches' Council for Covenanting had agreed to join in making the Covenant. A leading article in the Church Times on 2 July urged members of the Synod to accept the proposals:

> If the Synod agrees to covenant with Methodism and the United Reformed Church, surely the overwhelming and correct impression left on the public will be of Churches agreeing to bury the quarrels of the past in order to get on with their mission…'*Towards Visible Unity*' (after improvements) is best understood as one step on the road which would lead towards a Catholicism which was truly scriptural and universal.[62]

Ominously, the same edition reported that 218 priests had a signed a declaration that they could not, in conscience, accept the proposals or 'any new church' which would result from the implementation of the proposed Covenant.

---

[59] Memorandum of Dissent, paragraph 33.
[60] An earlier amendment in the Assembly that the vote on the Proposals should require a 75% majority was lost.
[61] The Assembly had received a report from its World Church and Mission Department indicating that the combined membership of churches reporting (97,856 members) represented only 66.42% of the Church's total membership of 147,337 members. The combined membership of 52,076 members either voting for or generally supporting the proposals was only 35% of the total membership of the United Reformed Church. See *Reports to Assembly 1982.*
[62] *Church Times*, 2 July 1982.

The Failure of the Covenant

On 7 July 1982 the Proposals were rejected by the General Synod. They were approved by sufficient majorities in the House of Bishops and the House of Laity, but in the House of Clergy failed to reach the two-thirds majority which was required for their acceptance. Less than a week after the Anglican rejection of the Proposals, the Council for Covenanting resolved not to meet again. The new hope for Christian Unity which had sprung from the pioneering work of the Churches Unity Commission had been extinguished. It was a devastating blow for a whole generation of church leaders who had given much of their time and energy to the cause of reunion. The Church Times declared that

> Last week's failure was a tragedy for English Christianity and for the Church of England. It will not be lightly redeemed. But some good will come of it if the lesson is learned that the Anglican majority must be sufficiently clear in its aims to be able to convert enough of those who at present find conviction elsewhere.[63]

Dr Kenneth Greet, a member of the Council for Covenanting and General Secretary of the Methodist Church, summed up the feelings of many on both sides of the debate when he remarked that:

> The way marked out by a whole generation of ecumenical leaders has proved to be a *cul de sac*. We must pray that a new generation will succeed where we have failed, for in the end a way must be found. The Holy Spirit does not declare a moratorium just because we have temporarily lost our way.[64]

But in the immediate aftermath of rejection, it was difficult for even those most deeply committed to the ecumenical vision to see any way ahead.

Who killed the Covenant? The immediate answer is that the Proposals were dealt the fatal blow by their rejection in the Church of England. The largest of the covenanting partners was caught standing by the corpse of the Covenant on 7 July 1982 with a smoking gun in its hand. The Anglo-Catholic wing of the Church of England had been most vocal in their opposition, but there were evangelicals and others who had also voted against the Proposals.

The Proposals failed because a sufficient majority in the House of Clergy were unable, in the act of covenanting, to accept the wider 'episcopal' ministry of United Reformed Church provincial moderators by virtue of their ordination as ministers of Word and Sacrament and without additional ordination to the historic episcopate. What was required, if the Covenant was to be made, was that those in ministries of oversight in the United Reformed Church and the other non-episcopal churches should be re-ordained to the *episcope* to which they had been appointed and inducted under the approved procedures of their churches. This would be in effect an act of reordination which pointedly singled out particular ministries as defective. Discussions in the

---

[63]   *Church Times*, 16 July 1982.
[64]   *Failure of the English Covenant*, op. cit. p. 30.

Council for Covenanting had made it clear that this was not acceptable to the non-episcopal participants. For a majority in the House of Clergy, as for the dissenting members of the Council for Covenanting, this was an area of irreconcilable difficulty.

The threat of failure hung over the Proposals from the publication of the Report with its Memorandum of Dissent in 1980. An editorial in The Times, welcoming the Proposals, had then warned of the dangers of their rejection.

> It must be said that when the three high churchmen find so much acceptable in this novel design for a slow motion merger, the ground upon which they reject it – that it entails the temporary toleration of a handful of moderators whose churches will have accepted bishops and episcopal ordination for the future and who are themselves willing to be made bishops, if wanted, on expiry of their current seven-year term of office – looks narrow.[65]

To many it seemed that narrowness had prevailed.

While it is clear that the Church of England delivered the *coup de grace,* can the entire blame for the failure of the covenant be laid at its door? The Methodist Church, which had accepted the Proposals without scruple, felt a deep sense of rejection. Within the United Reformed Church disappointment was tinged with some relief among those who had opposed the Proposals that the Church of England had saved the United Reformed Church from a potentially divisive situation. Even while agreeing to the Proposals, the General Assembly had forwarded to the Council for Covenanting a series of amendments, on which ensuing debate might have indefinitely delayed the Covenant's inauguration.[66]

It was apparent that the United Reformed Church in 1982 had little taste for the model of episcopacy outlined in the Proposals and its fundamentally Anglican ethos. The United Reformed Church hoped for a more Reformed understanding of episcopacy and there were even suggestions that, within the Covenant, the United Reformed Church might eschew the title 'bishop' in favour of some other title which might carry less historical baggage. It was unlikely that the United Reformed Church would confer upon their bishops any greater authority than that of their existing moderators. Perhaps there was a failure of imagination, an inability to see how, within the new relationships established by the Covenant, the role of a United Reformed Church moderator might be developed as an enabler of the Church's mission in the world. While in the past moderators had been sometimes jocularly referred to as 'our bishops', their effective role had been more restricted to the pastoral care of ministers and, to a lesser extent, of congregations. Former Congregationalists in the United Reformed Church had not seriously thought of their provincial moderators as having any special responsibility 'to maintain and further the unity of the Church, to uphold its discipline, and to guard its faith'.[67]

---

65   *Bishops All Round, The Times,* 26 June 1980.
66   *Record of Assembly,* (The United Reformed Church, 1982).
67   *Towards Visible Unity,* p. 18.

In United Reformed Church services of ordination and induction there was nothing corresponding to the Church of England's Oath of Canonical Obedience to the diocesan bishop. In some respects the office of provincial moderator in the United Reformed Church seemed to approximate more to that of an Anglican archdeacon than a diocesan bishop.

Misgivings concerning episcopacy within the United Reformed Church were outweighed by the commitment to the unity of the Church which was enshrined in its Basis of Union. This commitment persuaded a sufficient majority to support the Proposals, though the substantial dissenting minority in both the United Reformed Church and the Church of England (if that Church had voted in favour) might have made the Covenant unworkable in some areas. But bishop Woollcombe was emphatic in his insistence that the failure of the English Covenant was not ultimately due to the opposition of minorities, however substantial. 'In the end, in all the churches, even amongst those who voted in favour, there was a general lack of the enthusiastic heart to make the Covenant happen: and so it died.'[68]

The failure of the Covenant proposals closed a chapter in English church history. It showed that the vision of Christian unity, for which Jesus had prayed, could not be realised, at least for the foreseeable future in England, by the organic union of denominations. The failure dealt a serious blow to the United Reformed Church. In its short life it had understood itself as having been called into temporary existence to act as a catalyst for a wider union of separated churches. The wider Church had hailed its formation in 1972 as a sign of hope for the whole Church. It now faced an uncertain future as a relatively small denomination which had been robbed of its *raison d'etre*. The brave commitment of its Basis of Union – 'to go on praying and working, with all our fellow Christians, for the visible unity of the Church in the way Christ chooses' – seemed impossible to achieve. This commitment could not be abandoned if the United Reformed Church was to remain faithful to its foundation convictions that 'There is but one Church of the one God' and that the unity of the Church was given to the Church by God, not for its own sake but as a sign of hope for a broken and divided world. Failure to covenant did not contradict the reality that only a united body could offer a united witness. The Covenant may have lacked the flexibility and diversity in ministry which such a united body would require. The world – and the Church – had changed greatly since 1972. The long reign of modernity since the Enlightment with its emphasis on settled structures, hierarchy and obedience to authority was facing what Jurgen Habermas called 'a legitimation crisis'.[69] The assumption in *Towards Visible Unity* that hierarchy belonged to the Church's essential nurture was being contested by a new postmodern emphasis on relativity and consumer choice. While this was not the reason for the rejection of the Proposals, postmodernity provided the new context in which the Covenant would have had to operate. It is at least open to question whether such a clerically and male-dominated scheme could have worked for long without major transformation. The fundamental question which sooner or later would have to be resolved was whether the starting point in understanding the ministry of the Church should begin at the top, ie with the ministry of bishops, or at the level of the ministry of the local congregation. Bernard Thorogood, who as General Secretary of the United Reformed Church had been an active participant and supporter of the Covenant proposals, later observed that discussions on ministry had tended to focus on the concept of succession and its

---

68 *The Failure of the English Covenant*, op. cit. p. 25.
69 See David Lyon, *Postmodernity*, (Buckingham: Open University Press, 1994) Chapter 5.

implications for authority in the Church. An over-emphasis on the personalising of succession in an episcopal office carried the risk that authority would be concentrated in a limited circle. Similarly a stringent emphasis on the threefold ministry of bishops, presbyters and deacons, might have positive benefits in preserving good order, but be less effective in equipping the Church for the variety of ministries which it needed to serve the modern world. The ordained ministry was necessary but it was essential to avoid creating a gulf between ordained ministers and the ministry of the whole Church. His preference was to start with the ministry of the congregation:

> The service of the whole congregation is primary, and in that ministry we do not sense the barriers to unity that have proved so stubborn. It is only on the small proportion of the ministry of the church that we call the professional or ordained ministry that our diversities divide us.[70]

This suggests that in the traditions of the United Reformed Church, the local congregation is the starting point for its understanding of ministry and ordination.

The Future - Growing Together Locally?

A further consequence of the failure of the Covenant Proposals was a new emphasis in the search for Christian unity on growing together locally. Local expressions of ecumenism rather than laboured and time-consuming attempts to unite whole denominations or, as in the case of the Covenant, to reconcile episcopal and non-episcopal ministries, offered potentially greater rewards. Recent decades had seen massive growth in the number of local Councils of Churches following the formation of the British Council of Churches in 1942. Their number had risen from 126 in 1945 to 600 in 1970, and would rise to 1200 by 1993. In many areas they had acted as midwife at the birth of new Local Ecumenical Projects including a range of combinations of Baptist, Church of England, Methodist, Roman Catholic and United Reformed churches. By 1993 some 750 such Projects would be in existence. The search for unity was finding new forms of expression.

A significant moment on the ecumenical journey was the *Swanwick Declaration* which was adopted at a major national conference in 1987 of national and local leaders of the British and Irish churches. At the heart of the Declaration, which was an impassioned plea that the churches should see themselves no longer as strangers, but as pilgrims on a shared journey lay the affirmation –

> We now declare together our readiness to commit ourselves to each other under God. Our earnest desire is to become more fully, in his own time, the one Church of Christ, united in faith, communion, pastoral care and mission. Such unity is the gift of God. With gratitude we have truly experienced this gift, growing amongst us in these days. We affirm our openness to this growing unity in obedience to the Word of God so that we may fully share, hold in common and offer to the world those gifts which we have received and still hold in separation. In the unity we seek we recognise that there will not be uniformity but legitimate diversity.[71]

---

70   Revd B Thorogood, *One Wind, Many Flames*, (Geneva: WCC Risk Book Series No. 48, 1991) p. 51.
71   The full text of the Declaration is printed in *Called to be One*, (London: Churches Together in England, 1995) pp. 1-2.

The *Swanwick Declaration* represented the churches' determination to leave behind the painful memories of the past and to reach out towards the reconciliation in Christ of all that God had promised. There is an inference that the issues of ministry, which had bedevilled earlier attempts at unity, needed to be set in a wider context of pastoral care and mission.

The Declaration quickly led to the establishment by 1990 of Churches Together in England with parallel bodies in Scotland and Wales and the formation of the Council of Churches in Britain and Ireland. One of the principal aims of Churches Together in England was

> To promote, coordinate, support and service intermediate bodies in England, assisting them in their care for local ecumenical activity and representing their concerns at the national level.[72]

The thrust of Churches Together in England was to be at the local level. An immediate objective was the appointment of full or part-time ecumenical officers 'at the intermediate level' throughout England to foster ecumenical commitment in their areas and, where possible, to develop common missionary strategies. 'Intermediate' was understood to mean the administrative area of a county, or a large city, or, as in the case of Milton Keynes, a large new town. The intermediate level lay between the local and the national. The response to this initiative was swift, so that by 1995 nearly 50 intermediate ecumenical bodies had been formed. A development of great significance took place at Milton Keynes where in 1990 a Baptist minister, the Revd Hugh Cross, was appointed as Ecumenical moderator with responsibility for pastoral oversight of the town's churches and developing an ecumenical strategy.

The proposal to establish the intermediate bodies produced an inevitable reaction in some quarters that the churches were developing yet another layer of bureaucracy. Ecumenism was not free from its image problem, and for some it had negative connotations. Yet there were more positive hopes that the new bodies would stimulate the churches to engage together in adventurous mission, and, by breaking out of their past, would discover new and enjoyable ways of worshipping, praying, and responding to the gospel imperative for unity.[73]

Flora Winfield, Local Unity Secretary for the Church of England's Council for Christian Unity, has suggested that the concept of 'organic unity', which had pre-occupied 20th century ecumenism, needs re-examination. In church language it has been almost exclusively associated with the church's organisational structures, but in the everyday speech of the 21st century the word 'organic' has acquired new meanings of wholesomeness and growth. She commends therefore the concept of the 'ecology of unity'

> where unity is the natural state of the Church, and is something into which we grow together, as we grow towards God.[74]

---

[72]   R Nunn, *This Growing Unity*, (London: Churches Together in England, 1995) p. vii.
[73]   See Flora Winfield, *Growing Together – Working for Unity Locally*, (London: SPCK, 2002) p. xvi.
[74]   ibid. p. 17.

Local Ecumenical Partnerships, as they are now called, offer a sign and foretaste of the full visible unity of the Church. They cannot on their own resolve the issues of ministry and ordination which have divided the churches over the centuries. But by setting them in the practical context of Christians working together locally, they point to the Church's underlying faith that in the fullness of time the Church will be reconciled in God's service. There is little point in Christian unity unless it finds expression in mission.

Chapter Nine

Towards a New Millennium

TOWARDS A NEW MILLENNIUM

The failure of the proposals for a covenant between the churches in England seemed to bring to a halt the movement towards visible unity which had been initiated by the Lambeth Appeal of 1920. Enthusiasm for inter-church conversations with a view to organic union had evaporated, leaving widespread disillusionment with the ecumenical enterprise. Forty years earlier Nathaniel Micklem had claimed that in respect of the articles of the Christian Faith 'there is not, and there never has been controversy between the Church of England and Orthodox Dissent'.[1] Resolving differences of church order and issues surrounding ministry and ordination had however proved recalcitrant, in spite of much goodwill and strenuous endeavour. Some now saw a way forward in the growing number of local ecumenical projects in which Anglicans, Methodists and United Reformed were working in a variety of united or associated congregational experiments. There were hopes that the unity which had proved elusive at the national level might be achieved locally. It was clear above all that the churches could no longer engage usefully in sterile debates on specific schemes of union. The Methodist Church and the United Reformed Church, who had many shared congregations, studiously avoided the option of seeking to unite into one Church. For the foreseeable future in England, the pattern of separate national denominational structures was set to continue. For this to change, they would have to wait for a time when, in John Robinson's famous words to the departing Pilgrim Fathers, the Lord would have more light and truth to break forth from his holy Word. Inter-church discussions would have to be take place in a different context if they were to be fruitful.

This did not mean the abandonment of dialogue, or that the churches would cease to wrestle with the issues of ministry and ordination which had proved so divisive. In this chapter we examine three areas in which that dialogue would be maintained.

I. A World Church Dialogue – Baptism, Eucharist and Ministry

Baptism, Eucharist and Ministry was a report presented by the Faith and Order Commission to the World Council of Churches at Lima 1982.[2] Known as the 'Lima Text' it was the fruit of a fifty year process of study stretching back to the first Faith and Order Conference at Lausanne in 1927. It appeared at what its compilers described as 'a crucial moment in the history of humankind' when the churches growing into unity were asking how their understandings and practices of baptism, eucharist and ministry related to their mission in and for the renewal of human community and to their endeavours to promote justice, peace and reconciliation. It represented the significant

---

[1]   N Micklem, *The Doctrine of our Redemption*, (London: Eyre and Spottiswoode, 1943) p. viii.
[2]   *Baptism, Eucharist and Ministry*, (Geneva: WCC, Faith and Order Paper No. 111, 1982).

theological convergence which the Faith and Order Commision had discerned and formulated while not claiming that they had fully reached the 'consensus' which would be necessary to realise and maintain the Church's visible unity. Its primary purpose was to demonstrate the major areas of theological convergence which had been achieved, and to identify those areas which required further research and reconciliation.

The starting point for *Baptism, Eucharist and Ministry* was the calling of the whole people of God. This was the perspective from which the churches needed to understand and order their life. The Holy Spirit bestows on the Church a diverse range of complementary gifts for ministry, including communicating the Gospel, healing, praying, teaching, serving, inspiration and vision. The community's task is to help members to discover the gifts they have received and to use them for the building up of the Church and the service of the world. Ministry is to be understood as the service to which all God's people are called, whether as individuals, as a local community, or as the universal Church. The ordained ministry is called by God to help the Church fulfil its mission. The community needs ordained ministers who are publicly responsible for pointing to the community's fundamental dependence on Jesus Christ.

> Their presence reminds the community of the divine initiative, and of the dependence of the Church on Jesus Christ, who is the source of its mission and the foundation of its unity.[3]

The ordained ministry exists only in relation to the community. In the eucharistic celebration especially the ordained ministry provides a visible focus of the communion between Christ and the members of his body. 'In the celebration of the eucharist, Christ gathers, teaches and nourishes the Church.' The ordained minister represents the presidency of Christ, who as the true host invites God's people to the meal. 'The ministry of such persons, who since very early times have been ordained, is constitutive for the life and witness of the Church.'[4]

Baptism, Eucharist and Ministry understood the act of ordination in a threefold sense. In the first place its form must make clear that *the initiative in ordination lies with God*. The Church receives from God its ministry to announce the Gospel to the world. In the same way the Church does not create the ordained ministry but receives it from God as a gift. The central act in ordination is therefore the Church's prayer that the new minister be given the power of the Holy Spirit in the new relationship which ordination establishes between the particular person, the local Christian community and, intentionally, the Church Universal. In the ordination prayer the Church affirms the divine initiative by acknowledging its absolute dependence upon God for the outcome of its invocation.

Ordination is then *a sign that the Lord has answered the Church's prayer.* God's freedom is absolute, yet the Church ordains in confidence that in the act of ordination God enters sacramentally into contingent and historical forms of human relationship and uses them for his purpose.

> Ordination is a sign performed in faith that the spiritual relationship signified is present in, with and through the words spoken, the gestures made and the forms employed.[5]

---

[3]   *Baptism, Eucharist and Ministry,* M. 12.
[4]   ibid. M. 8.
[5]   ibid. M. 43 (b)

Thirdly, ordination is *an act of acknowledgement and commitment*. The Church acknowledges the gifts which the Holy Spirit has given to the one ordained for building up the body of Christ for its mission to the world, and declares its readiness to receive those gifts. In the same way those ordained offer their gifts to the Church; they commit themselves to their new responsibilities and, at the same time, enter into a collegial relationship with other ordained ministers.

The Lima Text recognised that it is no longer possible to deduce from the New Testament a single pattern of ministry by which all future ministry in the Church might be determined. The New Testament exhibits instead a variety of forms existing at different times and places. By the second and third centuries of the Christian era a threefold pattern of bishops, presbyters and deacons became established as the normal pattern of ordained ministry throughout the Church. While recognising many changes over the centuries, *Baptism, Eucharist and Ministry* affirmed this threefold ministry 'as an expression of the unity we seek and also as a means for achieving it'.[6] Churches which already maintained this pattern needed to ask how its potential might be more fully developed to make effective the Church's witness in the world. Churches not yet having the threefold pattern as it had developed needed to ask whether it did not have a powerful claim to be accepted by them.

On the vexed issue of Succession in the Apostolic Tradition, the Text took a traditional stance in affirming that

> the orderly transmission of the ordained ministry is ...a powerful expression of the continuity of the Church throughout history.[7]

The ordained ministry is entrusted with the task of preserving and actualising the apostolic faith. Those churches for whom orderly transmission was unimportant needed to re-assess, and perhaps modify, their understanding of continuity in the apostolic tradition. Yet historical succession could not by itself ensure faithfulness to the apostolic mission. Thus

> where the ordained ministry does not adequately serve the proclamation of the apostolic faith, churches must ask themselves whether their ministerial structures are not in need of reform.[8]

Episcopal succession could only be a sign, and not a guarantee, of the continuity and unity of the Church.

The United Reformed Church welcomed the Lima Text at its General Assembly in 1993 and encouraged Synods, Districts and local congregations to study the text and report their findings. While the subsequent response was generally welcoming, the section on ministry gave rise to a number of concerns. The main concern was that, while having acknowledged the variety of forms of ministry in the New Testament church and in more recent times, the Text nevertheless endorsed the threefold pattern of ministry as having more than historical significance.

---

6   ibid. M. 22.
7   ibid. M. 35.
8   ibid.

It is not clear why the Spirit might not have been as much at work in the breakdown of the threefold pattern in the sixteenth and seventeenth centuries as in the creation of it in the second and third.[9]

The criteria for judging the theological significance of historical developments were not self-evident. The pattern of ministry needed to be determined by the missionary task of the Church rather than by historical precedent, however impressive.

Concern was also expressed at the omission from *Baptism, Eucharist and Ministry* of any reference to the ministry of the ordained elder in the Reformed Churches. The Text referred to the ministry of deacons who 'represent to the Church its calling as servant in the world.'[10] The tasks assigned to deacons included reading the scriptures, preaching, leading in prayer, teaching, exercising a ministry of love and fulfilling administrative tasks. Many of these tasks, in the Reformed Churches, were undertaken by ordained ministers of Word and Sacrament. The commentary, which formed an important part of the Lima Text, implied that, as the Churches moved closer together, the ministry of deacons might come to include ministries which already existed under a variety of forms and names. It seemed to many in the United Reformed Church that any proposal to subsume the ministry of elders into the Diaconate might be driven more by a concern to maintain the threefold pattern of bishops, presbyters and deacons than to honour and affirm the ministry of elders as it had developed within the Reformed tradition.

In a similar way, while *Baptism, Eucharist and Ministry* emphasised the gifts exercised by the laity,[11] no suggestions were offered as to how those gifts might be recognised and authorised. 'There is no suggestion that lay people may be called by a congregation and ordained to exercise a particular ministry, which is a charisma in the same sense as that term is used for the ministry of word and sacraments.'[12] It did not follow that such ministries should be fitted into a single order within a threefold pattern. Further work was required on the concept and nature of diaconal ministries.

There was profound concern at the inadequacy of the Text's treatment of the ordination of women. A response from one Synod bluntly described it as 'evasive and unhelpful'. *Baptism, Eucharist and Ministry* recognised that differences on this issue raised substantial obstacles to the mutual recognition of ministries. It urged the Churches to face one another with an open-mindedness which might enable the Spirit to speak to the Church through the insights of another.[13] While urging the Churches to re-evaluate their attitudes to exclusion from the ordained ministry on grounds of handicap, race or sociological grouping,[14] the Text nowhere considered positive arguments for the acceptance of the ministry of both men and women. The United Reformed Church's response included the comment that 'we value the sense of wholeness in ministry experienced as a gift of the Holy Spirit through the ordination of women, which has been practised since 1917 in one of our constituent Churches.'[15]

---

9   See United Reformed Church Response in *Churches Respond to BEM*, (Geneva: WCC, Faith and Order Paper 129, 1986). p. 104.
10 *Baptism, Eucharist and Ministry*, M. 31.
11 e.g. ibid. M. 5.
12 *Churches Respond to BEM*, op. cit. p. 107.
13 *Baptism, Eucharist and Ministry*, M. 54.
14 ibid. M. 50.
15 *Churches Respond to BEM*, p. 107.

The general feeling within the United Reformed Church was that *Baptism, Eucharist and Ministry* had placed too great an emphasis on the ministry of the sacraments, which were often visible signs of division, and had insufficiently emphasised the awareness of the unity which transcended divisions. This imbalance might be redressed by a renewed search for a common expression of the nature of the apostolic faith and the renewal of human community. Bernard Thorogood later observed that *Baptism, Eucharist and Ministry* had tended to emphasise the traditions which enshrined the Church's difficulties – succession, authority, and orders of ministry – rather than focusing upon the Church's calling to become involved in the diverse activities of human society where a 'manifold ministry' would be more appropriate.[16] A missionary Church would need to develop a variety of orders of ministry to meet the needs of mission. The United Reformed Church offered such an example in the ministry of its Church Related Community Workers. Others might develop so that the ministry of the whole people of God might become a reality.

II. A Bilateral Dialogue - God's Reign and Our Unity

From 1981 to 1984 the United Reformed Church was also involved in bilateral conversations between Anglicans and Reformed at a supra-national level through the work of the Anglican-Reformed International Commission appointed by the Anglican Consultative Council and the World Alliance of Reformed Churches. The results of their enquiry were published in the report - *God's Reign and Our Unity.*[17] Dr John Huxtable was the first co-chairman of the Commission. Other United Reformed Church representatives were Dr Alan Sell, who acted as co-secretary, and Dr Lesslie Newbigin, who was responsible for drafting much of the final report.

The parameters of the enquiry were 'the relationship between the Church and the Kingdom of God, the priority of grace, the trinitarian and christological basis of ministry, the mission of the Church'.[18] The quest for Christian unity was inseparable from the question of the unity of humankind. God's purpose would not be achieved merely by creating a united Church. 'Our quest for Christian unity is seen steadily in the context of God's purpose to reconcile all people and all things in Christ.'[19] Church unity would be a false unity if it were not for the sake of the fulfilling of that promise in all its universal scope.

Asking what kept Anglicans and Reformed apart, the report recognised that the role of the bishop in Anglican churchmanship had no exact parallel in Reformed experience. A point of real difference was the importance to Anglicans of the bishop as the one who stood, in a more than functional sense, as a personal symbol of the catholicity and apostolicity of the Church. Reformed churchmanship on the other hand was open to the criticism that it offered nothing exactly comparable. Councils, synods and assemblies, while exercising pastoral and personal *episkope*, often appeared impersonal to the average church member. A postmodern society also, with its greater emphasis on the person, required significant figures to whom people could turn to discover the mind of the Church on particular issues. In the case of the United Reformed Church, the General Secretary, Assembly Moderator and synod moderators fulfilled an important role in giving the Church a human face.

---

[16]   Revd B Thorogood, *One Wind, Many Flames*, op. cit. p. 52.
[17]   *God's Reign and Our Unity*, (London: SPCK, 1984)
[18]   ibid. Preface.
[19]   ibid. p. 17.

Ministry in the Church and the Ministry of the Church

A fundamental conviction of *God's Reign and Our Unity* is that ministry in the Church and the ministry of the Church are inescapably entwined. Both have their source in God's action. The Father sent the Son into the world anointed by the Spirit to announce and embody God's blessed reign over all humankind and all creation. Jesus called others – in particular the Twelve – to follow him in the fulfilment of his mission. After his final victory, through death and resurrection, Jesus returned to reassure his disciples that he was still with them, and commissioned them to continue his mission. The scars of his passion, which he showed them on Easter evening, would be a reminder to them that the kingship of God and God's victory over the powers of evil could only be made manifest to the world under the sign of the Cross. The company of disciples gathered in that closed room was in embryo both the Church and the ministry. The first disciples were both the first followers and the first apostles. There was thus from the beginning a pattern of ministerial leadership in the life of the Church. Such an understanding of ministry served to protect the Church from two opposing tendencies; on the one hand it rendered untenable any tendency to regard the ordained ministry as a separate and independent body standing over against the Church. On the other, it ruled out the claim that the ordained ministry was created by the Church. The ministry of the Church and ministry in the Church were inseparable. *God's Reign and Our Unity* quoted approvingly the assertion of the Lima Text that 'The Church has never been without persons holding specific authority and responsibility'.[20] At the same time a variety of ministerial structures had evolved in the course of the Church's historical development, none of which could claim the direct authority of scripture. The time had come to recognise that the Church as a living body needed to 'combine continuity of tradition with adaptation to new situations under the guidance of the Holy Spirit'[21] Not all the developments which had occurred could claim divine sanction, and were neither to be treated as immutable nor to be rejected because they were not explicitly authorised by Scripture.

Priest or Presbyter?

The Report explored the issue of the different words which were used in the Anglican and Reformed traditions to describe the work of the ordained ministry. Anglicans made wide use of the word 'priest' which was foreign to the Reformed tradition. It was accepted that the New Testament nowhere designates any Christian minister as a 'priest'. The word first came into use to designate the bishop and was later extended to presbyters. At the Reformation this usage had been abandoned by the Reformers because of its association with the doctrine of the eucharistic sacrifice and its lack of explicit authorisation by Scripture. The Reformers re-affirmed instead the Scriptural understanding of the whole Church as a 'priesthood of all believers'. Within such a context the Report wished to affirm the priestly nature of the ministry by virtue of ministers being called 'to lead, enable and equip the Church for this priestly office'.[22] A statement from *Baptism, Eucharist and Ministry* was quoted in support of this view:

---

[20]   *Baptism, Eucharist and Ministry*, M. 9.
[21]   *God's Reign and Our Unity*, para. 77.
[22]   ibid. para. 79.

Ordained ministers are related, as are all Christians, both to the priesthood of Christ and to the priesthood of the Church. But they may appropriately be called priests because they fulfil a particular priestly service by strengthening and building up the royal and prophetic priesthood of the faithful through word and sacraments, through their prayers of intercession, and through their pastoral guidance of the community.[23]

The Anglican view in *God's Reign and Our Unity* is thus heard strongly insisting on the appropriateness of using the word 'priest' to designate those ordained to a ministry of word and sacraments, while recognising that other words such as pastor, presbyter and minister were no less appropriate.

Ordination and Presidency

God's Reign and Our Unity defines ordination as the act which constitutes and acknowledges the special ministry of representation and leadership within the life of the Church, both locally and universally, which is given to particular persons who have been specially called and equipped within the whole body of the faithful. While the Spirit empowers all members of the one body with gifts for many kinds of ministry, it was clear that from the earliest times ordination had been associated with the Eucharist.

> In the Eucharist Christ himself is present in his fullness, and the company which shares in it is therefore the catholic Church in that place.[24]

Yet even in New Testament times problems had arisen, as in the Church at Corinth, when a group of members proposed to celebrate the Lord's Supper in separation from their fellow members.[25] How then could the Church distinguish the celebration of a divisive group – which Paul described as 'not the Lord's Supper' – from a true Eucharist in which Christ is present in the midst of his universal Church? The answer to this practical question had been formulated by Ignatius of Antioch (c. 35-c.107 CE) who stipulated that a 'valid' Eucharist is one presided over by the one acknowledged as its leader by the congregation and by neighbouring congregations, or by a person authorised by that acknowledged leader.

Presidency in this sense is therefore a matter of good order. The one who presides does not stand in any different relationship to Christ from the rest of the body, but because – as a matter of good order – he (or *she* as the Reformed would now insist) have been so authorised in an act of ordination which by its intention carried the authority of the universal Church. Such order arose from a genuine concern that what was celebrated should be truly the Lord's Supper. Those who presided at the Lord's Table should affirm their oneness with the whole Body and not separate themselves from their fellow members either through an excess of fervent enthusiasm, or by a desire to exclude others from their fellowship. In this sense the function of the ordained minister is to act as a focus of unity for the whole Body, both within a particular congregation and in the ever-widening network of relationships between congregations.

---

[23]   *Baptism, Eucharist and Ministry*, M. 17.
[24]   *God's Reign and Our Unity*, para 81.
[25]   *I Corinthians 11. 17-22*

This is the context in which the Report considered the issue of Lay Presidency at the sacraments. On the Reformed side the practice of 'lay celebration' had sometimes been advocated as a witness to the Reformed belief in the 'priesthood of all believers'. The practice appeared to declare that a celebration of the Lord's Supper – or Eucharist – was no less 'valid' if the president were a lay person than an ordained minister. The compilers of *God's Reign and Our Unity* believed this view to rest upon a profound misunderstanding. By implying that the president alone is the priest it thus contradicted the doctrine which it was intended to support. In reality the whole body of the Church celebrates the Eucharist which enacts the union of Christ with his Church. Presidency by an ordained minister in no way 'validates' the sacrament, since only Christ can give himself sacramentally to his people. What ordained presidency does is to make effective the intention of a particular congregation to be in sacramental fellowship with the universal Church. The over-riding consideration is that of good order, not validity.

In particular situations circumstances may arise where, because of a shortage of ordained ministers, or rapid missionary advance, congregations may have to decide whether to celebrate the Eucharist without an ordained minister or have no Eucharist at all. Reformed churches have often taken the view that in exceptional circumstances a lay person should be authorised to preside in order that the congregation should not be deprived of the gift of the sacrament. Such a practice, on the ground of 'pastoral necessity', might be defended as an 'orderly modification' of normal practice. The Report preferred to affirm the general rule that the president at the sacraments should be the person who by ordination has been given authority to preside. Presidency by the ordained did not signify that ordained ministers possessed a priesthood which non-ordained members lacked.

> It depends upon the good ordering which is essential to the life of the Church as it exercises corporately the priesthood given to it by the one who is alone the good High Priest.[26]

Ordination, Authority and Continuity

God's Reign and Our Unity associated itself with the understanding of the threefold nature of ordination which had been developed in *Baptism, Eucharist and Ministry*.[27] Ordination was the means by which authority was entrusted to the ordained person to act 'locally and representatively' for the whole Church. Anglicans and Reformed both confessed one holy, catholic and apostolic Church. Their shared intention was to ordain to the ministry of the Universal Church, and that the authorisation which ordination conferred should be universally valid. In reality this was not the case.

Each communion also recognised the importance to the Church of historical continuity. The Church depended for its continuity on the scriptures, the sacraments of baptism and the eucharist, the ecumenical creeds and the transmission of teaching and Christian practice through the generations. The two communions held different views over the role of ordination in safeguarding that continuity. The Anglican communion regarded its public *episcopal* ministry as its primary safeguard that the Church's teaching was the authentic message of Jesus and the

---

26 *God's Reign and Our Unity*, para. 83.
27 See p above

apostles.   In their case episcopal ordination provided historical continuity The Reformed communion emphasised continuity through ordination to the presbyteral ministry of Word and Sacrament which included detailed public confession by those ordained of their adherence to the historic faith.   GRU did not attempt the task of reconciling these difference of emphasis but underlined the relevance to each communion of the historical continuity which ordination afforded. Any methods which sought to bring the two separated communions into unity would need to acknowledge unambiguously the reality of God's gift of ministry to the churches in their separation, and also to ensure that the continuity of succession in ordinations with the undivided Church was visibly restored and maintained.

Common Patterns Of Ministry

Underneath what appeared as considerable differences between Anglicans and Reformed in their patterns of ministry, *God's Reign and Our Unity* discerned a common pattern which derived from the early Church. In one of its least satisfactory sections from the Reformed viewpoint, it claimed that the early Church evolved the classic pattern according to which the work of the ordained ministry was carried out in the local church by a chief pastor (the bishop) working collegially with colleagues (presbyters/priests) and assisted by a staff of helpers (deacons) who carried out the church's ministry in the world.   Essentially these were ministries of the local church. As the Church grew and congregations multiplied in each place, the bishop became the regional leader of several congregations, while the presbyters became local shepherds of these congregations.

A Reformed interpretation of the ministry of the early Church gave greater emphasis to the *variety* of ministries which existed in the earliest period, while accepting that the threefold pattern eventually prevailed. The Reformers of the sixteenth century believed that they had re-introduced a threefold ministry in the local church comprising the pastor as preacher of the Word, surrounded by a group of elders and deacons, while regionally church government was exercised by representative councils or synods. It was perhaps surprising, in the light of the failed attempts of Anglicans and Reformed to covenant in England, that *God's Reign and Our Unity* should claim without qualification that the classical pattern should be accepted 'in some form for the sake of the unity and continuity of the Church, both locally and universally, and for the sake of its missionary calling.'[28] The fact remained that notwithstanding the high claims made by Anglicans for the threefold ministry, that pattern had been effectively truncated to a two-fold ministry of bishop and priest, since the diaconal ministry had long been reduced to a temporary apprenticeship for the priesthood. In the Reformed churches also the diaconate had often disappeared as a distinctive ministry.

God's Reign and Our Unity was on surer ground in emphasising the importance of the personal, collegial and communal aspects of ministry. All ministry required a *personal* character to provide in specific persons a focus for the unity and witness of the community. Its *collegial* character, in which responsibility is shared by colleagues working together, points to the nature of the Christian community as a reconciled fellowship. Its *communal* character is demonstrated by the enabling of every member of the community to exercise the gifts which the Spirit gives.[29] In considering how

---

[28]   *God's Reign and Our Unity*, para 92.
[29]   ibid.

these dimensions might be reflected in practice, *God's Reign and Our Unity* suggested that the Church needed to adopt a more inclusive approach to ministry, and to explore the contemporary relevance of the various ministries which were designated in the New Testament as, for example, 'prophets' and 'evangelists'. This should be extended to new ministries which had emerged in more recent times. The neglected role of theologians in the Church needed also to be re-considered in the light of the Reformers' historic emphasis on the doctors of the Church and the Anglican emphasis on the teaching role of bishops.

Women and the Ordained Ministry

God's Reign and Our Unity noted that the two traditions had not yet reached a common mind on the ordination of women to the threefold ministry which it envisaged as the Church's future pattern. Within the Church of England it was a matter of anxious debate. In general the Reformed churches saw no theological objections to the ordination of women, except for a minority within the World Alliance of Reformed Churches who objected on the grounds that biblical teaching emphasised the headship of the male. Over the previous half-century – and since 1917 in the case of the English Congregationalists – they had begun to ordain women to the ministry of Word and Sacrament out of conviction and not as a response to a shortage of male candidates. Women ministers had not always been accepted sociologically or emotionally. Nor had any serious and sustained consideration been given to the distinctive contribution that women ministers might make to the Church. The Report believed that this debate, which in the past had often been too narrowly church-based, should be carried on in the context of the mission of the Christian Church to the whole of humanity.

> The debate is not simply about the ministry. It concerns the nature of the Church and of Christ's salvation of humanity, and is indeed central to our understanding of the nature and being of God.[30]

Practical Suggestions

The section on practical suggestions followed as something of an anti-climax after the more theologically-based earlier chapters. It assumed that the Reformed Churches would accept some form of the threefold ministry and face the question of bishops. The bishop's role would be to provide ministerial leadership in the whole life of the Church in his area. It was suggested that Reformed Moderators of presbytery or synod should develop a role as 'bishops-in-presbytery'. They would need to hold office for a substantial period in order to develop a significant pastoral relationship with ministers and people and become publicly recognised as the representatives of the Church in their regional areas. Church order as envisaged in *God's Reign and Our Unity* perpetuated a 'top down' hierarchical structure. It was argued that a sustained personal leadership, rightly exercised, should not undermine the authority and effectiveness of a synod. Yet from a Reformed perspective significant safeguards would be needed to ensure that personal leadership did not become aggrandised to the detriment of the responsibilities of presbytery or synod for oversight and leadership.

---

[30]   *God's Reign and Our Unity,* para. 104.

Anglicans were asked to consider what they understood as the ministry of the diaconate. Exercised as a temporary and short-term apprenticeship to the priesthood, it was not a genuine diaconate in the biblical or classical sense. *God's Reign and Our Unity* recommended that Anglicans should adopt the eldership, as exemplified in the Reformed churches, by developing in every congregation a number of elders, who would be non-stipendiary and without intending to serve later as priests, to share in the pastoral care of the congregation. If this suggestion was to be taken forward, the issue would have to be grasped whether the eldership was to be understood as part of the Church's 'clerical' ministry, or, as most Reformed elders would see themselves, as a form of ordained yet 'lay' ministry. To Anglicans, of course, it often appeared that the Councils of the United Reformed Church were exclusively comprised of the ordained – ministers and elders - to the exclusion of the laity.

The Report also envisaged a greater involvement of the entire membership of congregations in the governance of the Church through regular meetings – the 'Church Meeting' of classic Congregationalism now enshrined in the Basis of Union of the United Reformed Church as a fundamental council of the Church - and the opportunity to choose representatives to act on its behalf in the governance of the congregation and of the wider Church.

United Reformed Church Response to 'God's Reign and Our Unity'

In its response to *God's Reign and Our Unity*[31] the General Assembly of the United Reformed Church warmly endorsed its dynamic understanding of the Church as God's pilgrim people 'called to a journey whose goal is nothing less than God's blessed Kingdom embracing all nations and all creation'. It welcomed its emphasis on the calling of the Church to be a sign, instrument and foretaste of God's reconciling purpose in Christ. It agreed that concerns for evangelism, social justice and church unity were not in conflict but were complementary aspects of God's mission.

The Assembly's overall support for the core chapter of *God's Reign and Our Unity* dealing with matters of ministry was at best lukewarm. The opportunity to explore the concept of priesthood, from both Anglican and Reformed perspectives, had been missed. Priesthood had not been satisfactorily defined and appeared to overshadow other understandings of ministry. This especially influenced the Report's understanding of ordination which focused too narrowly on the issue of presidency at the Lord's Supper to the exclusion of other key responsibilities of the ordained ministry. At the same time it assumed the ordained ministry, as then practised, to be normative for ministry and overlooked the growing awareness of the need for diaconal ministries focusing on mission and service to the world. At its heart the chapter on ministry perpetuated an uncritical acceptance of the so-called 'classic' threefold ministry of bishops, priests and deacons. It then appealed for Reformed acceptance of this pattern without providing any sustained arguments – apart from the appeal to history – why it should be accepted as the most appropriate pattern for the Church's ministry and mission at the end of the twentieth century.

To the suggestion that they should accept 'bishops in synod', the Reformed churches could justifiably argue that they had already begun to do this without benefit of what they believed to be dubious doctrines of apostolic succession. To the complementary suggestion that Anglicans should reform their ministry of deacons by introducing elements of the Reformed eldership, the Reformed might

---

[31]   United Reformed Church, General Assembly Reports 1986, pp. 95-96.

have wondered why Anglican colleagues – and sometimes Methodist colleagues also – had been so slow to recognise and provide for the ministry of elders in the growing number of local ecumenical parishes and projects in which the United Reformed Church was a fully engaged and committed participant. Nearly two decades after the publication of *God's Reign and Our Unity* the Reformed eldership has still not been more widely received and adopted as a Reformed contribution to the ministry of the whole Church. A significant omission from *God's Reign and Our Unity* was any in-depth theological exposition of the meaning of the ordained eldership and its potential for the Church's ministry and mission. The United Reformed Church, because it needed to reconcile tensions between the traditions of ministry which had grown from its Congregational, Presbyterian and Churches of Christ roots, had also been slow to discover how the gift of the eldership which it had received from its Presbyterian inheritance might be developed as a diaconal ministry to support the Church's witness to God's reign over all creation.

God's Reign and Our Unity represented an important stage on the journey towards greater understanding between Anglican and Reformed pilgrims. However it did not bring closer the prospect of unity between the two communions. Its central chapter on ministry left unchallenged too many assumptions and failed to explore other avenues which might have proved fruitful. Bishop Lesslie Newbigin's biographer later posed the question whether Newbigin had been right to fear the futility of bilateral dialogues between Christian world communions. Few would disagree with his conclusion that 'their record of providing an enabling structure for local, national, or regional unions is not strong'.[32]

III. An Internal Dialogue – Patterns of Ministry

A Time for Radical Change

In its response to *Baptism, Eucharist and Ministry* the United Reformed Church had stated its conviction that 'the pattern of ministry today should be determined by the missionary task of the Church. The commission of our Lord and the consequent enabling gifts produce a manifold ministry which is apostolic.'[33] By the early 1990s the United Reformed Church was confronted by radical changes which had taken place in church and society since its formation. Membership had declined by 42% since 1973 (from 192,000 to 110,000), while the number of congregations had fallen by only 13%. The number of stipendiary ministers had fallen by 34% between 1974 and 1993 with the result that the ratio of churches (as communities and centres of mission) to stipendiary ministers had increased from 1.8:1 in 1974 to 2.3:1 in 1993. While the recruitment of 201 non-stipendiary ministers had improved the ratio of churches to ministers to 1.9:1, their availability and geographical distribution varied greatly. In practice 1800 churches, over 500 with less than 50 members, were being served by 740 full-time stipendiary ministers The stark reality of the situation was that the United Reformed Church could not provide more than one ordained minister of Word and Sacrament for every two congregations. The single pastorate could no longer be regarded as normative. Yet to spread ministers even more thinly in ever enlarging group pastorates would not provide a satisfactory response.

---

[32]   G Wainwright, *Lesslie Newbigin – A Theological Life*, (Oxford: 2000) p. 127.
[33]   M Thurian (ed) *Churches Respond to BEM*, (Geneva: WCC 1986) p. 108.

One solution would have been a sharp reduction in the number of congregations by the amalgamation of contiguous congregations of the closure of small congregations whose size and generational 'mix' offered insufficient opportunities of fellowship and Christian experience. A more hierarchically structured Church might have been able to achieve such changes, and to have faced the pain and hurt which hard decisions would have entailed. The United Reformed Church still retained a strong memory of the autonomy of local congregations. There would have been strong resistance to the implementation of proposals which would have been regarded, however mistakenly, as being imposed by external authority. Yet in the allocation of scarce ministerial resources, it is impossible to avoid decisions based upon criteria of mission potential and 'kingdom value'. The test of a conciliar Church is how to maintain its unity while taking unpopular decisions.

These domestic issues were set within a wider context of social change. A paper prepared for the Ministries Department of the United Reformed Church[34] pointed out that the context for ministry was more far-reaching than the local church. It was the Church's missionary calling in a nation where Christianity had become a minority faith. Ministry was properly concerned with building up the community of faith but its goal was the Church's witness to the wider communities of village, town, district or nation. The context for mission – 'urban and rural, sophisticated and simple, wealth and poor, sympathetic and hostile, black and white, young and old' – required varied ministries which would be familiar with and involved in the many areas of social life where power was exercised. This missionary calling should be the over-riding consideration, to which the Church's domestic needs, though necessary, should be subordinated.

Restructuring for Mission

It was clear by 1991 that the United Reformed Church needed to re-examine its patterns of ministry for a rapidly changing context in church and society. This task was entrusted to a Working Party which first produced an interim report[35] which after revision in the light of comments from churches, districts and synods came as a final report to the General Assembly in 1995.[36]

Patterns of Ministry underscored the mission context of the Church.

> The Church exists for the sake of God's world, and its ministry is focused in the world, for the world, for God's sake (2.1)

The United Reformed Church gladly understood itself to be part of God's global mission and ministry. Its first task was to discern the will of God for mission in each place and to provide ministry appropriate to its needs and opportunities. Allocation of ministerial resources should be in response to the needs of local congregations and to enable them to develop their forms of ministry and leadership.

The core recommendation of the 1991 paper had been that each local church, of whatever size, should nominate from among its eldership those whom the District Council might recognise as 'Presiding Elders' and authorise them to preside at all services and meetings of the local church. This would obviate the need for District Council to give special authorisation for presidency at the sacraments and, more significantly, would be a means of developing local leadership. This recommendation was based on the long experience of Churches of Christ in placing continuous responsibility for presidency within each local fellowship.

---

[34]   *Patterns of Ministry 1991* (United Reformed Church).
[35]   *Patterns of Ministry – Interim Report 1994* (United Reformed Church).
[36]   *Patterns of Ministry –* (United Reformed Church Reports to General Assembly 1995) pp. 114-33.

The Interim Report 1994 rejected this suggestion on the grounds that, while it affirmed the importance of local leadership, it might cause unnecessary division with the eldership of a local church, and tend to the creation of a new 'tier' of Elders.[37] It over-emphasised the Presiding Elder's sacramental role as president at the sacraments rather than in the provision of lay leadership to the congregation. The final report recommended instead that in each church there should be one or more *Moderating Elders* who would provide continuous and identifiable local leadership. Their role would be to provide stimulus, leadership and initiative within the congregation, to focus the pastoral care of the church, and to act on behalf of the congregation as an identifiable local representative. Their sacramental role was diminished, though it was recognised that some Moderating Elders might, according to their gifts, lead worship and chair elders' and church meetings. By so doing they would help to reduce an over-exclusive focusing of the expectations of congregational leadership upon the ordained minister. *Patterns of Ministry* recognised that in some churches elders were already undertaking *de facto* some of the roles of the proposed Moderating Elders, and argued that it would be beneficial for them to be formally recognised and extended to other congregations.

The framework for the proposal for Moderating Elders was the belief that the United Reformed Church needed to recognise a 'spectrum' of ministries, both lay and ordained. This spectrum might include stipendiary ministers, non-stipendiary ministers, local ministers, ministers in secular employment, church-related community workers, moderating elders, elders and lay preachers. It was essential that these should not be seen as a status-laden hierarchy, but should embody the reality that the Church needed to embrace different functions and styles of ministry. Local leadership needed to be rooted in the eldership working collaboratively with ministers of Word and Sacrament.[38] Since it was now clear that the United Reformed Church had accepted that it could not provide a full-time stipendiary minister for every congregation, *Patterns of Ministry* recommended that it should draw further on the pattern of Churches of Christ and expand what had been its 'Model I' for non-stipendiary ministry.[39] This would in future be understood as *Local Ministry*. Congregations would be challenged to discover whether God was calling some of their members to become ordained ministers within their local congregations and pastorates on a non-stipendiary basis. Ordination to Local Ministry, as envisaged, would carry an authorisation restricted to the designated congregation or pastorate.[40]

Included also in the 'spectrum' were those ministers who, not in pastoral charge, saw their ministry being fulfilled through their work in the world. Their relationship to the councils of the Church was sometimes uncertain and ill-defined. *Patterns of Ministry* recommended that these should be re-named *Ministers in Secular Employment* in order to recognise their service in the secular world as an indentifiable ministry within the mission of the Church.[41]

---

[37] *Patterns of Ministry (Interim Report 1994)* 5.5.1.
[38] The Report recommended that, except for internal administrative purposes and since the distinction between stipendiary and non-stipendiary ministers carried no theological significance, the term 'minister of Word and Sacrament, should be used of all ministers in order to emphasise the unity of the ministry.
[39] Model 1 was defined as 'service in a congregation as part of a team'. It is of a pastoral nature and is shared with others and with stipendiary ministers.
[40] *Patterns of Ministry*, 4.5.4, 4.5.5.
[41] ibid. 4.5.10, 4.5.11.

These recommendations were not intended to diminish the importance of the full-time stipendiary ministry as a major resource for ministry and mission. Nor were they seen as a panacea for numerical decline. *Patterns of Ministry* emphasised that the United Reformed Church would continue to need stipendiary ministers, and that far from contracting, the need for stipendiary ministry would continue to increase. Stipendiary ministers were of central importance for developing strategies of ministry and mission. Unlike other forms of ministry in the spectrum, they were in principle available to the whole Church as a national and mobile resource.

The Report equally affirmed the crucial roles of *Lay Preachers* and *Church Related Community Workers*. Lay Preachers united the Word and the world, and made a vital contribution to maintaining and invigorating the worship of local churches. It was hoped that some might become Moderating Elders or Local Ministers, or become members of local leadership teams. The Report recommended that the title of 'Lay Preacher', which tended to reinforce a distinction between lay and clerical ministries which was foreign to the United Reformed Church's understanding of the *laos*, should be replaced by that of 'Local Preacher' as used in the Methodist Church and the former Churches of Christ. This recommendation was to be defeated, an indication perhaps that the theology of the *laos* as the whole people of God had not yet been fully accepted by the membership of the Church as a whole.

In a wry note the Working Party recorded their disappointment that few United Reformed Church members seemed to be aware of the diversity of patterns of church life outside their home congregations.[42] It was not surprising therefore that the General Assembly rejected by a large majority the core recommendation of *Patterns of Ministry* to appoint Moderating Elders for every congregation. The failure of this central recommendation of the Report suggested that the United Reformed Church as a whole was not yet ready to take seriously the need for a local ministry working collaboratively within the spectrum of ministries which Patterns of Ministry had envisaged.

The Rejection of the Proposals

The debate over *Patterns of Ministry* revealed considerable misgivings among many of the Church's ordained ministers of Word and Sacrament who felt threatened by the proposal to appoint Moderating Elders in their pastorates. Most serving ministers at that time had not been trained for collaborative ministry. The recent introduction of the non-stipendiary ministry had not been free of tensions which the proposal for Moderating Elders seemed likely to aggravate. *Patterns of Ministry* failed to allay the fears of stipendiary ministers, some of whom felt that their commitment to life-long service and their acceptance of the requirement to face periodically the emotional and domestic upheavals of moving to new pastorates had been insufficiently valued. The consequence of the rejection of the proposal for Moderating Elders was that stipendiary ministers would find themselves under ever-increasing pressure to extend their ministries to larger groupings or clusters of congregations. A further unspoken consequence was that without the development of some form of Moderating Eldership, the elders as a whole would have to take increasing responsibility for providing stimulus, leadership, pastoral care and initiative within their congregations.

---

[42]   ibid. 7.1.

Patterns of Ministry failed in its intention to provide new forms of ministry which would strengthen the Church in its mission. With hindsight the proposal for Moderating Elders may have been based on too optimistic an estimate of the number of likely candidates. The rejection of the proposal, which owed much to the experience of the ministry of Elders in Churches of Christ, may have been a sign that the United Reformed Church had not yet fully assimilated this element in its tradition. Nor was it certain that the non-stipendiary ministry could be expanded to provide the churches with a significantly increased number of local ministers.[43] The Report however should not been seen as a failure. Its challenges could not be ignored, and the issues which it had highlighted of the development and deployment of ministerial resources would continue to occupy the councils of the Church.

Presidency at the Sacraments

In other respects also *Patterns of Ministry* was a significant theological milestone for the United Reformed Church. It included important statements on Presidency at the Sacraments and on the Meaning of Ordination which summarised the Church's understanding of ministry and ordination as the twentieth century neared its close.

On the matter of Presidency, *Patterns of Ministry* took up the practical issue that each local church needed to make provision for someone to administer the sacrament of Baptism and to preside at the Lord's Supper. There were deeply held differences of conviction within the United Reformed Church which both reflected and transcended its diverse traditions. Lay presidency was valued by some as a means of blurring any supposed distinction between ministers and members. Others would prefer not to celebrate the sacraments rather than have a non-ordained president. The Basis of Union had endeavoured to provide a framework within which different views could be held without doing violence to members' consciences. District Councils were authorised to recognise some of their members as those who might be invited by local churches to preside at baptismal and communion services 'where pastoral necessity so requires'.[44] This provision was subject to periodic review and it was clearly stated that only such recognised persons might be invited. The emergence since 1972 of a variety of regional interpretations of 'pastoral necessity' had not been helpful to the overall unity of the Church. Ecumenical considerations were of increasing importance when more than 10% of United Reformed congregations were participating in joint United Reformed and Methodist churches. The growing number of local ecumenical partnerships and projects, in which the United Reformed Church was involved, highlighted the need for an agreed and uniform policy for presidency at the sacraments.

Patterns of Ministry affirmed two principles to guide the Church in what had become a perplexing and sensitive area. The first was that Baptism and the Lord's Supper were sacraments which linked the local congregation to the whole Church, past, present and future. They were not private observances of a local congregation or denomination but acts in which the one holy, catholic and apostolic Church was made present. These sacraments were Christ's gift to the whole Church.

---

[43]   The number of non-stipendiary ministers, 207 in 1995, rose in the following year to 219, but by 2002 had declined to 159. See United Reformed Church Year Books (1983-2002).

[44]   Basis of Union, para. 25.

It followed as a second principle that, in the ordering of their sacramental life, local congregations of the United Reformed Church should be sensitive to the ecumenical dimensions of their worship and life.

> The first principle means that no congregation should ever be deprived of the sacraments, and that there must always be someone available and authorised to preside. The second principle implies that those normally authorised to preside should be ministers of Word and Sacraments.[45]

A pattern of presidency was thus proposed in which an ordained minister of Word and Sacraments should preside when available, but in situations of 'pastoral necessity' where no minister was available, the District Council should make provision for lay presidency. The authorisation of lay presidents, who might normally come from within the congregation concerned or be a lay preacher familiar to the congregation, should not be given for a period longer than one year without consultation and a review of the needs of the congregation. These recommendations, which were agreed by General Assembly, were advocated as congruent with the spirit of the Basis of Union. They were far removed from any claim that unordained members of the Church possessed any inherent right to preside at the sacraments. It was because the observance of the sacrament of the Lord's Supper was central to the Church's worship and pilgrimage, and its neglect would be ecumenically irresponsible, that lay presidency might need to be authorised in situations of pastoral necessity. In making this judgement the United Reformed Church did not reject that strand in its tradition which had believed that, in the interests of good order, sacraments should not be administered in a church which was not 'furnished with officers'. That concern however should not lead to the neglect of the sacrament. *Patterns of Ministry* was no less concerned with church order when it affirmed that the ministry of Word and Sacrament was God's gift to the Church, and that in normal circumstances presidency at its sacraments should normally be by those who had been ordained to that ministry.

Ordination

An appendix to *Patterns of Ministry* included a statement on the Theology of Ministry arising from the engagement of the United Reformed Church with the issues which had been raised in *Baptism, Eucharist and Ministry* and *God's Reign and Our Unity*. The Lima Text had emphasised the new relationship which ordination establishes between the minister, the local church and the Church universal. This relationship was important in resolving the centuries' long debate over whether the ministry was to be understood in *ontological* or in *functional* terms, on which depended whether ordination conferred upon the person ordained a different kind of character. The commentary in *Baptism, Eucharist and Ministry* had noted[46] that the New Testament normally used for ordination the Greek word *cheirotonein* , derived from its secular use of appointment by extending the hand or to cast a vote.[47] The terms *ordo* and *ordinare*, derived from Roman law, were used to describe a special class of persons distinct from the *plebs*. *Cheirotonein* seemed to designate those who were to serve within the *Laos*, while the cultural and social significance of

---

[45] *Patterns of Ministry*, 5:1.4.
[46] *Baptism, Eucharist and Ministry*, M. 40.
[47] e.g. Acts 14:23, II Corinthians 8:19.

ordo and *ordinare* pointed to a class of people who were either separated from, or superior to, the *Laos*. It was clear in the Reformed tradition that ordination did not create a class of people with superior status. It did however create a new relationship between those ordained and the Church. While particular tasks were appropriately assigned to the ordained ministry – preaching the Word, celebrating the gospel sacraments, pastoral care and leadership – public ministry was more than an aggregate of discrete tasks. On necessary occasions the tasks of ministry, including as we have seen presidency at the Lord's supper, might be undertaken by those who were not ordained to the ministry of Word and Sacrament. The difference was that they did not stand permanently in that relationship to the local community and the universal Church which is established by ordination.

> The distinctive identity of the minister, like the distinctive identity of every Christian, is created by relationships rather than tasks.[48]

'Relationships' are to be understood here in broad terms. They include a minister's relationship to a particular congregation and the special bond which exists between minister and people. They also extend more widely to embrace the relationships which exist between congregations in different places. The mutual recognition of ministries of Word and Sacrament and their celebrations of the sacrament of the Lord's Supper was a historic sign of the unity of many different congregations in the one Body.

Ordination is therefore to be understood in terms of authorisation rather than power. It serves the good order of the Church, in the sense of orderliness, by ensuring that those who exercise the functions of ministry do so with the authority of the whole Church and not by self-appointment or as a means of self-aggrandisement. Ordination confers no powers or rights which can be exercised apart from the Christian community. The status which it confers is not social, but, in a Christian context 'the status of the servant of all, following the example of Christ himself'.[49] Ordination is always to 'representative servanthood'.[50] The theology of ministry expounded here was opposed to models of ministry which had seemed too often to have exhibited an unattractive arrogance and enjoyment of status. The opposite extreme needed also to be avoided. The concept of servanthood itself needed to be delivered from secular notions of the minister as an employee of the Church. As a servant of the Word, and also a member of the *Laos*, the minister's task includes representing the independence of the Gospel over against the community. The Church's Lord stands among his people as one who serves, but his Word also calls the Church to repentance, faith and renewed discipleship. The fundamental principle of Reformed ecclesiology that the Church is constituted by the Word of God needed to be safeguarded within the Church's understanding of ordination to servanthood. Ordination is the Church's recognition that God has taken the initiative in calling particular men and women to ministry. It is the act whereby they are commissioned to be servants of that Word and celebrants of the gospel sacraments. It is then the act in which the Church, as God's *Laos*, commits itself to receive and respond to the ministry as God's gift to the Church. This 'high' view of ministry has nothing to do with payment and applies equally to stipendiary and non-stipendiary ministries.

---

48   *Patterns of Ministry*, Appendix A, 3.13.
49   ibid. 3.9.
50   ibid. 3.13.

Ordination to Other Ministries?

The perception of ordination in *Baptism, Eucharist and Ministry*, and *God's Reign and Our Unity* was primarily that of a setting apart to a preaching and sacramental ministry within the Church together with pastoral responsibilities. The United Reformed Church with other Reformed churches also used the term ordination to denote the setting apart of those who were called to be Elders. The use of the term 'ordination' for both orders of ministry had at times been a cause of public and ecumenical confusion. The distinction between ordained ministers and ordained elders was not always clearly understood. One strand within Presbyterianism had used the term 'elder' for both orders of ministry, distinguishing them as 'teaching' and 'ruling' elders, though that had largely disappeared in modern times. *Patterns of Ministry* offered clarification in suggesting that

> the act of ordination has to be understood in terms of the intention of the ordination prayer which defines the character of the ministry exercised.[51]

In the case of elders, the intention of their ordination was to pastoral oversight and leadership of the local church, and to be associated with ministers in all the councils of the Church.[52]

But should other ministries in the Church, for example, those of lay preachers and church-related community workers be similarly authorised by ordination? The answer to this was partly pragmatic and traditional. The ministries of lay preachers and, more recently, those of church related community workers, had arisen relatively recently in response to particular needs. A case could be made for ordaining church-related community workers to a diaconal ministry in the world as a witness to the ministry of Christ as servant. Diaconal ministry might also include special appointments to hospital and industrial chaplaincy. It could also be argued that those who were regular lay preachers should be ordained to a non-stipendiary ministry of Word and Sacrament, especially if their ministries were exercised in several congregations within their district councils. The question of the ordination to other ministries need not be a closed issue. What was important in the statement on the Theology of Ministry was the 'sense in which ordination has been reserved for those ministries which most closely recall us to the foundational ministry of Christ himself.'[53] The statement provided a benchmark for determining which of the varied ministries in the Church should be recognised by ordination.

IV. The Continuing Dialogue

As the 20th century reached its end, issues surrounding ordination and ministry remained a source of disagreement in the Church. The goal of visible unity, envisaged as the organic union of divided churches, remained elusive. Yet during the century relationships between the separated churches had changed beyond all recognition. Dialogue had become established as the normal pattern of communication and, in spite of disappointments and setbacks, its momentum showed no sign of

---

[51]   ibid. 3.7.
[52]   Basis of Union, 7.(22).
[53]   Patterns of Ministry, op. cit. 3.10.

slackening. The newly formed, for example, Churches Together in England (CTE) published *Called To Be One* in 1996 as a means of exploring how their communion with Christ and with one another in the Church might be deepened and expressed by common witness and service in the world.[54]

In 1994 the Methodist Church invited the Church of England to explore through informal conversations the possibility of formal conversations with a view to organic unity. As these informal approaches progressed to formal conversations, the United Reformed Church, which now shared nearly 200 local congregations with the Methodist Church as well as three areas uniting United Reformed Church District Councils and Methodist Circuits, became directly involved in Trilateral Informal Conversations. In the year of the Millennium, by uniting with the Scottish Congregational Union, the United Reformed Church became for the first time a church in the three nations of England, Scotland and Wales.

Dialogue was not restricted to the British mainland. Since 1975 the United Reformed Church had been a member of the Leuenberg Fellowship which, formed in 1973, brought together European Lutheran, Reformed and United churches. The *Leuenberg Agreement* offered mutual recognition of ordination, and what has been described as 'a pragmatic approach to ministry and *episcope*',[55] which recognised that the development of diocesan bishops as the normal leadership pattern in the church in Europe had been an adaptation of the Roman imperial order to the needs of the Church in the new national states which emerged from the collapse of the Roman Empire.

The United Reformed Church also had observer status at the bilateral dialogue between the Church of England and the Evangelische Kirche, Deutschland (EKD) which led to the *Meissen Common Statement* of 1989. Here two national churches committed themselves to sharing a common life and mission, but did not remove restrictions on sharing in ordinations. The episcopal succession of Anglican orders continued to be distinguished from the ordinations of the German Church.

The *Poruoo Agreement* (1993) between the British and Irish Anglican Churches and some of the Nordic and Baltic Lutheran Churches was able to offer interchangeability of ministry through their agreement 'to welcome persons episcopally ordained in any of our churches to the office of bishop, priest or deacon...'[56] The *Poruoo Agreement* offered a 'fresh approach to understanding apostolic succession in terms of a corporate succession of the whole Church, expressed and focused, but neither guaranteed nor exhausted, by the succession in the episcopal sees'.[57]

Consultations on new questions about *episcope* were arranged by the Faith and Order Commission of the World Council of Churches at Strasburg in April 1997 and Crêt-Bérard in the following November. These urged renewed ecumenical study of this theme in the light of the emergence of new forms of episcopal oversight and new questions about *episcope*[58].

---

[54]   *Called To Be One*, (London: CTE, 1996)
[55]   M H Cressey, *Three Games in a Long Ecumenical Set*, in Peter C Bouteneff and Alan D Falconer (eds), *Episkope and Episcopacy and the Quest for Visible Unity*, (Geneva: WCC, Faith and Order Paper No.183, 1999) p.123.
[56]   Quoted in United Reformed Church *Reports to Assembly 2002*, p. 223.
[57]   M H Cressey, op. cit. p. 124.
[58]   See *Episkope and Episcopacy and the Quest for Visible Unity*, op. cit.

The twentieth century ended in a ferment of ecumenical discussions in which the United Reformed Church was fully engaged. In its short life since 1972 it had evolved a theologically mature understanding of ministry and ordination, which may be recapitulated thus:

The starting-point for its understanding of ministry was encapsulated in the phrase, 'the ministry of the whole people of God', though the phrase may not have come naturally to the average church member. This ministry was a sharing by all the baptised in the mission to the world which God had initiated through the life, death, and resurrection of Jesus. Yet the phrase was ambiguous. Some took it to express the responsibility of all church members to share the work of the ordained ministry, but was this sufficient? Did it refer to the Church's corporate offering of worship and obedience, or to individual acts of service and witness, or to a combination of both? By what forms should it find expression? Was it to be exercised in the Church or the world? How would it be identified? Would those exercising particular ministries within the 'whole people of God' require authorisation and, if so, by whom? Clarification was needed of the questions raised by the phrase if it was not to be misunderstood, or to lose its relevance.

The United Reformed Church supported the consensus which had found expression in *Baptism, Eucharist and Ministry* that the Church required for its mission a special ministry of leadership. This ordained ministry was rooted in the ministry of Jesus and the common ministry of all the baptised. Differences of view remained on whether the threefold ministry of bishops, presbyters and deacons should be accepted for the sake of unity. Some were willing to accept an episcopally ordained ministry provided it could be accepted as a human design and not a divine law. It was almost certain that a condition of the acceptance of episcopacy would be that women should be equally eligible with men for appointment to episcopal office.[59] A contrary trend could also be discerned in the United Reformed Church of a deepening attachment to its long tradition of Reformed practice and the conviction that its conciliar and participatory form of government encapsulated something of value to the whole Church. It was not clear which view would prevail in the new century.

Ordination was understood as commissioning in the name of Christ for public office in the Church by invocation of the Spirit and the laying on of hands. The initiative in every ordination lies always with God who calls and equips men and women for ministry. The risen Lord is the true ordainer who calls to ministry and bestows gifts for ministry. Those who ordain do so as representatives of the whole Church.

The act of ordination involves *invocation* to God that the ministry be empowered by the Holy Spirit, *acknowledgement* by the Church that the Lord has answered the Church's prayer by granting the gifts of the Holy Spirit to the one ordained, and *commitment* by the Church and the ordained to the new relationships established by ordination.

---

[59]   The General Assembly 2002 reluctantly voted for the appointment of an ecumenical bishop in Wales who could not, at least in the first instance, be a woman.

It was axiomatic that the ministry created by the solemn act of ordination did not constitute a superior order in the Church. Reformed churchmanship could never be hierarchical if it were to remain faithful to its traditions. The gifts which the Holy Spirit poured upon God's people created 'a circle of service and praise rather than a pyramid of status and power'.[60]

On the basis of this understanding of ministry and ordination, the United Reformed Church was ready to enter the new millennium committed to continue its ecumenical dialogue with its Christian partners as it sought, in the words of its Basis of Union –

> To work for such visible unity of the whole Church as Christ wills and in the way he wills, in order that people and nations may be led more and more to glorify the Father in heaven.[61]

---

[60]　*Patterns of Ministry*, 2.5.
[61]　Basis of Union of the United Reformed Church, Schedule D, para. 9.

Bibliography

BIBLIOGRAPHY

Printed Books and Articles

Ainslie, J L. *Doctrines of Ministerial Order in the Reformed Churches.* Edinburgh: T & T Clark, 1940.

Anglican-Reformed International Commision, *God's Reign and Out Unity*, London:SPCK, 1984.

Bate, H N. (ed) *Faith and Order,* Lausanne 1927. London: SCM Press. 1940.

Bell, G K A. (ed) *Documents on Christian Unity 1920-24.* Oxford: 1924.

Bell, G K A. (ed) *Documents on Christian Unity, Second Series 1924-30.* Oxford: 1930.

Bogue, D and Bennett, J. *History of the Dissenters.* London: 1808.

Bouteneff P C. and Falconer A D. (eds) *Episkope and Episcopacy and the Quest for Visible Unity.* Geneva: WCC Publications, Faith and Order Paper No 183. 1999.

Cadoux, C J. *The Congregational Way.* Oxford: 1945.

Calvin, John. *Institutes of the Christian Religion.* London: SCM Press, 1961.

Clague, W J. *The Principles of Church Organisation in Primitive Christianity and Their Application to Present-Day Church Life.* Churches of Christ Conference Paper, 1937 and 1938. Churches of Christ Year Books 1937 and 1938.

Cornick, David. *Under God's Good Hand: A History of the Traditions which have come together in the United Reformed Church in the United Kingdom.* London: The United Reformed Church. 1998.

Countryman, L W. *The Language of Ordination - Ministry in an Ecumenical Context.* Philadelphia: Trinity Press International. 1992.

Chadwick, Owen. *The Victorian Church 1829-1859.* London: SCM Press, 1966.

Dale, R W. *History of English Congregationalism.* London: Hodder and Stoughton, 1907.

Dale, R W. *Manual of Congregational Principles.* London: Congregational Union of England and Wales. 1884.

Davies, Horton M. *The Worship of the English Puritans.* London: Dacre Press, 1948.

Davies, Horton M. *The English Free Churches.* Oxford: 1952.

Dunkerley, R. (ed) *Ministry and Sacraments.* London: SCM Press. 1937.

Forsyth, P T. *Positive Preaching and the Modern Mind* (first published 1907). London: Independent Press. 1949.

Forsyth, P T. *Faith, Freedom and the Future.* London: Hodder and Stoughton. 1912.

Forsyth, P T. *The Church and the Sacraments.* London: Longmans, Green, 1917. (Re-published by Independent Press. 1947).

Goodall, N. *A History of the London Missionary Society 1895-1945.* Oxford: 1954.

Gray, J. (ed) *Towards Christian Union.* Leicester: Churches of Christ Union Committee. 1960.

Hanson, A T. and R P C. *The Identity of the Church.* London: SCM Press. 1987.

Hodgson, L. (ed) *Convictions.* London: SCM Press. 1934.

Huxtable, John. *The Ministry.* London: Independent Press. 1943.

Huxtable, John. *Christian Unity – Some of the Issues.* London: Independent Press. 1966.

Huxtable, John. *A New Hope for Christian Unity.* London: Collins. 1977.

Huxtable, John. *Ordination: Aspects of a Tradition.* Journal of the United Reformed Church History Society. Vo.2. No.4. 1979.

Huxtable, John. *As It Seemed to Me.* London: United Reformed Church. 1990.

Jenkins, D T. *The Nature of Catholicity.* London: Faber and Faber. 1942.

Jenkins, D T. *The Gift of Ministry.* London: Faber and Faber. 1947. (re-issued as *The Protestant Ministry.* London: Faber and Faber. 1958.)

Jenkins, D T. *Congregationalism - A Restatement.* London: Faber and Faber. 1954.

Jones, R. Tudur. *Congregationalism in England 1662-1962.* London: Independent Press. 1962.

Kaye, E H, and Mackenzie, R. *W E Orchard, A Study in Christian Exploration.* Oxford: 1990.

Kaye, E H. *Mansfield College - Its Origin, History and Significance.* Oxford: 1996.
Kirk, K E. (ed) *The Apostolic Ministry.* London: Hodder and Stoughton. 1946.

Luther, Martin. *Reformation Writings of Martin Luther, Volume I, The Basis of the Protestant Reformation,* trans. B. Lee Woolf. London: Lutterworth Press. 1952.

Macarthur, A L. *The Background to 1972.* Journal of the United Reformed Church History Society, Vo.4, No.1. 1987.

Manning, B L. *A Layman in the Ministry.* London: Independent Press. 1942.

Manson, T W. *The Church's Ministry.* London: Hodder and Stoughton. 1948.

Manson, T W. *Ministry and Priesthood: Christ's and Ours.* London: Epworth Press. 1958.

Matthews, A G. (ed) *The Savoy Declaration of Faith and Order 1658.* London: Independent Press. 1959.

Micklem, N. *What is the Faith?* London: Hodder and Stoughton. 1936.

Micklem, N. (ed) *Christian Worship.* Oxford: 1936.

Micklem, N. *The Doctrine of our Redemption.* London: Eyre and Spottiswoode. 1948.

Moberly, R C. *Ministerial Priesthood.* London: John Murray. 1910.

Newbigin, L. *The Reunion of the Church.* London: SCM Press,. 1948.

Nunn, R. *This Growing Unity.* London: Churches Together in England. 1995.

Nuttall, G F. *The Early Congregational Conception of the Ministry and the Place of Women Within It.* Congregational Quarterly, Vol. XXVI, No.2. 1948.

Nuttall, G F. *Visible Saints.* Oxford: 1957.

Oman, John. *Vision and Authority.* London: Hodder and Stoughton, Second Edition. 1928.

Paul, R S. *Ministry.* Grand Rapids, Michigan, Eerdmans. 1965.

Paul, R S. *The Assembly of the Lord.* Edinburgh: 1985.

Payne, E A. *The Free Church Tradition in the Life of England.* London: SCM Press. 1944.

Peel, A. (ed) *Essays Congregational and Catholic.* London: Congregational Union of England and Wales. 1931.

Peel, D R. *Reforming Theology.* London: United Reformed Church. 2002.

Robinson, W. *A Church Order, Reformed and Catholic.* The Presbyter, Vol.2, No.8, 1944.

Sell, A P F. *Saints: Visible, Orderly and Catholic.* Geneva: World Alliance of Reformed Church. 1986.

Simpson, P Carnegie. *Church Principles.* London: Hodder and Stoughton. 1923.

Simpson, P Carnegie. *The Evangelical Church Catholic.* London: Hodder and Stoughton. 1934.

Simpson, P Carnegie. *The Character of Presbytery.* Congregational Quarterly. Vol. XXII (1944-45), pp.306-316.

Taylor, J H. *Ordination Among Us.* Transactions of the Congregational Historical Society. Vol. XX. No. 7. 1968.

Thompson, D M. (ed) *Stating the Gospel – Formulations and Declarations of Faith from the Heritage of the United Reformed Church.* Edinburgh: 1990.

Thompson, D M. *Let Sects and Parties Fall.* Birmingham. Berean Press. 1990.

Thorogood, B. *One Wind, Many Flames.* Geneva: WCC. 1991.

Thurian, M. (ed) *Churches Respond to BEM.* Geneva: WCC. 1986.

Torrance, T F. *Royal Priesthood – A Theology of Ordained Ministry (Second Edition).* Edinburgh: 1993.

Wainwright, G. *Lesslie Newbigin – A Theological Life.* Oxford: 2000.

Watts, M R. *The Dissenters: from the Reformation to the French Revolution.* Oxford: 1978.

Whale, J S. *The Protestant Tradition.* Cambridge: 1955.

Whale, J S. *Ordination to the Ministry.* The Presbyter, Vol.2, No.6. 1944.

White, B R. *The English Separatist Tradition.* Oxford: 1971.

Watters, A C. *How We May Increase Whole-time Ministry and at the same time preserve Mutual Ministry among us.* Churches of Christ Conference Paper 1944. Churches of Christ Year Book and Annual Report 1944.

Winfield, Flora. *Growing Together – Working for Unity Locally.* London: SPCK. 2002.

Wollaston, E P M. *The First Moderators 1919.* Journal of the United Reformed Church History Society, Vol. 5, No. 5. 1994.

World Council of Churches, *Baptism, Eucharist and Ministry,* Faith and Order Paper No.III: Geneva, 1982.

Journals, Periodicals and Reports

Called to Be One. London: Churches Together in England. 1996.
Church Times.
Churches of Christ Year Books and Annual Reports.
Congregational Year Books.
Congregational Quarterly, Vols. I-XXXVI, 1923-1958.
Expository Times.
Journal of the United Reformed Church History Society.
Presbyter, The (1943-1949).
REFORM – The magazine of the United Reformed Church.
The Times.
Churches' Council for Covenanting. Towards Visible Unity: Proposals for a Covenant. 1980.
Churches' Council for Covenanting. The Failure of the English Covenant. London: British Council of Churches, 1982.
Transactions of the Congregational Historical Society.
United Reformed Church, Reports to Assembly.
United Reformed Church, Records of Assembly.
Year Books of the United Reformed Church.

Manuals and Directories of Public Worship

A Manual For Ministers. London: Independent Press. 1936.
A Book of Services and Prayers. London: Independent Press. 1959.
A Book of Public Worship, compiled for the use of Congregationalists. Oxford: 1948.
Directory for Public Worship. London: Publications Committee of the Presbyterian Church of England. 1921.
The Presbyterian Service Book. London: Publications Committee of the Presbyterian Church of England. 1948.
The Presbyterian Service Book. London: Publications Committee of the Presbyterian Church of England. 1968.
A Book of Services (Doctrine and Worship Committee of the United Reformed Church in England and Wales). Edinburgh: St Andrew's Press. 1980.
Service Book (The United Reformed Church in the United Kingdom). Oxford: 1989.

Copyright acknowledgements

Index

A

B

C